ARTISAN BAKING ACROSS AMERICA

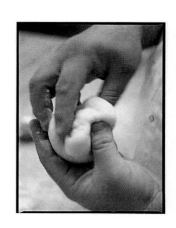

ARTISAN
BAKING
ACROSS AMERICA

THE BREADS, THE BAKERS		THE BEST RECIPES

MAGGIE GLEZER

PHOTOGRAPHS BY BEN FINK

Artisan · New York

Published by Artisan
A Division of Workman Publishing, Inc.
708 Broadway
New York, New York 10003
www.workman.com

Library of Congress Cataloging-in-Publication Data
Glezer, Maggie.
    Artisan baking across America : the breads,
    the bakers, the best recipes / Maggie Glezer;
    photographs by Ben Fink.
        p. cm.
    Includes index.
    ISBN 1-57965-117-8
    1. Baking. 2. Bakers and bakeries. I. Title.

TX763 .G557 2000
641.8'15—dc21   99-056544

Printed at Arnoldo Mondadori Editore, Verona, Italy

10 9 8 7 6 5 4 3 2 1

Book Design by Dania Davey

To Ari, my great love and lodestar

CONTENTS

Scaling dough into correctly proportional loaves on a balance scale at The Acme Bread Company

INTRODUCTION

Couches folded on a shelf

Baguettes proofing in
a folded couche

Freshly baked bread

LONG BEFORE I EVEN IMAGINED WRITING THIS BOOK, I watched my first artisan baker in action in Grenoble, France. It was very early in the morning, well before dawn, and I stood chatting with a young journeyman baker in a bakeshop so tiny I had to sit on the counter next to his beautiful old brick oven to avoid being bludgeoned by his jerking peel. Over the course of the morning, that cramped space produced a mind-boggling array of old-fashioned French breads, the kind seldom seen in France anymore. I was fascinated by his oven, fronted with brick and ornate cast-iron doors and grates, the vast, brightly lit hearth heated from below with a fire-box that he stoked intermittently. In went his peel, and out came the golden breads, slipped directly into a tub-sized basket, where they began crackling almost immediately. He knew that oven's every secret—where to set the delicate croissants, where to place the longer-baking pain au levain, and how to slip his long-handled peel into the mosaic of slowly browning loaves to retrieve only the finished breads. When dawn broke, after the market workers had come to collect their baskets of baguettes and petits pains to sell later that morning, his work finally slowed, and he had a moment for coffee, taken leaning against the well of the cool back doorway. When we said good-bye, he plied me with fragrant breads to take back to my still-sleeping husband. I can't remember his name, but I remember him and his bread, and how real it tasted back in our curtain-darkened hotel room.

That experience marked me, and ever since, I have done all I could to learn more about the craft. I eventually joined the Bread Bakers Guild of America, an organization of artisan bakers, and discovered that craft baking is experiencing a rebirth on these shores, that some of the best bread in the world is made right here, in American bakeries with bakers just as devoted to and passionate about superb bread as that Grenoble baker. I have studied with the guild both here and in France, eventually writing technical columns for it as well, and in the process have made many good friends, and learned that bakers are the most grounded, interesting, generous, inspiring, and energetic people I know.

This is the world I want to open to you, to walk into the backdoor and enter these warm bright bakeshops smelling of toast and fermentation, to see the flour flying, to sink up to your elbows in warm wet dough, to feel the heat of the oven, and to appraise the shelves crowded with carefully, speedily, and perfectly made loaves. I want you to meet the men and women who have devoted their lives to mastering this intricate and complex craft, to know more about bread's primary ingredient—flour—and how bread gets baked at a variety of different artisanal bakeries, and, finally, to get a sense of the baker's challenges and rewards.

To bring all these people and places to you, Ben Fink, the superbly talented photographer whose photographs illuminate this book, and I went on tour together, visiting millers, scientists, farmers, and some of this country's best bakers—often unheralded because of their single-minded focus on their craft. I realized early on that I couldn't possibly visit every great bakery, write about every step, or elucidate every baking technicality, so I tried to concentrate on the people, places, methods, and events that especially interest me or are particularly underrepresented or misunderstood.

We begin at the foundation—with flour, bread's most important ingredient—not only what makes flour important and special, but also how wheat is grown and bred, and the different methods of milling it. Processing that flour into bread follows, and we learn about the hallmarks of artisanal production—sourdough baking and pre-ferments; the contrasting production methods between a very small and a very big bakeshop; and one baker's focus on his brick wood-fired oven. Next, we go to four of the best American specialty bakeries to study the production of some of my favorite breads—dark rye breads, Neapolitan pizza, pandoro, and bialys. I think you will be amazed at how well the best professional methods learned there work at home. Finally, we examine the baker's life, at the training undertaken to achieve mastery, at the stories that anchor a lively neighborhood bakery, and at a baking competition, where we learn how baking skills and connoisseurship are honed.

Woven into the tour are the recipes and baking advice I learned from the bakers. All recipes are scaled-down versions of the original bakeshop formulas; if some seem rather complex, it is because I have unwaveringly adhered to professional techniques and ingredient ratios. Each recipe is categorized by skill level to help steer less-experienced bakers away from the trickier recipes.

So whether your interest in the craft of bread baking is vocational, avocational, or epicurean, I invite you to tour with me, to see the intent, devotion, and mastery that go into the making of our best daily bread.

WHAT IS "ARTISAN BREAD"?

When I tell people that I have written a book about artisan bread baking, I always get a quizzical look—what is artisan bread (as it has come to be called, no one being able to pronounce artisanal)? The dictionary, saying the term "artisan" refers to a person working in a skilled trade or a craftsman, offers little clarity. So I decided to conduct a poll among some well-respected bakers to see what their definitions might offer. While I got a variety of answers, they all agreed on one thing: For bread to be considered "artisan," at least one part of its production must be performed by hand. Beyond that, artisan bread is *most likely* to be crusty European-style bread, sometimes sourdough, sometimes not; hopefully weighed, rounded, shaped, and slashed by hand; and baked directly on a hearth in a "deck oven." More difficult to define is the level of quality implied by the term, the concern for the color and flavor of the bread's flour, and for the naturally arising flavors conjured by careful craftsmanship.

ARTISAN BAKING ACROSS AMERICA

BAKING BASICS

INGREDIENTS,

EQUIPMENT, AND

TECHNIQUES

FOR THOSE UNFAMILIAR WITH THE INGREDIENTS, EQUIPMENT, OR TECHNIQUES used in these recipes or just needing a little handholding, this is the place to come. Read through these sections carefully, then go on to the recipes. Some instructions will become much clearer when you are actually trying them out on the dough.

Baking is a craft mastered only through years of trial and error, and recipes alone can take a baker only so far. I can't emphasize enough how important it is to let yourself try and fail—it's only flour and water and time. Remember, success is a poor teacher. I have tried to think of every provision, and the recipes have been repeatedly tested both by my excellent tester, Rita Yeazel, and myself. However, conditions in your kitchen and ingredients in your part of the country will be different from ours, and you will have to make your own adjustments.

Professional bakers expect to adjust yeast amounts and water temperatures with the seasons, to control the fermentation rates of their doughs, and there is no reason that home bakers shouldn't do the same. If your dough is fermenting too slowly, next time add 25% more yeast or use warmer water. If your kitchen is really hot, use ice water or use 25% less yeast. Don't be timid about fiddling with the yeast; it is just a simple adjustment.

The most important thing to remember is to get in the kitchen and have a good time. I once heard Lionel Poilâne, the famous Parisian baker who has inspired so many of the bakers featured in this book, speak about being invited for dinner at a family's home. The hostess set a basket of bread on the table and immediately apologized for it, saying she had made it herself and of course, it didn't compare to his masterful loaves. But M. Poilâne said on the contrary, this bread was far better than anything he had ever sold, for she had made it to feed her family—with her own two hands and all her heart.

INGREDIENTS

Flour, water, salt, and yeast—these are the basic ingredients of bread. While at first glance nothing could be simpler, a closer look proves that this impression is wrong. For home bakers trying to replicate professional-style bread baking at home, the most frustrating part will be trying to find the right flour. The varieties and types of flour available to professional bakers are tremendously greater than those available to the home baker. Yet, for the most part, home bakers can manage if they are intelligent about their substitutions. All recipes have been tested with the most common types and brands of flour whenever possible, but some breads require very specialized flours that usually can only be mail ordered (see Sources, page 222). Another problem source is yeast, as most professionals use compressed or instant, while most home bakers use active dry. Read through this section for more detailed information about these topics and the rest of the ingredients called for in the recipes.

wheat flours

White Flour Almost all the recipes in this book were tested with national brands of flours, unless special flours are specified. Organic flours are preferable, not necessarily because they taste or perform better, although they often will, but simply because they are better for the environment.

Recipes specify unbleached flour: either all-purpose flour or bread flour or a mixture of the two. I should add that "bread" flours are always *un*bleached, unless specified on the bag, but "cake" and "all-purpose" flours are usually bleached—with chlorine gas—unless otherwise specified on the bag. Some artisan breads require a flour with 11.5% protein, or at least a flour that acts like it. In these cases, I have mixed all-purpose flour with bread flour in the recipes (most bread flour is about 12.5% protein [4g per 30g serving] and most all-purpose is 10.5% protein [3g per 29g serving]). If you are already using an 11.5% protein flour (King Arthur all-purpose flour is in this range), you can just substitute it for the combined flours.

Whole-wheat Flour Be sure to use freshly milled whole-wheat flour that is clearly meant for bread making. Much grocery store whole-wheat flour is meant for muffins and pancakes and is thus milled from soft wheat—a poor performer in bread doughs. Soft whole-wheat flours have a protein content of up to 11% (3g per 30g serving). One trick for telling what kind of whole-wheat flour you are buying is to look at the recipes on the flour bag: If they are for pancakes or muffins, chances are the flour is milled from soft wheat. Other whole-wheat flours are milled from dark Northern spring wheat and are too strong; they have a protein content of

up to 16% (5g per 30g serving). Hard red winter wheat, not spring, with a protein content of around 13% (4g per 30g serving), is best for artisan-style breads.

High-Extraction Flour This is a superb white flour with a little of the bran and germ left in, resulting in a light tan, richly flavorful flour. The category can vary from flours containing between 77% and 90% of the wheat kernel, meaning that 77% to 90% of the kernel has been extracted during milling. Typical white flour contains only 72% of the wheat kernel. The best flours in this category are bolted stone-ground flours, but these are currently available only in Europe. Even the roller-milled versions are rare and must be mail-ordered in fifty-pound bags (see Sources, page 222).

If you don't want to mail order this much flour, you can make your own by sifting coarsely ground, hard winter whole-wheat bread flour through a sifter or strainer (use the bran remaining in the strainer for muffins or for dusting your peel). It is a little more effort than just mixing whole-wheat and white bread flours, but the resulting golden-hued flour is worth it.

High-Gluten Flour A very strong bread flour with a high protein content, about 14%, milled from dark Northern spring wheat. There is no substitute.

Durum Flour When durum flour is called for, be sure to use the "extra fancy" patent durum flour, sometimes called "extra fancy pasta flour." This product is as fine as flour, not coarse and granular like semolina, which is also milled from durum wheat (hence the confusion). While durum flour can make wonderful strong bread dough, semolina won't. Your bread will not rise very high and will be quite dense if semolina is used (great for North African breads, but not right here). Unfortunately, durum flour usually is available only through mail-order sources (see Sources, page 222).

Diastatic Malted Barley Flour While this is not an ingredient called for in any recipe, you may need to use it to correct a problem with your flour. If you are buying flours directly from small mills, you will need to ask if malted barley flour or fungal amylase has been added to the flour, or if the flour is "enzymatically balanced." The large national mills always make sure their flours are balanced, and you will see malted barley listed as an ingredient, but smaller mills, especially organic mills, will sometimes leave this step up to the bakers. You will know you have a problem if your bread has a pale crust, despite adequate baking. Other symptoms of enzyme deficiency include sluggish fermentation and a smaller-than-normal size.

In order for the starch in the flour to become available to the yeasts for fermentation, two enzymes are needed—alpha and beta amylase. Beta amylase is abundant in most flour, but alpha amylase is often lacking. Many mills will test their flour and supplement it with precise amounts of either fungal amylase or malted barley flour to enzymatically balance the flour.

If you are cautious, you can easily supplement the flour yourself with diastatic malted barley flour (see Sources, page 222). Start by adding ½ teaspoon (enzymatically active) diastatic malted barley flour per 1 cup flour. If your breads are still very pale, double the amount. If you add too much, your bread's crumb will be damp and gooey, so be careful.

STORING WHOLE-GRAIN FLOURS AND MEALS
The unsaturated fat in the germ and bran of milled whole-grain products, such as flours, meals, and cracked grains, is susceptible to rancidity; however, unmilled intact grains can be stored for years. Once rancid, these products have a distinctly unpleasant, stale, bitter flavor, very noticeable to sensitive palates. The key to avoiding rancidity is to buy only freshly milled products, preferably directly from the mill so you know the milling date, or from a reputable distributor who stores these products properly and has a high turnover.

Bay State Mills, one of the largest rye millers in the United States, gives a ninety-day shelf life to all whole-grain products stored below 75°F. They suggest storing whole-grain products in the refrigerator up to fourteen weeks or, better yet, in the freezer for even longer. I like to store my flours in their original bags sealed inside Ziploc bags in the freezer, letting them come to room temperature before using them. Just be sure to keep flours stored in the refrigerator or freezer very tightly sealed, as they readily pick up odors.

rye products

All grades of rye flour have higher extraction rates than wheat flour, which means that more of the rye kernel is extracted, or included in the final flour. Containing more bran and germ, rye flours tend to be darker as well. Many good rye bakers will tell you that the secret to rye baking is to use really fresh rye flour and meal, that is, rye products that have been recently milled. Rye flavor apparently dissipates as the flour ages, similar to ground spices. Also, oils in the germ and bran contribute unsaturated fat to the flour, which can quickly spoil, giving the flour a discernible rancid flavor.

The following products are industry standards:

White rye flour is the purest of the flours and the only one that is sometimes bleached (with chlorine gas). Milled from the very center of the rye endosperm, with the least amount of bran, it contains 7.5% to 9.5% protein, depending on the year, and about 0.65% ash. It has very little rye flavor and is the equivalent of a patent-grade wheat flour.

Medium rye flour is made of the entire rye endosperm, so it is much darker and more flavorful than white rye. It contains 9% to 11% protein, depending on the year, and about 1.2% ash. It is the equivalent of a straight-grade wheat flour.

Dark rye flour is not, as is commonly thought, a whole-grain flour, but it does contain ample bran. Milled from the outer portions of the endosperm, with 14% to 17% protein, depending on the year, and about 2.5% ash, it is the flour left when the white rye flour is removed, making it the equivalent of a clear-grade wheat flour and the most intensely flavored of the rye flours.

ABOUT BAKER'S PERCENTAGES FOR INGREDIENTS

In addition to calling for ingredients by volume and by weight, I have used the professional system called "baker's percentages" to list ingredients. If you bake a lot, you would do well to learn this system, for it allows you to convert any recipe easily into any desired yield, and more experienced bakers to assess recipes quickly on an apples-to-apples basis. For advanced bakers, it is the best tool to formulate bread recipes. This is the system I used to convert the huge professional formulas into manageable sizes for home bakers while maintaining the same ingredient ratios.

This weight-based system works by expressing all ingredients as a ratio of the total flour weight. Thus, if a recipe uses 1,000 grams flour, 700 grams water, 20 grams yeast, and 20 grams salt, the baker's percentages would be 100% flour, 70% water, 2% yeast, and 2% salt.

If several different flours are used, their total should add up to 100%. Thus, if a recipe uses 1.6 ounces rye flour, 6.4 ounces whole-wheat flour, and 8 ounces white flour, the baker's percentage would read 10% rye flour, 40% whole-wheat flour, and 50% white flour. The total flour weighs 16 ounces: $1.6 \div 16 = 0.1 = 10\%$ rye flour; $6.4 \div 16 = 0.4 = 40\%$ whole-wheat flour; $8 \div 16 = 0.5 = 50\%$ white flour.

When a pre-ferment is used, different bakers handle the percentages in different ways. I have decided to call the total flour in the pre-ferment recipe 100%, but in the final dough I express the total weight of the pre-ferment as a percentage of the flour weight.

TO USE BAKER'S PERCENTAGES TO CHANGE A RECIPE'S YIELD

Follow the following four steps. To illustrate these steps, let's say that a recipe makes one 500-gram loaf, and you want to make one 750-gram loaf. The recipe calls for 50% pre-ferment, 70% water, 100% flour, 2.4% salt, and 0.6% instant yeast.

1. Determine your desired final weight of dough (most bakers add about 10% to the weight to account for weight loss during baking), expressing it as kilograms, grams, pounds, or ounces. Remember that all ingredients will be expressed in the same units. The total amount of dough will be:

   750 x 1.1 = 825 grams dough (1.1 is used to add 10% more).

2. Add up the recipe's percentages (50% pre-ferment, 70% water, 100% flour, 2.4% salt, and 0.6% instant yeast):

   50 + 70 + 100 + 2.4 + 0.6 = 223   Next, divide them by 100:   **223 ÷ 100 = 2.23**

3. Divide the desired dough weight (825g) by the sum obtained in step 2. This will be the total weight of flour needed to make your desired quantity of dough.

   825 ÷ 2.23 = 369.9 (rounded up to 370)   **370 grams flour**

4. Multiply the flour weight obtained in step 3 by each ingredient's percentage to get the ingredient's new weight. You can check your calculations by adding the new ingredient weights together. They should add up to the desired total dough weight in step 1.

370 x 0.5 = 185	**185 grams pre-ferment**
370 x 0.7 = 259 (rounded up to 260)	**260 grams water**
370 x 0.1 = 370	**370 grams flour**
370 x 0.024 = 8.8 (rounded up to 9)	**9 grams salt**
370 x 0.006 = 2.2 (rounded down to 2)	**2 grams instant yeast**
	826 grams dough

Rye meal is milled from the entire rye kernel in a range of different particle sizes. In the finest granulation, it is the equivalent of a whole-rye flour, but the coarser granulation can be anywhere from one sixteenth to half of the whole berry. Some smaller mills and distributors call their fine meal "pumpernickel flour," while others label it "dark rye flour."

salt

All the salt in this book is ordinary table salt, to ensure consistency, so your 1½ teaspoons salt will be the same as my 1½ teaspoons salt. It is extremely important to use salt correctly, for undersalting results in insipid flavor, while oversalting alters flavor and impedes fermentation. If you prefer to use sea salt or kosher salt, you will have to weigh it to make sure you are using the correct amount. Each brand of salt has a different size crystal and thus a different volume-to-weight ratio; only weighing it will ensure that you are using the correct amount.

water

I use tap water for my baking, even in sourdough starters—the chlorination is not really strong enough to inhibit the fierce sourdough microflora. Unless you are living in an area with extraordinarily soft water, which causes doughs to be sticky and slack, use tap water. I lived and baked in Tucson, Arizona, which has very hard water, and never had a problem. In the case of excessively soft water, which I personally have never encountered, you could use bottled water for your bread baking.

The myth about water quality affecting bread quality (you often hear this in New York City, where people claim their water, and hence their bread, is better) started hundreds of years ago, before the advent of municipal water systems, when bakers drew their water from private wells. If the water in the well was bad, so was the bread, obviously. Today, almost all tap water is fine for all types of bread baking.

yeast

In their sealed original packages, active dry, instant active dry, and special instant active dry yeasts will last for one year. However, once they are opened, all dry yeasts have a shelf life of just two to three months if stored in the coldest part of the refrigerator in an airtight container. Be sure to mark the opening date on

the jar so you can keep track of the yeast's freshness. Freezing yeast is not recommended because it damages the yeast cells. While it is least expensive to buy yeast in 1-pound packages, realize that you will probably end up discarding most of it. If that disturbs you, buy only as much yeast as you will use in a three-month period.

Here are the different types of yeast available to home bakers:

Active Dry Yeast is the yeast most familiar to home bakers. It is commonly available in ¼-ounce (7-gram) three-envelope strips and must be rehydrated before use in 105° to 110°F water (the temperature of bathwater too hot for your baby but heaven to you) for 5 to 10 minutes. (Lately many writers have said this step is unimportant, but that is only because most recipes contain such an overabundance of yeast that it really doesn't matter. I prefer to use the minimum amount and handle the yeast carefully to draw out its maximum potential.) Active dry yeast produces the least amount of carbon dioxide per yeast cell, and it is the slowest and most cumbersome type of yeast to use.

Instant Active Dry Yeast This is the yeast that many food writers have taken to calling "rapid-rise" yeast, just like some people call tissues Kleenex. RapidRise™ is a trademarked name used by Fleischmann's for the instant active dry yeast packaged in ¼-ounce three-envelope strips and is not a distinct type of yeast. This same yeast, with the addition of ascorbic acid as a dough strengthener, is sold by Fleischmann's as Bread Machine Yeast when packaged in a 4-ounce jar, and as Instant Yeast when packaged in a 1-pound foil pack. Red Star calls its instant active dry yeast QUICK·RISE™ when packaged in three-envelope strips. SAF is another popular company; amazingly, they call their product Instant Yeast. The important thing to understand is that *this is all the same yeast*.

Instant yeast is really wonderful for home bakers because it does not need to be rehydrated before it is added to the dough unless the dough is water-poor, because its cell membranes are very porous and easily absorb water. However, because this yeast does take about 20 minutes to activate fully, I recommend adding it before the autolyse, or rest, so that the yeast does not remain in pellets in the dough and you get the maximum level of activity from it. Also, dough temperatures need to be between 70° and 90°F for the yeast to rehydrate properly, so that using lukewarm to warm water in the dough is best. (Ignore the manufacturers' silly suggestion to add very hot water when mixing doughs.) In those cases where dough contains very little water or very cold ingredients are added, rehydrate the yeast separately in warm water, about 105°F. In some of the recipes, the yeast is rehydrated separately simply as a means of measuring a very tiny quantity of yeast.

Because instant active dry yeast produces more gas per yeast cell than active dry yeast, *less* of it needs to be used. The most common mistake in recipes written for home bakers is using too much instant yeast. In an interesting marketing ploy (and manufacturing decision), Fleischmann's and Red Star package ¼ ounce (7 grams, 2¼ teaspoons) yeast for both instant active dry and active dry yeasts, even though less instant yeast is needed in recipes. This gives consumers the idea that instant yeast ferments dough faster than active dry yeast. The truth is that instant yeast can be used for very slow fermentations, as long as amounts are moderated for the activity level desired.

Osmotolerant Instant Active Dry Yeast This is a type of instant yeast that has an excellent tolerance to sugar and performs brilliantly in sweet doughs, which often contain very low amounts of water (in the form of milk or eggs) and high amounts of sugar. Its advantage is that it can be used in normal amounts in very sweet doughs, which otherwise require huge amounts of active dry yeast or instant yeast for the same fermentation rate. As of this writing, the only widely available osmotolerant instant yeast is SAF's Instant Gold, available through mail-order sources (see Sources, page 222).

Compressed Yeast This is the most active yeast; it produces the most gas per yeast cell, and many artisan bakers prefer its strong and steady performance. However, it is unavailable to home bakers in many parts of the country, so I seldom call for it and always offer an alternative.

Professional bakers crumble it into a dough as it is mixing, but most home bakers dilute it in warm water first.

The drawbacks are that it is highly perishable and has a shelf life of only about eight weeks from packaging. To store it properly, never let it warm past 45°F. Warmer temperatures will cause it to begin breaking down, while freezing temperatures will damage yeast cells (the ice crystals formed during freezing are believed to puncture fragile cell walls). Yeast allowed to warm will produce off odors and a slack and sticky dough that will bake into foul-tasting bread.

EQUIVALENTS BY YEAST TYPE

There is no reason not to switch from one type of yeast to another as long as you account for the different activity levels. For an active fermentation in doughs without sugar, use the following equivalents:

Compressed yeast: For every 1 cup (5.3 ounces, 150 grams) flour in your recipe, use ⅙ cake (0.1 ounce, 3 grams) compressed yeast. One 0.6-ounce cake compressed yeast will ferment about 6 cups (32 ounces, 900 grams) flour.

Active dry yeast: For every 1 cup (5.3 ounces, 150 grams) flour in your recipe, use ½ teaspoon (0.05 ounce, 2 grams) active dry yeast. One ¼-ounce envelope active dry yeast will ferment about 4⅔ cups (25 ounces, 700 grams) flour.

Instant active dry yeast: For every 1 cup (5.3 ounces, 150 grams) flour in your recipe, use ⅓ teaspoon—that is, a heaping ¼ teaspoon or ¼ teaspoon plus ⅛ teaspoon—(0.04 ounce, 1 gram) instant active dry yeast. One ¼-ounce envelope instant active dry yeast will ferment about 6 cups (32 ounces, 900 grams) flour.

PROOFING VERSUS REHYDRATING

I never proof my yeast, but I often rehydrate it. What is the difference? When you proof yeast, you add sugar while rehydrating it, causing the mixture to foam up as the yeast begins to ferment the sugar. This is a good step for beginners who wonder if the yeast is truly active, but it is totally unnecessary if the yeast has been properly stored and has not exceeded its expiration date. When you rehydrate yeast, you are simply soaking the yeast in water—no sugar—to activate it—105°F water for instant yeast or 105° to 110°F water for active dry yeast. I often rehydrate instant yeast if a recipe is particularly low in water, as many sweet doughs are, or to allow me to portion off a very small quantity of yeast.

EQUIPMENT

To make good bread, hardly any equipment is necessary and most of it can be improvised as long as you have a reasonably well-equipped baker's kitchen that includes baking sheets, loaf pans, wooden spoons, rubber spatulas, hot pads, dry and liquid measures, cooling racks, and a large bowl or two (stainless-steel bowls are particularly nice because they are so light and easy to clean). A heavy-duty, large-capacity food processor or stand mixer is optional in most recipes but really can lighten your load.

Committed bread bakers may want to add the following pieces of specialized bread-baking equipment:

A NOTE ABOUT MEASURING SPOONS

Measuring spoons vary significantly from one brand to another; that is, one's 1 teaspoon is another's 1¼ teaspoons. The only way to be certain that your measurements are accurate is to weigh your ingredients. The biggest problem I have found has been with salt. The inaccuracies can make bread taste either too salty or too pallid, so if you are having such results, consider that your measuring spoons might be the culprits. I have found an excellent set of stainless steel measuring spoons available in some high-end kitchenware stores. "Endurance" measuring spoons, made in China, are truly and correctly calibrated, meaning that the tablespoon measures 15 ml, the teaspoon 5 ml, etc. Additionally, they have narrow scoops, so they fit easily into spice jars, and have a good, heavy feel (see Sources, page 222).

Baking Stone

A large baking stone that fits into your oven, leaving a 2- to 3-inch gap for airflow on all sides, is an essential piece of equipment. The preheated stone delivers an immediate jolt of heat to your bread, allowing it the best possible oven spring, and then continues to offer slow, even heat throughout the bake for a crunchy, not burned, crust, even at very high temperatures. Look for a thick rectangular stone or go to a marble fabrication store and bargain for a scrap of untreated marble, granite, or slate, cut to size (these are often treated with sealers, which are toxic, so be sure to ask). Hint: Baking stones can be cleaned in the cleaning cycle of your oven.

Kitchen Scale

This invaluable piece of equipment will help you to perfect and streamline your ingredient measuring. Home bakers often blame the weather for dough variations (the dough is sticky, so it must be too humid), but inaccurate measuring is usually the cause. I would recommend an electronic scale with a calibration of 0.1 ounce and 1 gram and a capacity of at least 80 ounces or 2,000 grams. Spring scales are either finely calibrated with small capacities or coarsely calibrated with large capacities, neither of which is very useful for bread baking.

Ball-bearing Rolling Pin

If you love making sweet yeast doughs, a solid-wood ball-bearing rolling pin at least 15 inches long is indispensable for rolling out the often-resistant doughs. While French pins may be great for short pastry doughs, this workhorse transfers your strength directly to the dough for smooth, even sheeting.

Bencher, a.k.a. dough scraper, pastry scraper, bench knife

This is an incredibly handy piece of equipment; if you buy one, you will wonder how you ever got along without it. It aids in moving and kneading very slack doughs, cleanly cuts dough, incises decorative marks, and even cleans your work surface. It should be made of a heavy metal and have good sharp corners and a comfortable handle. If you are really concerned about kitchen hygiene, use one made of a single piece of metal.

Hint: To clean off a really messy countertop after kneading one of the very wet doughs, wet down the area by squeezing a spongeful of water over it, then evenly distribute the water with your hands. Let soak for about 10 minutes, or until the dough debris gets really loose; then scrape off the mess with a bencher and wipe it clean with a sponge.

Single-edged Razors

Buy these at an art supply store for slashing and decoratively marking breads before they are baked.

Plant Mister and Pressurized Garden Sprayer

Moistening dough with a plant mister before it is baked will create a somewhat shiny, very well opened crust. A pressurized garden sprayer will provide an even deeper shine.

Proofing Baskets, a.k.a. Bannetons

These are woven or coiled willow baskets used to support shaped dough as it proofs. Some are lined with the same raw linen used for couches, while others are unlined and meant to imprint a pattern on the dough. The French and German baskets can be incredibly expensive, and really one of the last purchases a home baker should make, but there is no reason why you couldn't make your own. If you lack a banneton, you can line a basket or colander with a floured tea towel, or, better yet, a piece of couche material, for round loaves; for long loaves, just use a couche. Baker Kathleen Weber of Della Fattoria buys plastic chips baskets (the sort used in Mexican restaurants for serving tortilla chips) at restaurant supply stores and swears they are just as nonstick and even easier to care for than the imported baskets. She leaves them unlined.

Couche

Couche means "layer" in French (also "diaper," but not in this sense) and refers to the heavy raw-linen cloth used to support freestanding breads, such as rolls and baguettes, as they are proofing. Unlike cotton tea towels or burlap, the heavy raw linen is nonstick, even if unfloured, because it wicks away moisture from the surface of the dough, creating a thin, elastic skin while preventing crusting. Its stiffness also helps to shore up spreading doughs. To care for the cloth, just shake it out well after each bake and hang it up to dry thoroughly. (I don't believe these ever get washed in bakeries, only replaced.) You can buy either the same cloth used by professional bakers (see Sources, page 222), or raw linen at a fabric store, which will be nonstick but lack the heft of the professional cloth.

Peel

If you are a baking hobbyist, you may want to buy a short-handled peel to load proofed dough onto a hot baking stone just for the fun of it. However, any flat light, rimless baking sheet will do the job just as well. As an alternative to the very expensive peels sold in upscale kitchenware catalogs, try the fiberboard pizza peels available at kitchen supply stores.

WOODEN FLIPPING BOARDS

If you are a frequent baguette maker, you will want this thin, light, narrow board to extract proofed baguettes from the folds of the couche, transfer them onto the peel, and straighten them. Most professional bakers cover their boards with a sheath of pantyhose to prevent the dough from sticking (see Sources, page 222).

A Note About Bread Machines

I have tested some of these recipes in a Zojirushi bread machine, which was lent to me by the company. I found it to be a great mixing and fermenting tool, although somewhat hampering because of its small capacity. I found I could easily program this machine to mix a bread dough for as long as I wanted, then to hold it—really very convenient. I retrieved the dough to turn it, if necessary, and to shape it, then baked it in my oven. Because all the breads in this book are hand shaped, I never used it to bake the bread. While I wouldn't buy a bread machine just for this purpose, you can use it as long as you cut down recipes to fit the machine's capacity.

TECHNIQUES

The techniques presented here are either professional techniques learned directly in the bakeshop or at seminars, or modifications and tricks that will allow you to make the best bread you possibly can. The best advice to help improve your baking is to pay attention and to try to remember exactly what you did at each step along the way. Take notes. Then, as you evaluate your breads, connect the dots from your baking technique to the result. Dough has an incredible memory, and everything you do to it will show up in the finished bread. For bread baking especially, God is in the details.

Measuring Ingredients

I strenuously recommend weighing your ingredients to be sure you are measuring accurately. Flour is especially important to weigh, as is the salt if you are not using table salt. Not only is weighing more accurate, but also easier, cleaner, and faster, especially for larger quantities.

However, if you are measuring by volume, know that these recipes are based on the dip-and-sweep measuring technique. To dip and sweep, scoop up the ingredient with your measuring cup or spoon, heaping it up with more than you need, then sweep off the excess with a metal spatula or the back of a knife. When measuring flour, do not stir it or spoon it into the measuring cup; your measurements will be too light.

Increasing or Decreasing the Recipe's Yield

I have based almost every recipe's yield on the maximum amount of dough that can fit in an ordinary home oven without overcrowding. However, you can increase or decrease the yield by doubling, tripling, halving the ingredients, (also see About Baker's Percentages, page 6).

Resting

Some recipes call for a resting period or autolyse in the middle of mixing. During this time, you quickly combine the recipe's flour and water and let this rough dough sit covered with plastic wrap for 15 minutes to 1 hour. After the rest, add the salt, yeast, pre-ferments, and any other ingredients and finish kneading.

Making Pre-ferments

Pre-ferments, often called sponges or starters, are partial doughs made of flour, water, yeast, and sometimes salt that are quickly mixed and allowed to ferment, often overnight, prior to mixing the main dough (see pages 101–107).

A very choppy and craggy-looking dough before the autolyse

A dough after autolyse; notice how smooth and extensible it has become.

AUTOLYSE, a.k.a. RESTING

The term "autolyse" (pronounced AUTO-lees and used as both noun and verb) was adopted by Professor Raymond Calvel, the esteemed French bread-baking teacher and inventor of this somewhat odd but very effective technique. During the rest time, the flour fully hydrates and its gluten further develops, encouraged by the absence of: compressed yeast, which would begin to ferment and acidify the dough (although instant yeast is included in autolyses lasting no longer than 30 minutes because of its slow activation); salt, which would cause the gluten to tighten, hindering its development and hydration; and pre-ferments (see pages 101–107), which would also acidify the dough. The flour's improved hydration and gluten development shorten the mixing time, increase extensibility (the dough rips less during shaping), and ultimately result in bread with a creamier colored crumb and more aroma and sweet wheat flavor.

At the end of the autolyse, the once-rough dough will have greatly smoothed out and become much more extensible. Salt, compressed yeast, and pre-ferments are now added and the mixing is continued. While it may seem strange to add salt directly to a dough, as long as it is finely granulated, it will quickly dissolve. If you are hand kneading, you can actually feel the dough tighten and dry when the salt dissolves.

(I often use Diamond kosher salt and have no trouble with it dissolving.)

Here is the technical explanation of what's happening during autolyse: The term "autolyse" means "self-destruction," referring to the proteolytic—or protein-attacking—enzymes that Professor Calvel believes help to break down the gluten during this hiatus. While it might seem contradictory to want to dismember gluten when it is supposed to be developing, it is, in fact, one of mixing's primary steps. When gluten first forms, it is jumbled together in an uneven manner. During mixing, the gluten is pulled apart and rebonded into a stronger and more uniform network. The autolyse facilitates that step without mechanically altering the dough. The reason acid-producing ingredients like pre-ferments and compressed yeast are avoided is because these proteolytic enzymes work more effectively in a more neutral pH environment.

Finally, the bread's color and flavor are improved because the dough is mixed less, so that less air is beaten into it and, thus, less oxygen. Oxygen is believed to oxidize the flour's unsaturated fats and bleach its yellow pigments. The fats are a source of vitamin E and an important source of flavor. Oxidizing them destroys their vitamin E content and unpleasantly alters the flavor of the bread.

mixing and kneading

"Mixing" is the professional term for kneading and not really a separate step, although in home-baking parlance, bread dough is first "mixed" and then kneaded.

Mixing by Hand Kneading dough by hand is the reason many people bake—it is such a peaceful and productive activity. The best surface to knead on is one that is easily cleaned and the same height as your palms with your arms extended straight down. Countertops are about right, if slightly too high for most of us, while most tables are too low, causing you to hunch over your work and strain your lower back.

To knead dough in the traditional manner, *use no extra flour;* instead use a bencher or a metal spatula to help maneuver the dough. (Extra flour will not only coat the dough, preventing you from feeling it properly, but will also stiffen it.) Turn the dough out onto your work surface. Using a bencher if necessary, fold the dough topside down, digging the heels of your hands into the dough. Give the dough a push to seal the fold. Again using a bencher if necessary, rotate the dough a quarter turn and repeat the folding and sealing. Continue to fold, seal, and turn the dough until it is very smooth and shiny.

The key to kneading very wet doughs without being entrapped by them is to handle the dough very quickly, almost flinging it from your hands after each contact. This takes some practice but is worth mastering.

Traditional kneading: LEFT, fold the dough down into the center. RIGHT, give the dough a push to seal it.

A FRENCH KNEADING TECHNIQUE

If you are an experienced baker, you may be interested in learning a kneading technique for soft doughs (it does not work on very firm doughs) taught to me by Lionel Vatinet, a French master baker and former teacher at the San Francisco Baking Institute who is now co-owner of La Farm Bakery in Cary, North Carolina. Lionel had to learn how to hand knead very large doughs as part of his apprenticeship, and this is the technique he was taught. It does require some practice to master and is definitely not for the beginner, but it is an extremely efficient (and fun) way to mix dough and, once conquered, will allow you to knead even large batches of dough much more quickly and thoroughly than by the traditional method.

Turn the dough out onto the work surface, again using no extra flour, and pick up the end closest to you. Grasping the dough with both hands, squeeze it through your thumbs and fingers, making two opposing holes. Release the dough with a quick flicking

Lionel's kneading: LEFT, squeeze the dough through your thumb and forefingers to make two opposing holes. RIGHT, fold the near end of the dough over the far end to create a smooth surface.

motion and move up the dough, making another set of opposing holes. The quick release prevents the dough from sticking to your hands but is the hardest part to master. Continue moving up the dough, hole punching all the way to the top. (You will notice what a workout it gives your hands!) Now hold the closest end of the dough with both hands and fling its far end onto the work surface. Fold the close end over the far end, folding away from you, to form a (hopefully) smooth surface over the dough. Fling and fold the dough a few more times, or until it is smooth again. Now hole punch the dough, making a set of opposing holes up the length of the dough again. Repeat the hole punching and flinging until the dough is very smooth and strong. (Strange as it seems, squeezing the dough is what actually develops the dough. The flinging just gives you a clean slate.)

Mixing in a Large-Capacity Food Processor The food processor is excellent for mixing firm to moderately soft doughs; its most serious drawback is the size of the batches it can handle. If a recipe is too large for your processor, you can first mix the ingredients together in a bowl, then process the dough in batches. Be sure to fit the processor with the steel blade and not the plastic so-called dough blade (which doesn't seem to work).

Food processors quickly overheat dough during processing (due to the friction of the dough spinning in the workbowl at very high speed), making it feel hot and runny. Such dough is just hot, and rarely overmixed, as other food writers have imagined; it will quickly firm up once it has cooled. (Not until dough is heated past 115°F, which is really hot, will it be irreversibly damaged.) To prevent overheating but still thoroughly develop the dough, I recommend processing the dough at intervals, removing it from the workbowl between intervals, and hand kneading it on the work surface until it cools down and firms up. This sequence might seem rather labor intensive, but it is still faster than doing it by hand or in a stand mixer.

Very wet doughs will creep under the sleeve of the blade and gum it up before becoming fully mixed, so I don't recommend putting them in a processor. Hint: If you do end up with dough in the sleeve of the blade, remove it from the workbowl (this will be difficult), immediately fill it with vinegar, and scrape a skewer around in it to loosen the dough. Let it sit for about 30 minutes, then flush it out with warm water.

Mixing in a Stand Mixer Almost every recipe has separate stand mixer instructions, so I will not elaborate much here. I tested these recipes in my KitchenAid KSM5 with great success, but occasionally my tester, Rita Yeazel, who owns a lighter KitchenAid, had trouble with the mixer rocking. Placing the mixer on a towel helps, as does just leaning on the machine. In general, the dough hook is preferable for mixing, but it doesn't pick up all doughs. In that case, switch to the paddle and increase the mixing speed to help fling the dough off the paddle so the dough doesn't end up just spinning around on the paddle.

MAKING A GLUTEN WINDOW

How can you tell how developed your dough is? Many professionals can judge just by looking at the dough, but others will grab a piece of dough and make a gluten window with it. To do this, take a small fistful of dough and stretch it out between your fingers. If the dough rips into thick strands, it is barely developed. If it forms a lumpy sheet that rips easily, the dough is moderately developed. If it forms a smooth, even, translucent sheet without ripping, the dough is highly developed. All doughs can and should be highly developed. But a highly developed dough is not created just in the mixing, for the longer a dough is mixed, the more oxygen is incorporated, which bleaches the flour's color and destroys the wheat's flavor. Many bakers will mix a dough just to moderate development, then give the dough a full fermentation and several turns (see page 16) to complete the development.

A very soft dough

A soft dough

A firm dough

ADJUSTING THE DOUGH'S CONSISTENCY

The dough's appearance and texture will tell you all you need to know about its consistency. A **firm dough** should sit up in a high, pert mound, and not be sticky but stick to itself if folded in half. A **soft dough** should spread out in a low mound and readily stick to your hands and to itself when folded in half. A **very soft dough** should spread into a flat pancake and be extremely sticky.

A number of factors could cause your dough's consistency to deviate from what is described in the recipes. Flour loses moisture as it ages, so that older flour, or flour stored on a warm shelf, will absorb more water, creating a stiffer dough. If you have not accurately measured ingredients (see Measuring Ingredients, page 11), your dough's consistency may be off. Home bakers usually make doughs that are too dry, but kneading in a tablespoon or two of water usually will be enough to restore the dough's consistency.

More developed doughs, that is, doughs mixed for a longer time or more intensely, are drier even if they are very wet to begin with. If your dough seems too wet and sticky, rather than add more flour, you might just need to mix it longer, or preferably give it an extra turn or two (see page 16).

To improve your consistency judgment, make a mental note about how the dough feels at the end of kneading, then compare that with the finished bread. If the crumb of your bread is tightly grained, with small air cells, and the loaf sits up high, the dough was too dry; next time add more liquid. On the other hand, if the bread is flat and spread out, with poorly opened, flat cuts, and thick-walled air cells, the dough was underdeveloped; next time allow the dough to ferment fully and turn the dough a few extra times during fermentation.

Retarding or Refrigerating the Shaped Dough to Bake Later

Sometimes you may run into a time, energy, or attention jam and need to put your baking on hold. A great way to stop your bread making is to refrigerate your dough immediately after shaping it and placing it either on a board, pan, basket, or couche. This is done by carefully wrapping the just-shaped dough in plastic wrap to prevent crusting, and placing it in the refrigerator for up to 12 hours. When you are ready to bake again, take the dough out and allow it an hour or two to warm up to room temperature. Then finish proofing and baking the dough as usual.

This works because, in the cold, the enzyme activity is greatly reduced, so the dough ferments at a very slow rate. However, as the dough chills, it does pass through the 50° and 60°F temperature range, which is optimal for acetic acid production. Therefore, doughs that have been chilled taste more acidic than those that have been proofed at room temperature and will often have many blisters on their crusts. This increased acidity is a good thing for some breads and bad for others (sourdoughs, especially, can become almost unbearably sour).

Fermenting

"Fermenting" is the professional term for what home bakers often call the "first rise." Professionals use the term "fermentation" to distinguish this rising period from the one after the dough is shaped, which home bakers call the "second rise" and professionals call the "proof."

Doughs can be fermented at any temperature from 33° to 105°F. At lower temperatures the fermentation will be extremely slow and much acetic acid will form, causing a sour flavor. At very high temperatures the dough will ferment very quickly and off-flavors will be produced. All these recipes were tested at about 75°F, which is a temperature that works especially well for sourdough-based breads (we happened to test in the summer, so this was the ambient temperature). Fermentation and proofing temperatures between 72° and 85°F are ideal. In the winter, when many homes are kept at 68°F, you may need to find a warmer place to ferment and proof your bread if you want it in the time given in the recipe. A good warm place is in a closed oven with a pan of hot, not boiling, water. A heating pad set at low and wrapped in towels is another possibility. I have heard of people fermenting dough on a water heater but have never tried it myself. You *can* ferment your doughs at colder temperatures; they will ferment fully but more slowly than indicated, and sourdough-based breads will ferment especially sluggishly.

The fermentation is complete when the dough has risen to about double its former size, is full of carbon dioxide, and is still bouncy when pressed and *not* at the point of collapsing. You want the dough to be resilient enough to retain its airy structure during shaping. Underfermenting is always better than overfermenting.

Turning

This is the term preferred by professionals for a step more commonly known as "punching down the dough." Its purpose is not to degas the dough but to develop the gluten by folding the dough. Professional bakers turn their doughs to minimize the amount of mixing necessary, while still achieving really thorough gluten development. (Excessive mixing bleaches the flour's color and degrades the flavor; see Autolyse, page 12.)

The dough can be turned from one to five times during fermentation, but figure that the dough will need at least 15 minutes between turns and about 30 minutes after the last one to relax adequately before being shaped.

To turn the dough, sprinkle the top of the dough and the work surface with flour, then scrape the dough out of its rising container and onto the floured work surface. Sprinkle the dough with flour again, then gently spread the dough out, trying not to deflate bubbles. Fold it up into a tight bundle by folding the left side into the center, followed by the top, the right side, and the bottom. Turn the dough over so that the smooth side is up, and fold it in half again if it still feels loose. Place it, smooth side up, back into the rising container, and cover it tightly.

Flouring the Work Surface

If you want to flour like a real pro, take a handful of flour, holding it in your fist, and, as if you were skipping stones on a lake, open up your index finger and shoot the flour horizontally over the work surface. You are aiming for a very light, even veil of flour in the way that professional bakers flour even large areas.

Dividing the Dough

Dividing means to cut the dough into pieces of the correct weight with a bencher. Many of the more practiced professionals divide their doughs by cutting them into correctly sized pieces the first time (practice makes perfect), thereby avoiding hacking the dough into little pieces and destroying its texture, then checking the weight on a balance scale (by the speed of the platform's

LEFT TO RIGHT: A very soft dough, fully kneaded and ready to ferment; turning the dough by folding it into a square; turned dough that has tightened and smoothed.

fall). At home, only perfectionists like me need to weigh out each dough piece. Rolls, however, do look very professional when sized (and weighed) identically.

Rounding and Resting

After the dough is divided, the dough pieces need to be rounded to surround them with a smooth dry skin, which prevents the loss of gas and prepares the dough to be shaped. Turn the dough piece skin side up (this is the dry, smooth side), tucking any extra dough pieces underneath; using your hands to cup and pull the dough, push under the raw edges to create a smooth, slightly taut skin all around the dough piece. Dough to be shaped into a round should be left like this, but dough to be shaped into a long loaf should then be nudged into a fat log shape by pushing against one side. The rounded pieces are then allowed to rest for 15 to 30 minutes, until they are again filling up with carbon dioxide and are very soft and extensible. In bakeries, this resting step tends to evaporate because, by the time the last pieces in a batch have been cut and rounded, the first pieces have already had their rest. At home, however, a conscientious effort must be made to allow the dough an adequate rest period so it will not rip during shaping.

Shaping

Artisan-style breads frequently require considerable skill to shape, which only practice will gain. Some of the best bakers I know consider themselves to have grown rusty when they are not baking daily. Luckily, even if your bread doesn't look like the pictured bread, it will taste just as good.

Instructions for individual shapes are included in each recipe. Instructions to form additional French shapes are detailed on pages 34–35.

Arranging a Couche for Rolls, Baguettes, or Bâtards

To arrange the couche, use a tray with high sides or a large baking sheet as a base, so that you can move the proofing breads around if you need to. Then, roll up one side of the couche, leaving the selvage edges on either side. Place a baguette, bâtard, or row of rolls against the roll and fold up the free end of the couche to more than double the height of the dough. This fold will keep the dough in each valley separate from its neighbor even after it is fully proofed and prevent any plastic wrap from touching the dough. Continue to fill and fold the couche until you run out of dough, then roll up the remaining fabric. Both ends of the couche should be supported by the baking sheet or tray to prevent the couche from unrolling. Drape the folded couche with plastic wrap and set it in a warm area to proof.

Proofing

Professionals often proof bread in "proofer-retarders," which look like big computerized refrigerators; they first chill the dough to slow the proof, then slowly warm it up to get it ready for baking. The long cold proof creates a lot of acidity, leading to large blisters on the crust, which many consider to be a flaw. At home, I think it's best to proof most breads in a warm area, ideally between 75° and 85°F.

Judging a full proof is another difficulty for beginning bakers. In general, a dough that underwent a short proof will expand more and open its cuts more during baking than a dough that underwent a long proof. However, you do not want the dough expanding wildly or remaining too tight to fully open, so it is important to proof the bread long enough. But even worse than underproofing is overproofing. Although the dough might not collapse in the oven, it will open lethargically if at all, be paler, and contain odd tastes from the excessive fermentation.

Generally, you can use a "press test" and your eyes to check the proof of your bread. For the press test, lightly flour your index finger, then gently press it against the dough. If you have just shaped it, the indentation should pop back into shape immediately. The more proofed your dough is, the more slowly the indentation will spring back. If you have not shaped your dough very tightly, you will probably want to proof it for less time to get more of a jump in the oven. In this case, your dough will be ready to bake when it looks well risen but still springs back pretty quickly. If you are a very fine shaper, you can let your dough proof much longer. Your dough will be ready to bake when it is very well expanded and the indentation almost remains.

Removing Breads from Proofing Baskets

Dough can seem very recalcitrant if you are trying to remove it from a proofing basket, especially a sourdough that has been proofing for a long time. If the basket is linen-lined, the dough *will* release if, while holding the basket upside down, you gently work your fingers between the dough and the basket, nudging the dough with your fingers. If a bit of the dough sticks, or pulls excessively as it releases, don't worry about it; just reshape the dough as best as you can. Removing dough from baskets with tea towel or cotton liners is difficult, so remember to use enough dusting flour.

Doubling Baking Sheets

Baking on doubled baking sheets goes a long way to prevent scorching, especially with doughs containing a lot of sugar. A more expensive but equally effective alternative is to use insulated baking sheets.

Misting the Bread to Create Steam

Creating steam in the oven seems to be every amateur baker's dream. Steam slows crust formation, allowing for the best possible oven spring and gelatinizing the starch on the surface of the bread to create a thin, glossy crust. However, achieving this requires steam under pressure, which is impossible in home ovens. I would just like to point out that bread baked in old-fashioned brick ovens, like the one in which I got to bake in the mountains of Auvergne, comes out matte, with no shine at all—a truly rustic look.

The easiest way to create a somewhat shiny but well-opened crust is to mist the dough or paint it with water *just before* it is peeled onto a hot baking stone. The business of repeated mistings once the bread is in the oven is a waste of effort and precious heat (at least 50°F each time the door is opened).

Using a Pressurized Garden Sprayer to Create Steam

For a higher shine, Atlanta baker Lynne Sawicki, who helped me with a portion of the testing, discovered that pressurized garden sprayers fill the oven with more steam than any other nonprofessional method. Just before loading the bread into the oven, barely crack open the door (to minimize heat loss), insert the spray nozzle, and pump in mist for about 30 seconds or until the oven is so full of steam that it is escaping out the door.

Slashing

Many breads are slashed with a single-edged razor before they are baked. This slash not only is decorative but also helps the bread to expand fully and evenly, improving the bread's crumb structure and ensuring that the bread expands symmetrically. A little trivia: The inside portion of the cut, which is webbed and often paler than the rest of the crust, has a name— grigne (green-YIH).

Long slashes across long breads are usually made about ¼ inch deep with the razor held at an angle to the dough, about 30°, creating more of a flap under the skin of the dough than a gash straight into the dough. On round breads, the razor is often held vertically, although not always (see Della Fattoria's Polenta Bread, page 118). Take your time making slashes; they need not be done with professional speed. If you feel that a slash is not deep enough, just go over it again until you are pleased with it.

Peeling the Bread onto the Hot Baking Stone

To transfer proofed bread to the hot baking stone, use a peel or any rimless, lightweight board. Gently set the proofed bread directly on the well-floured peel and jerk it onto the hot stone. If it was proofed on parchment paper, slide it in *paper and all* (the paper will not ignite!). If you would feel more comfortable, use hot pads and pull the stone out about halfway before peeling the bread (but you tend to lose more oven heat this way).

Baking

In the recipes, I have specified the shelf height at which to bake your breads. The point is to provide even top and bottom heat to the bread for even coloration. Generally, you want to get the breads as high in the oven as possible, so shorter breads can be baked at higher positions than taller ones. If your bread is browning unevenly—your oven and baking stone are, after all, different from mine—move the bread up a shelf if the bottom is browning too quickly, or down a shelf if the top is browning too quickly. The exception is bread baked in pans or molds, which I find are always best baked on the bottom shelf, no matter how tall or short they are, to ensure adequate bottom browning.

I tested these breads in an electric oven; if yours is gas, you might need to lower the oven rack by one rung to get an even bake. Be sure to rotate your breads from front to back and side to side once during the baking to ensure even coloring. All home ovens will be hotter in the back and some even on one side.

If your baking times are very different from mine, check your oven temperatures with a reliable oven thermometer.

Finally, most bakers, not just home bakers, under-bake their bread. Professor Calvel once told me—eyes twinkling—that it is impossible to overbake bread. While he may have been exaggerating just a teensy bit, he made his point. As long as your oven temperature is correct and you are using a baking stone, it *is* very difficult to overbake bread.

A good portion of bread flavor comes from the chemical reactions taking place in the crust. Underbaked bread will taste insipid, even if fortified with the best pre-ferments and crafted with the best techniques. On the other hand, really plain bread dough can be redeemed by an intense bake. I would just advise new bakers to bake the bread until you judge it to be done, then give it 5 more minutes!

Cooling the Bread

Allow the baked bread to cool on a rack or in a spot that allows good air circulation. It will be releasing plenty of steam, and you do not want it recondensing on the crust, destroying its brittleness. Let the bread cool completely before slicing it.

Slicing the Bread

If you have worked hard to achieve a beautiful, open texture, do show it off by slicing the bread, not ripping it, when you offer it at a meal.

Storing the Bread

I store fresh bread at room temperature for only one day. I set it unwrapped and cut end down on the bread board in my second, and rarely used, oven. A breadbox is an excellent alternative. When I lived with a family

in France, they kept their daily bread in a muslin bag, hanging on the kitchen door, replenishing it every morning after breakfast when my French mother went marketing. Most breads are at their best at room temperature for only a day, although some of the whole-grain sourdough breads will last for a few days. The biggest danger of keeping bread at room temperature for more than a day is mold.

For longer storage, I wrap bread in a plastic bag, using Hefty brand Baggies (these don't seem to impart an off-flavor to the bread, which other brands of plastic bags do, especially the heavy Ziploc bags) and refrigerate it. The bread does become firmer in the cold but is quickly revived in the toaster or the oven. It will not get moldy, however, and will keep in stable condition for a week.

For even longer storage, the freezer will keep breads in good shape for a month or two. The biggest danger is in it picking up odors from the freezer or wrapping and in the constant fluctuation of temperature, which frequently opening and closing the freezer door will cause. Wrap the bread first in a Baggie, sealing it well, then in large Ziploc freezer bags. I sometimes slice the bread, especially bialys or sandwich bread, first, and then pull out just what I need. Store the bread in the back of the freezer, away from the door.

BREADS BY CATEGORY

Breads on display behind the counter at The Acme Bread Company

STARTING WITH

STRAIGHT GRADE

R2 R3

ORGANIC

FLOUR

Flour

BS. (22.68 kg)

OUR MILLING L.L.C.

eville, Colorado 80651

1110

FAX: (970) 785-0575

R4

ROC
40

R5

Samples showing colors of flours produced by Rocky Mountain Milling. R2 is the very light, almost bran-free flour of the first set of breaking rolls. R3 is from the second set. Markedly darker are R4 and R5, bran-laden flours from the end-of-the-line rolls. Straight grade is a mixture of R2 to R5.

THE SOUL
OF BREAD

THE ACME BREAD COMPANY

BERKELEY, CALIFORNIA

FLOUR MUST SEEM LIKE BREAD'S MOST BANAL INGREDIENT—just a bag of dusty, off-white processed wheat—but flour is to bread what grapes are to wine and milk is to cheese. Flour is not only bread's backbone, but also its heart and soul.

If you want to know a bakery, buy a baguette, for every twitch of the baker's hand and every nuance of the flour is manifested in the finished bread. One of my favorite baguettes is baked at The Acme Bread Company in Berkeley, California. Founded in 1983 by Steve and Susan Sullivan, this bakery is a mecca for serious bread lovers from around the world. Their Rustic Baguette has a soft, creamy-yellow crumb almost frothy with huge gas cells, and a lightly floured crust that is brittle eggshell thin. Its flavor is pure sweet wheat, with just enough acidity to open all the flavor notes.

I spent one morning shuttling between Acme Division I, "Div. I," where I ducked around the tiny crowded bakery watching Rustic Baguettes being made, and Acme Division II, "Div. II," observing the making of Herb Slabs, a focaccialike flatbread with a butter-yellow crumb flecked with chopped fresh rosemary. In between and afterward, I got to interview Rick Kirkby, the vice-president/production manager for all three Acme facilities, responsible for quality control and recipe development, and to discuss Acme's almost quixotic pursuit of fine flour.

So what about a flour might make it superb, or even terrible? The answer involves two separate elements—function and aesthetics—about which I will attempt a simplified discourse.

Concerning function, gluten is the key. Gluten is derived from a special combination of proteins found only in wheat that happen to link up into a 3-D web or network when moistened. Possessing a quality that scientists call viscoelasticity, gluten exhibits both viscous flow (it will spread all over a table and on down to the floor if allowed) and elasticity (if not stretched too far, it will spring back into its original shape). So gluten can flow into a new shape or snap back into its old, depending on how it is handled.

Steve and Susan Sullivan, who founded The Acme Bread Company in 1983

This network of gluten forms when flour is mixed with water. At the same time, air is being beaten and squeezed into the dough in minuscule air bubbles. When the dough is fully mixed, the tangle of gluten makes it very difficult for the air bubbles to rise to the top of the dough and escape, as they would in a gluten-free cornmeal batter, for example. During fermentation, yeast releases carbon dioxide (as well as a few other byproducts), which dissolves into the liquid portion of the dough. Eventually the carbon dioxide saturates this liquid and evolves into the trapped air bubbles (and out of the dough completely). The air bubbles expand, and the gluten accommodates them, stretching around them, allowing the dough to be leavened. The ability of wheat protein to link or bond into a viscoelastic network and, hence, to leaven bread, is one of nature's great miracles and mysteries.

While this simplified model of gluten's activity sounds predictable, in everyday production, bakers meet many variations. Gluten is not a uniform substance, and neither is the dough that is created. Bakers use many different terms to describe different characteristics. For example, some gluten is "tough," meaning that the dough takes a long time to mix and is difficult to stretch out. Some gluten is "extensible," meaning that the dough will stretch out beautifully during shaping without ripping. Some gluten loses extensibility as the dough ferments, making the dough "bucky," meaning that it will rip during shaping.

What causes the variability? Gluten can be made up of many different proteins, and its quality—that is, its tenacity, extensibility, its volume potential, and so on—depends on the particular assortment of proteins present in any given flour. Different wheat varieties develop specific assortments of proteins, and weather and growing conditions, such as irrigation and fertilization, heavily influence the gluten's protein quality. The blend of wheat varieties in a given flour and how those wheats were grown also affect the flour's behavior in a dough.

TOP TO BOTTOM: A worker turning fermenting dough inside tubs; Acme vice-president Rick Kirkby; placing proofed rolls on an oven loader. RIGHT: A close-up on the dough showing its creamy yellow color and long strands of gluten.

ASH

Flour color is often gauged by its percentage of ash. This ash is not actual ash in the flour but rather the ash that remains after a controlled burn of a sample of the flour, representing minerals that resisted combustion. Most of wheat's minerals are concentrated in the bran and germ layers, so this procedure tells something about how much bran and germ are left in a flour after milling. Rich in oils, amino acids, nongluten-forming proteins, enzymes, and sugars, the bran and germ greatly contribute to the flour's taste, color, and aroma. The vast taste differences between white and whole-wheat bread illustrate it best. The straight-grade flours Rick Kirkby uses typically have higher ash percentages; he asks for an ash content between 0.55% and 0.65%. By comparison, a patent flour might have an ash content of around 0.45%, and whole-wheat flour an ash content of around 1.5%.

Acme's Rustic Baguettes (page 30), whole and sliced, showing their exquisite crumb structure

So how can bakers like Rick be assured that a flour possesses the qualities they desire? For the most part, they can't. They can only roughly indicate their perfect flour by specifying to their miller or flour distributor the range of percentages of protein and results from laboratory tests.

Protein percentage is a fairly crude way to describe a flour, because it only describes the amount of protein and not its quality, but it does provide a ballpark estimate of the flour's quality. Rick says that flour with a range of 11% to 11.5% protein is safe, but flour with more than 12% protein creates problems. For artisan bakers, 11% to 11.5% protein is the most frequently specified range, and most of the bakers included in this book try to stay within it. Home bakers using grocery-store flour have to combine their bread flour, which is too high in protein, with all-purpose flour, which is too low, to get within this range (I have given these proportions in the recipes). A few widely available flours, such as King Arthur all-purpose flour, are already in that protein range.

Yet function is just half the battle. To win the war, a flour will also need pleasing flavor, color, and aroma. Rick looks for flour with a creamy yellow color, as opposed to white or gray; "a very clean, unfettered aroma that's sweet and what I think to be wheatlike"; and flavor that is "sweet and nutty, tasting of the grain." Rick believes that these three attributes—color, flavor, and aroma—are related, and color is the critical component. When the color is dead white, flavor and aroma will be lacking too. He finds that straight-grade flours (flours including all the endosperm), rather than patent flours, tend to possess the best color, flavor, and aroma.

Finding all the functional and aesthetic requirements in one flour is very rare, something like finding a beautiful horse that runs very fast *and* has a sweet disposition. Even if all the baker's wishes come true in one perfect flour, the stroke of midnight comes when the miller runs out of that particular bin of wheat and has to buy more, most likely a different variety grown in a different area, with very different performance characteristics. Part of Rick's mastery is being able to make consistently wonderful bread with a flour palette that is forever in flux.

Acme's Rustic Baguettes

- Makes two 8-ounce (250-gram) mini baguettes and one 1-pound (500-gram) boule or bâtard
- Time: About 18 hours, with about 30 minutes of active work

This recipe uses all the tricks in Acme's bag and contains two separate pre-ferments (see page 103)—a scrap dough or *pâte fermentée,* for acidity, and a poolish for extensibility and wheaty flavor. Acme uses a 4-hour poolish, but I have converted it to a 12-hour poolish to make the schedule more reasonable for home bakers (the original would have required at least a 14-hour baking day!). Acme bakes this dough into baguettes, but at home it makes more sense to make a few different things out of it.

Because real baguettes cannot be made at home—our ovens are not wide enough for their length—I have scaled down the classic to a mini baguette that fits nicely in an ordinary oven. Still, making pretty baguettes is one of the most difficult jobs in all of baking, so expect to put in some practice time.

This is really a gussied-up ordinary French dough, so you could make rolls, *couronnes, boules, bâtards,* or any shape you please with it (see pages 34–35).

RECIPE SYNOPSIS THE EVENING BEFORE BAKING: Mix the scrap dough and let it ferment for about 3 hours at room temperature, then refrigerate it. Mix the poolish and let it ferment overnight for 12 hours. **THE NEXT MORNING:** Mix the final dough, giving it a 15- to 20-minute rest, then let it ferment for 3 hours, giving it 3 or 4 turns. Shape the bread, let it proof for 1 to 2 hours, and then bake it for as long as is appropriate for its size, up to 45 minutes.

	Scrap Dough	volume	weight	metric	baker's percentages
THE EVENING BEFORE BAKING MAKING THE SCRAP DOUGH	**Instant yeast**	¼ teaspoon			(eventually 0.5%)
	Water, 110° to 115°F	½ cup			(eventually 65%)
	Unbleached all-purpose flour, preferably organic	¾ cup	4 ounces	115 grams	100%
	Salt	¼ plus ⅛ teaspoon			2%

Sprinkle the yeast over the warm water in a glass measure, stir, and let it stand for 5 to 10 minutes. Mix the flour and salt in a bowl and add ⅓ cup of the yeasted water (reserve the rest for the poolish). Knead this soft dough until smooth, about 5 minutes. Cover it tightly with plastic wrap. Let it ferment at room temperature for about 3 hours, then refrigerate it until the next morning.

	Poolish	volume	weight	metric	baker's percentages
MAKING THE POOLISH	**Instant yeast**				(eventually 0.07%)
	Unbleached all-purpose flour, preferably organic	1 cup	5.3 ounces	150 grams	100%
	Water, lukewarm	⅔ cup	4.8 ounces	135 grams	(eventually 110%)

Add 1 tablespoon of the yeasted water from the previous step to the flour (to measure $\frac{1}{32}$ teaspoon yeast), then beat in the lukewarm water. This will be a very gloppy batter. Cover the poolish with plastic wrap and let it ferment overnight for 12 hours, or until the bubbles are popping and the top is just starting to wrinkle and foam.

	Dough	volume	weight	metric	baker's percentages
BAKE DAY **MIXING** **THE DOUGH**	**Unbleached all-purpose flour, preferably organic**	2¼ cups	12 ounces	340 grams	100%
	Instant yeast	¼ teaspoon			0.2%
	Water, lukewarm	¾ cup plus 2 tablespoons	6.4 ounces	180 grams	53%
	Fermented poolish				93%
	Fermented scrap dough				55%
	Salt	1¾ teaspoons	0.3 ounce	9 grams	2.7%

by hand: Mix the flour and yeast together in a large bowl. Pour the water into the poolish, stir to loosen it, and pour it into the flour mixture. With a wooden spoon or your hand, mix the dough just until combined. Turn the dough out and knead it a few times just to combine the dough well. Return the dough to the bowl, cover it with plastic wrap, and let it rest (autolyse) for 15 to 20 minutes.

Break up the dough into smaller pieces and add it along with the salt to the autolysed dough. Turn the dough out of the bowl and knead it without adding extra flour but using the dough scaper to help you, until it is smooth and strong, about 10 minutes.

by stand mixer: Mix the flour and yeast together in the mixing bowl. Pour the water into the poolish, stir to loosen it, and pour it into the flour mixture. With a wooden spoon or your hand, mix the dough just until roughly combined. Mix the dough on low speed with the dough hook just until the dough comes together on the hook, about 1 minute. Cover the bowl with plastic wrap and let it rest (autolyse) for 15 to 20 minutes.

Break up the scrap dough into smaller pieces and add it along with the salt to the autolysed dough. Mix the dough on low to medium speed until it is smooth and strong and cleans the bowl, about 10 minutes.

by food processor: Mix the flour, yeast, and salt together in the workbowl. Pour the water into the poolish, stir to loosen it, and pour it into the flour mixture. Process just until the dough comes together, about 30 seconds. Let the dough rest (autolyse) in the workbowl for 15 to 20 minutes.

Break up the scrap dough into smaller pieces and add it to the autolysed dough. Process the dough until the workbowl fogs, about 30 seconds. Remove the dough and knead it by hand to cool the dough and redistribute the heat (use a dough scraper, not extra flour, to help you). Process the dough for 30-second intervals, hand kneading it between intervals, until it is very smooth and strong, 5 or 6 intervals.

The dough should be soft and smooth, slightly dry to the touch, with a very smooth gluten window and with bubbles forming under the surface when it is fully kneaded. Add 1 to 2 tablespoons water if the dough feels too stiff during mixing.

continued

FERMENTING AND TURNING THE DOUGH

Place the dough in a container at least 3 times its size and cover it tightly with plastic wrap. Let it ferment until light and bubbly and about doubled in bulk, about 3 hours. Turn the dough (page 16) 3 times in 20-minute intervals, that is, after 20, 40, and 60 minutes of fermenting. Turn it a fourth time (at 80 minutes) if you think you did not knead the dough enough. Then leave the dough undisturbed for the remaining time.

ROUNDING AND RESTING THE DOUGH

Cut the dough in half, then cut one of the halves in half. Gently round the two quarters for baguettes into stubby cylinders (photograph 1), and the half for a boule into a ball. Lightly sprinkle the pieces with flour and cover them with plastic wrap. Let rest until puffy with gas and very soft, about 30 minutes. Do not skimp on this rest period, for it is one of the keys to successful shaping.

PREHEATING THE OVEN

After the dough has rested, arrange an oven rack on the oven's second-to-top shelf and place a baking stone on it. Clear away all racks above the one being used. Preheat the oven to 450°F (230°C).

SHAPING THE DOUGH

Shaping Acme's Rustic Baguettes is a two-step process, with the dough first shaped into a short cylinder, then stretched out to its full length after a rest. If the following shaping instructions sound difficult, it is because the baguette is the hardest shape to master, and I have gone into as much detail as possible so that you can get it right. Remember that this whole sequence takes just a minute or two.

The trick to this shape is to handle the dough "gently but meaningfully," in Rick's words, so that you have not pressed out all the air bubbles or made it too long and still have a tight, very even cylinder. This can take months of practice, but don't despair; whatever you make will taste wonderful.

Heavily coat a cookie sheet or a wooden proofing board with a sifting of flour, and lightly coat your work surface. It's good to have a ruler or even your baking stone nearby so that you can keep track of the length of your baguette.

For the first step of the shaping, take one of the rested pieces of dough for baguettes and place it *skin side down* on the lightly floured work surface. Lightly flatten out the dough into a vaguely rectangular shape, pressing very gently to preserve the bubbles. Fold the bottom long edge up just past the middle of the dough (photographs 2 and 3), then fold the top edge down to the middle. You should now have a rectangular piece of dough that looks a little like a business letter.

Make a shallow trough along the seam with the side of your hand, sealing the dough at the same time (photograph 4). Now fold the top edge down, folding the dough in half into a cylinder. At this point, the cylinder should be no longer than the span of your hands with your thumbs extended.

Seal the bottom edge and tighten the cylinder at the same time by pushing your thumbs into the dough at the seam and gently pushing the cylinder back away from you with your thumbs (photograph 5). The dough should grip the work surface and resist your pushing, thus tightening, and the seam should be well sealed. If your cylinder is still flabby or if your seam is barely sealed (if you are new to this, it will be), you can tighten and seal the cylinder by folding it in half around your left thumb and sealing the edges with the heel of your right hand (photograph 6).

Next you will narrow and lengthen the cylinder to about half the width of your baking stone.

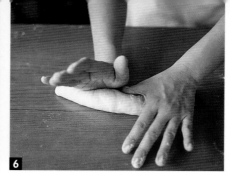

Roll the dough so that the seam is on the bottom. The cylinder will need to grip the work surface lightly but not stick, so you should have just the lightest veil of flour on it. Place one hand over the other in the center of the dough, palms down (photograph 7). With the heel of your hand and your fingertips in constant contact with the work surface, push the dough back and forth, narrowing the cylinder in the center. As soon as the center thins down slightly, place both hands, palms down and thumb to thumb, in the center of the dough and, still keeping the heel of your hands and fingertips in constant contact with the work surface, continue to push the dough back and forth, narrowing the cylinder (photograph 8). As the dough narrows from the center out, keep moving your hands apart, but do not stretch the dough laterally; rather let the dough narrow first, then move your hands gradually to the thicker ends. Slowly move your hands apart until you have reached the ends, then apply a little extra pressure while pushing the dough back and forth to make points on each end (photograph 9). Lengthen the cylinder of dough to about half the width of your baking stone, about 8 inches. Place it seam side up on the floured cookie sheet or wooden board. Repeat with the other dough piece.

Shape a *boule* or a *bâtard* with the larger piece of dough (see pages 34–35 for instructions) and put it in a basket or couche to proof.

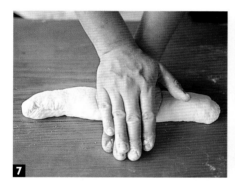

PROOFING THE DOUGH

After shaping your baguettes, cover them with plastic wrap and let proof on the floured sheets until light and very extensible, for 30 to 45 minutes.

While the baguettes are proofing, prepare a couche with two troughs. Pull out each baguette to be just long enough to fit on your baking stone, about 14 inches for a standard stone. Place the baguettes floured side up in the troughs and loosely cover them with plastic or a flap of the couche. Let proof until the dough is very light, well expanded, and slowly springs back when gently pressed with a floured finger, 30 to 60 minutes.

BAKING THE BREAD

Transfer the proofed baguettes to a sheet of parchment paper, using a baguette board or another thin lightweight board if you have one (just pick them up gently if not), and arrange them floured side up, making them very straight by edging the board against them. If desired, just before baking, fill the oven with steam (page 18). With a single-edged razor, make 3 angled cuts down the length of each baguette, holding the razor at a 45° angle to the dough and being sure to overlap the cuts. Slide the breads, still on the paper, onto the baking stone. Bake until the edges of the cuts are very dark brown and the whole bread is golden brown, 30 to 35 minutes, rotating the bread halfway into the bake. Let the bread cool completely on a rack.

To bake the *boule* or *bâtard*, reduce the oven heat to 425°F, and steam the oven again if desired. Move the *boule* or *bâtard* to a piece of parchment paper and slash it as desired. Bake until the bread is browned all around, 40 to 45 minutes, rotating it halfway into the bake. Let it cool completely on a rack.

A FEW BASIC FRENCH BREAD SHAPES

One trick to making pretty shapes with great crumb structure is to allow the rounded dough plenty of time to rest before you shape it, so that it is very extensible and filled with taut air bubbles. After shaping, place the dough either in a couche or in linen-lined baskets or colanders. Be sure to cover the dough with plastic wrap to prevent a crust from forming. For a floured crust, sift flour over the linen and proof the breads topside down. For a shiny crust, proof the dough without flour, topside up or down.

Boule (or *miche* or round loaf)

There are many ways to form a round, but the goal for all is to get a very taut skin to stretch evenly around a perfect dome of dough while not disturbing the large bubbles within. This takes some practice. Skid the dough across the work surface, with cupped hands nudging the base of the dough, rotating it as you are nudging it. The work surface should grab the bottom of the dough and force it to tighten, while the rotation should give you an even and not lopsided round. Let the dough rest for about 10 minutes on the bottom seam to seal it.

Couronne (or crown)

Make a baguette shape (page 32) but leave the ends stubby. For a full-sized crown, using about 1½ pounds (750 grams) dough, the dough cylinder should be about 30 inches. Proof the dough. Just before baking, place the dough on a piece of parchment paper, slash the dough in any desired pattern, and bring the ends together, forming a circle. Pinch the ends together firmly; they will overlap, but that is part of this shape's charm.

Rolls

This is a shape that also needs some practice. Cut the dough into equal pieces; for a really professional look, weigh them to make sure they are equal. Dinner rolls usually weigh about 2 ounces and large sandwich rolls weigh 3.5 to 4.5 ounces. Place the rolls skin side up on an unfloured work surface. Cup your hand over a roll with the palm resting on top of it. Rotate your hand around in a circle, lightly pressing on the top of the dough, until the dough tucks itself up into a tight ball with a little puckered seam on the bottom. If you get really good, you can do 2 rolls at once using both hands!

Bâtard (or long loaf)

This is almost identical to a baguette, just thicker and stubbier. Place the dough skin side down on a lightly floured work surface. Lightly flatten out the dough into a vaguely rectangular shape, pressing very gently to preserve the bubbles. Fold the bottom edge up just past the middle of the dough, then fold the top edge down to the middle. You should now have a rectangular piece of dough that looks a little like a business letter. Make a shallow trough with the edge of your hand, sealing the dough at the same time. Starting from the right side of the cylinder, fold the upper edge of the dough down to meet the lower edge, creating a cylinder. Press the edges together very hard with the heel of your hand to seal them. Go down the length of the dough, folding and sealing, until you have formed a tight cylinder. Smooth, even, and lengthen the cylinder by rolling it under your hands until it is as long as you desire. Ten inches will fit easily on most baking stones.

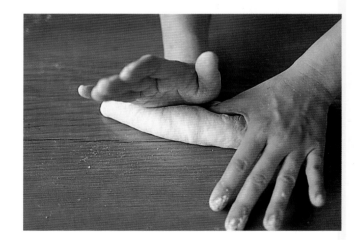

Acme's Herb Slabs

- Makes 2 large flatbreads, just over
  1 pound (500 grams) each
- Time: About 23 hours, with 20 minutes of active work

A stylized version of focaccia, this rosemary-flecked bread has an unusual crust. Just before baking, it is stippled all over, then baked for five minutes on one side. It is then flipped over to finish baking on the other side. This keeps the bread very flat and squared off, like a stone tablet.

The dough is based on a poolish and undergoes a stately fermentation and proof, giving it a very rich flavor. (In this recipe also, I have converted Acme's original 4-hour poolish to a 12-hour poolish to ease the baking schedule.) It is uncomplicated to make, and if started the evening before, it can be ready for dinner the next day.

continued

RECIPE SYNOPSIS THE EVENING BEFORE BAKING: Mix the poolish and let it ferment overnight for 12 hours. **THE NEXT MORNING:** Mix the dough and let it ferment for 6 hours. Shape the bread, proof it for 3½ hours, and then bake the bread for about 25 minutes.

	Poolish	volume	weight	metric	baker's percentages
THE EVENING BEFORE BAKING MAKING THE POOLISH	**Instant yeast**	¼ teaspoon			(eventually 0.07%)
	Water, 110° to 115°F	I cup			
	Unbleached all-purpose flour, preferably organic	2 cups	10.6 ounces	300 grams	100%
	Water, lukewarm	1⅓ cups	10.6 ounces	295 grams	(eventually 118%)

Whisk the yeast into the 110° to 115°F water and let it stand for 5 minutes. Add ¼ cup of the yeasted water to the flour (to measure ¹⁄₁₆ teaspoon yeast), then beat in the lukewarm water. This will be a very gloppy batter. Cover the poolish with plastic wrap and let it ferment overnight for 12 hours, or until its bubbles are popping and the top is just starting to wrinkle and foam.

	Dough	volume	weight	metric	baker's percentages
BAKE DAY MIXING THE DOUGH	**Unbleached all-purpose flour, preferably organic**	3 cups	16 ounces	450 grams	100%
	Salt	I tablespoon plus ¼ teaspoon	0.6 ounce	16 grams	3.5%
	Fresh rosemary leaves, chopped	I tablespoon plus I teaspoon			1.5%
	Instant yeast	¼ teaspoon			0.2%
	Water, lukewarm	¾ cup	6 ounces	170 grams	38%
	Olive oil	2 tablespoons	I ounce	30 grams	6%
	Fermented poolish				145%

by hand: Combine the flour, salt, rosemary, and yeast in a large bowl. Add the water and oil to the poolish, stir to loosen it, and pour it all into the flour mixture. Stir the mixture with your hand until it forms a rough dough. Turn it out onto your work surface and knead it briefly, without adding extra flour, until it is well combined. Cover the dough with a bowl and let it rest for 10 minutes to allow the yeast to rehydrate. Knead the dough, without adding extra flour, until it is very smooth, about 10 minutes.

by stand mixer: Combine the flour, salt, rosemary, and yeast in the mixing bowl. Add the water and oil to the poolish, stir to loosen it, and pour it all into the flour mixture. Mix with the dough hook on low speed just until a rough dough forms. Cover the bowl with a plate and let it rest for 10 minutes to allow the yeast to rehydrate. Mix the dough until it is very smooth, about 5 minutes.

by food processor: Combine the flour, salt, and yeast in the workbowl fitted with the steel blade. Add the water and oil to the poolish, stir to loosen it, and pour it all into the flour mixture. Process the dough just until it forms a ball, about 30 seconds. Remove the dough from the workbowl, set it on your work surface, cover it with a large bowl, and let it rest for 10 minutes to allow the yeast to rehydrate. Process the dough in four or five 30-second intervals, hand kneading it to cool it off between intervals. Remove the dough from the workbowl and knead in the rosemary by hand.

The dough should feel soft and tacky. Add 1 to 2 tablespoons water if the dough seems too firm.

FERMENTING AND TURNING THE DOUGH

Place the dough in a container at least 3 times its size and cover it tightly with plastic wrap. Let the dough ferment until light and doubled in bulk, about 6 hours. Turn the dough (page 16) 3 times in 20-minute intervals, that is, after 20, 40, and 60 minutes of fermenting, then leave the dough undisturbed for the remaining time.

SHAPING AND PROOFING THE DOUGH

Cut the dough in half. Round the pieces (page 17) and let rest for about 20 minutes. Lightly press one piece of the dough into a rectangle. Loosely fold it into thirds like a business letter by folding the bottom short edge up and the top down. Place it seam side down on a couche and cover it with a flap of the couche. Repeat with the other piece. Let them proof for about 1½ hours.

Cover a peel or rimless baking sheet with a large piece of parchment paper. Remove the dough from the couche and gently press each piece into a 12 x 6-inch rectangle with your hands (the workers in the bakery use a small wooden ruler to get the dimensions just so). Press your fingertips deeply into the dough to stipple it all over. Move the rectangles of dough to the parchment paper and resquare them. Cover them with plastic wrap and let proof until very soft and well expanded, about 2 hours more. The total proof time is about 3½ hours.

PREHEATING THE OVEN

About 45 minutes before the bread is fully proofed, arrange a rack on the oven's second-to-top shelf and place a baking stone on it. Clear away all racks above the one being used. Preheat the oven to 450°F (230°C).

BAKING THE BREAD

Poke the dough all over with a toothpick or a skewer, pushing all the way through. If desired, just before baking, fill the oven with steam (page 18). Slip the breads, still on the paper, onto the hot stone and bake for 5 minutes. Carefully flip the breads over onto the stone and remove the paper. Continue baking until they are well browned, about 20 minutes more, rotating them after 10 minutes. Let the breads cool on a rack.

INTO THE
WHEAT FIELDS

HARVEY COUNTY FIELD DAY
_____

MANHATTAN, KANSAS

WE DROVE BETWEEN GREEN-GOLD FIELDS ALL DAY, taking the long way to the station. It was late May in Kansas, and the billowing wheat had arrived at what the growers call the soft-dough stage—bright emerald grains, still soft and milky, releasing a surprising sweetness when chewed. The vast landscape was now flat, now gently hilly, prairie uniquely suited for growing this engineered grass. The few trees interrupting the horizon circled farmhouses or edged fields, immigrants like the settlers who planted them, as respite from the unremitting sun. We arrived in Harvey County in the late afternoon, joining the growers to attend a field day at the Kansas State University Agricultural Extension Farm.

Field days are seminars held right in the field, where university scientists introduce new wheat varieties, discuss experimental results, and dispense general agriculture advice. Dr. Rollie Sears, a wheat breeder from Kansas State University in Manhattan, Kansas, met us in front of a large outbuilding. He introduced us to Dr. Gina Brown-Gvedira, a wheat geneticist with the USDA whose main interest is the ancient ancestors to modern wheat. She explained to me how modern bread wheat came to be: Thousands of years ago, one of the first farmers planted an ancient wheat in his garden, a type of grass called einkorn wheat. At the garden's edge, some of the einkorn wheat interbred with a patch of wild grass. During the harvest, the farmer noticed an unusual new variety of wheat growing. Instead of eating this hybrid, the farmer saved the seed and planted it the next season. In successive harvests, emmer wheat, or farro, as some call it, went on to parent durum wheat, that hard, amber-colored wheat prized for pasta making. It took emmer wheat one more natural hybridization, with another wild grass at the edge of a farmer's field, to produce our bread wheat, *Triticum aestivum*.

Dr. Brown-Gvedira describes these hybridizations as "genetic bottlenecks," where a relatively few plants contributed the genes to a very long line of hybrids. The genes that squeezed through often proved valuable, enabling those ancient strains to resist drought, disease, or insect

OPPOSITE, CLOCKWISE FROM TOP: Wheat geneticist Dr. Gina Brown-Gvedira; growers viewing wheat varieties; an experimental field. ABOVE: Plant pathologist Dr. Robert Bowden checking for wheat diseases.

infestation or to increase yield. Her job is to retrieve seed from these ancient grasses and pass them on to wheat breeders like Dr. Sears.

The university plot at the Harvey County Extension is an excellent one for testing drought tolerance, because the fields are not irrigated, and this year has been particularly dry. On this "million-dollar day," so called because of the cost of bringing a new variety to market, breeders and growers alike would get to see how these new varieties fared in the face of disease, heat, and drought.

Dr. Sears filled in some of the background for the day. The breeder needs to address four basic qualities when developing a new wheat variety: insect and disease resistance; agronomics, that is, being short enough not to topple in the wind, being winter hardy, being tolerant to high temperatures, and so on; good milling and baking quality; and high yield, that is producing abundant bushels of wheat per acre. "As a breeder, I use wheat lines from all over the world and make crosses with all of those things in mind to try to combine and select something out that is going to be useful," Dr. Sears said. The process is incredibly lengthy and painstaking, and new wheats take many years and hundreds of thousands of dollars to bring to market.

Wheat ancestors, ancient grasses especially adept at surviving, are often an excellent source of genes. "I tell our producers, plants don't have legs, they can't run away; so they've been very ingenious in developing mechanisms to cope with disease and insects in order to continue to reproduce," he said. "All we are doing basically is looking for some of these new genes. Actually moving these new genes into a cultivated species is what Gina does. That's a five- to ten-year project, to actually take those genes and, through breeding and selection, move them from a wild ancestor into a cultivated species. Once she gets the resistance gene into a cultivated species, she releases that [seed] to someone like myself. We then cross that with our elite material that has already been refined for all the other components that we are looking for, to ultimately come up with a new variety."

After a brief introduction in the Extension outbuilding, we climbed on tractor-pulled hay wagons to visit the fields. Our first stop was at the Extension test plot, where over thirty different wheat varieties had been planted,

Tam 107, a popular wheat variety with artisan bakers

some old, grown as checks, and some new, developed by university breeders and seed companies. The plot is quite large and planted every few yards with a different variety, each clearly marked with a posted sign. From the top of the wagon, the field looks like a striped quilt, with each variety displaying a different height, head shape, and color. Some of the heads had long awns, the slender filament that extends from the hull, while others were awnless and looked almost naked.

Plant pathologist Robert Bowden had gone through the plot earlier and pulled out examples of the diseases. He mounted these examples in a green plastic frame and passed them around for the growers to examine: leaf rust, tan spot, speckled leaf blotch, wheat streak mosaic, powdery mildew, take-all, scab, and loose smut. Growers need to identify diseases correctly in order to take appropriate action.

Drs. Sears and Bowden walked along the wheats and commented about individual varieties in detail, pointing out things like level of maturity, height, and insect, disease, heat, and drought resistance. White wheats, which have a tan seed coat instead of a red one, are the breeders' darlings and have generated a lot of interest among growers, millers, and bakers. Three new hard whites were planted this year, and all looked well. The university plans to gradually replace the hard red wheats with the whites in Kansas; in fifteen years, Kansas may be planted entirely in hard white wheats. Many prefer white wheats: Millers can extract more white flour from the grain, making them more profitable, and bakers find the whole-grain flour looks lighter and tastes sweeter and less astringent than the whole-grain flour milled from red wheats.

After every wheat variety was addressed, we hopped back on the hay wagon to examine the other plots. These plots focused more on the crops grown in rotation with wheat: corn, soybeans, and milo or sorghum. Marion County grower Glenn Ensz explained to me, "With any crop grown in the same field year after year after year, you get a disease buildup. So rotating to other crops is a way of spreading the risk. It would be very risky to put all your farm in one crop, no matter what it is."

We slipped out early, to try to capture the look of the wheat fields in the last and best burst of light, fields whose harvests are the distant beginning to the bread we put on our tables.

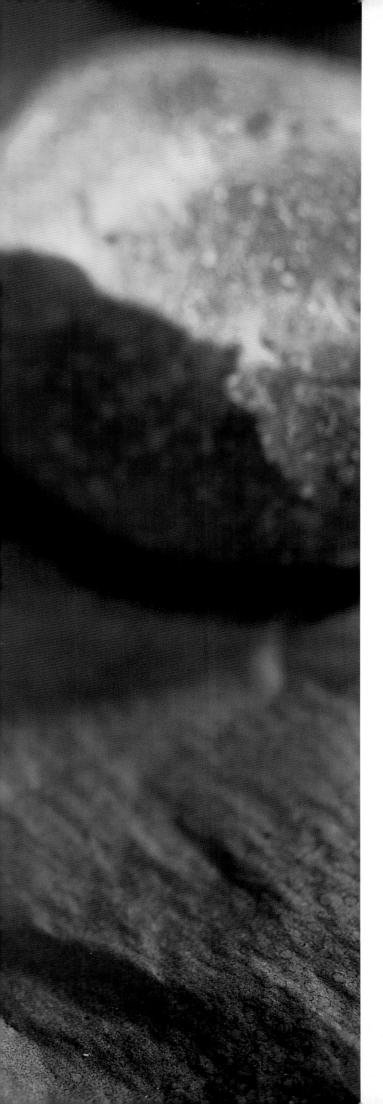

THE QUEST FOR NEW WHEAT

When asked why breeders constantly have to develop new varieties, Dr. Rollie Sears explained, "As we introduce new varieties, for example, that have [insect or disease] resistance, we are basically giving the organisms that attack that plant two options: Either they go extinct, because they cannot feed on that plant species now, or they develop genetic options to overcome and defeat the resistance. The first choice is unacceptable, so the organisms then unleash a Pandora's box of strategies to overcome the genetic resistance.

"When we release a resistant variety, it's not too long, say five or six or maybe ten years, it depends on how popular the variety is, before organisms start to defeat that resistance. So varieties that were resistant at one time become susceptible, and that affects not only their yield, but also their quality.

"The other reason is that we are making anywhere from half a bushel to three-quarters of a bushel per year progress on yield. For example, we will harvest Turkey [the wheat variety brought to Kansas by the Mennonites in 1874] this year in our plots and Turkey will average eight bushels per acre. And we will harvest Jagger, [which was planted] right next to it and received the same moisture, fertility, and all the other components added to the soil, and Jagger will yield about sixty-five bushels per acre. Farmers, since they are paid by the bushel, are interested in planting the highest-yielding varieties they can."

Just-baked White-Wheat Rolls (page 46) still on parchment

White-Wheat Rolls

- Makes eighteen 1.8-ounce (55-gram) rolls
- Time: About 6 hours, with about 30 minutes of active work

I developed this recipe after coming back from Kansas with a bag of Hudson Cream white-wheat flour (see Sources, page 222). The flavor of the white wheat really is different from hard red winter wheat; it is noticeably sweeter and has a much lighter color, more yellowish tan than dark brown. These simple rolls have become a favorite with my family, especially my kids, who normally shun whole-wheat anything.

This recipe calls for a small amount of sourdough starter, which is optional but highly recommended. I have found that it adds a wonderful complexity to bread without adding much actual sourness, besides being a good way to use up the scrap. Just save any leftover starter in a jar in the refrigerator and use it within the week.

RECIPE SYNOPSIS Mix the dough and let it ferment for 2 hours. Shape the rolls and let them proof for 2 to 3 hours before baking them about 25 minutes.

	Dough	volume	weight	metric	baker's percentages
BAKE DAY **MIXING** **THE DOUGH**	**Unbleached all-purpose flour**	2 cups	10.6 ounces	300 grams	50%
	Whole white-wheat flour	2 cups	10.6 ounces	300 grams	50%
	Instant yeast	1 teaspoon			0.5%
	Water, lukewarm	1¾ cups plus 2 tablespoons	15.3 ounces	435 grams	72%
	Salt	2¼ teaspoons	0.4 ounce	12 grams	2%
	Fermented firm sourdough starter (pages 91–94)	¼ cup	2 ounces	60 grams	10%

by hand: Combine both flours and the yeast in a large bowl, then add the water. With a wooden spoon or your hand, mix the dough just until well combined. Cover the dough and let it rest (autolyse) for 10 to 20 minutes.

Knead the salt and the starter, if using it, into the dough. Turn it out of the bowl and, without adding extra flour, knead it until it is smooth and strong, 5 to 10 minutes.

by stand mixer: Combine both flours and the yeast in the mixing bowl, then add the water. Using the dough hook, mix the dough on low speed just until it is well combined and gathered around the hook. If the dough is not catching on the hook, add 1 to 2 tablespoons water. Cover the dough and let rest (autolyse) for 10 to 20 minutes.

Add the salt and the starter, if using it, and continue mixing on medium speed until the dough is smooth and strong, about 5 minutes.

by food processor: Follow the instructions for mixing the dough by hand up to kneading the dough. Divide the dough in half and process half at a time in the food processor fitted with the steel blade. Process the dough for 15 to 30 seconds, remove it from the workbowl, and knead it by hand to cool it down and redistribute the heat. Repeat this procedure twice (a total of 3 times for each half), or until the dough is very smooth and strong. Then, briefly knead the 2 pieces of dough together.

FERMENTING THE DOUGH

Place the dough in a covered container at least 3 times its size and cover it tightly with plastic wrap. Let it ferment until it is light, well expanded, and about doubled in bulk but not to the point of collapsing, about 2 hours.

This is a soft dough.

SHAPING THE ROLLS

Line 2 baking sheets with parchment paper. Lightly flour the top of the dough and your work surface and turn the dough out. Lightly flour the top surface, then flip the dough so that its skin side is up. Cut the dough into 18 equal pieces, each 2 ounces (60 grams). Round the pieces into smooth balls (page 35). Place them well spaced on the baking sheets and cover them well with plastic wrap. Let them proof until they are very soft and well expanded, 1½ to 2 hours.

PREHEATING THE OVEN

About 30 minutes before the rolls are fully proofed, arrange the racks on the top and lower third positions and clear away all racks in between. Preheat the oven to 450°F (230°C).

BAKING THE ROLLS

Slash or snip the rolls decoratively if desired. Or, if the rolls are too soft, leave them uncut. Bake until the rolls are dark brown all around, 20 to 25 minutes. Halfway into the bake, rotate the baking sheets and switch their positions on the top and bottom racks halfway into the bake. Let cool on a rack.

WINTER VERSUS SPRING, HARD VERSUS SOFT WHEAT

In Kansas, wheat is a winter crop, meaning that it is planted in the fall—in Harvey County around October 1—and harvested in the early summer—in Harvey County, mid-June to late June. Farther north, where winters are harsher, wheat is planted in the spring and harvested in the fall. Common wisdom among artisan bakers holds that hard winter wheats are best for artisan-style breads, because their protein levels tend to be more moderate. Hard spring wheats typically have protein levels that are too high (upward of 14%) for quality artisan-style breads, although they are sometimes used as blending wheats to bolster weaker wheats. Hardness refers to the wheat kernel's resistance to chewing, with harder wheats tending to have higher protein levels.

THRESHING DAYS

GOESSEL, KANSAS

THE LAST WEEK OF JULY EVERY YEAR BRINGS THRESHING DAYS TO GOESSEL, KANSAS, a festival celebrating the wheat harvest and Mennonite heritage. First learning about the event from a highway billboard in Kansas, I became curious about it and made a point of stopping there. So one hot Saturday in July we found ourselves in the very quaint town of Goessel, standing with Mennonite families on the side of a country road, watching as seemingly half the town passed by in an antique tractor parade. The tractor drivers—young men, old men, women, boys, girls, and even a few lap-riding toddlers—rode proudly, smiling and waving and throwing candy to the children, who came with small boxes to collect the windfall. A few entrants led unusual livestock breeds, and one older couple drove a restored turquoise blue Metropolitan.

When the parade ended in a line of backed-up traffic, most of the crowd left to line up for the German lunch in the local elementary school or the barbecue outside on picnic tables. We bypassed the lines to explore the festival grounds. At the children's exhibition in a restored barn, a craftsman carved long-maned rocking horses, while the children gathered in the stable to pet rabbits, piglets, and kittens in hay-strewn pens. Around the corner, row upon row of shiny restored tractors rested in concentric arcs. Men in farmer hats walked around the crayon-colored machines, praising their assets and trading restoration advice.

Behind this tractor lot, flying chaff heralded the wheat-threshing demonstration, where a small crowd had already gathered. Crew leader Russ Hamm, a member of the Wheat Heritage Engine and Threshing Company, the festival's copresenter with the Mennonite Heritage Museum, stood above us on deep piles of wheat bundles, called shocks, in an old wagon, pitching the wheat into the thresher with an antique pitchfork. The thresher is a long, narrow steel-cased machine that separates the bundled wheat into clean wheat, blowing the straw and chaff into a big pile. Another man sat on the spit-polished green tractor that powered the thresher through a long flat belt, while onlookers circled around a small high-wheeled wagon, running

OPPOSITE: A threshing volunteer holds aloft a shock of wheat before tossing it into a thresher. ABOVE: Onlookers to the antique tractor parade.

their fingers through the cleaned wheat as it poured down the chute like gold nuggets.

In the fields behind the thresher, Herman Richards, attending the festival from McPherson, Kansas, watched with his son and small, blond grandson. "My father's family had a threshing crew in the area they were in. You know, there weren't that many of them around. There were just certain families that had the equipment, and they'd go around and do the threshing for everybody else.

"[The wheat] was shocked up in bundles like that, and they'd stand them up in the fields. There would be a crew doing nothing but gathering in the shocks. There'd be another crew doing nothing but run the machines. And there was another bunch that just hauled the grain to town, and then the bunch at the threshing machines. Each one had their labor for the threshing.

"All the wagons were horse drawn, and the only machine usually was a steam engine. Families in the district would work together, and it would take them all summer to do all the farms. They'd just start at one farm and take care of the shocked grain. They'd thrash it out and get it all hauled into town and get it all

binned, and then they'd move to the next farm. And they'd do it all summer long."

By one o'clock, we were pretty parched, so we headed over to one of the outbuildings where an antique steam engine was churning homemade ice cream with grand overkill. A dollar got me a Styrofoam cup full of cold, sweet vanilla purity.

Outside, the tractors got one more shot at glory. One by one they catwalked through the festival ground's main thoroughfare while an emcee announced their critical statistics: their ownership, provenance, and restoration details. Judging by the people filling the stadium seats and tent-covered bales of hay, this display is the festival's main draw, luring farmers and wannabes from all over the state.

As the midsummer Kansas sun was peaking, we joined the group of mostly older people in the Immigrant House, the only air-conditioned building at the festival. This section of the Mennonite Heritage Museum honors the area's first settlers, Mennonites from the Caucasus who escaped the tsar's persecution by buying up the Santa Fe Railroad company's cheap prairie land in 1874. Glass cases archived the founding families' old photographs, cloths, and household items.

Many filing by were searching for names of relatives or a glimmer of a distant childhood—a grandmother's scarf, a great-uncle's picture, a cousin's eyeglasses.

A few of the first settlers' houses have been restored and moved behind the Immigrant House, making quaint venues for traditional homemaking demonstrations. In the Krause House, Judy Unruh, a Krause descendant, was making zwieback, not a rusk but a kind of sturdy dinner roll that looks like a flattened-out brioche, with her husband, Darrell, and her two daughters. In the bright kitchen, a brick oven, narrow to conserve floor space but with a deep hearth, warmed the home's only interior wall. These ovens were designed to be fired not with wood, which was nonexistent on the prairie, but with shelp grass, a tall oily grass found in ditches. Darrell monitored the oven while Anne Harvey, Judy's daughter, shaped little top-knotted rolls out of the dough that Judy had mixed earlier. Next to the towel-covered trays of rising rolls was a cloth-lined large tin pail full of warm zwieback. All afternoon, the smell of the baking zwieback lured people in, then the rolls delivered a taste of their past.

OPPOSITE, LEFT TO RIGHT: An antique tractor on parade; crew leader Russ Hamm near the mouth of a thresher. ABOVE, LEFT TO RIGHT: A wagon filled with newly threshed hay; Judy Unruh's Zwieback rolls (page 53) proofing in the doorway of Krause House.

Judy Unruh's Wedding Zwieback

- Makes 35 dainty dinner rolls or two 9 x 5-inch pan breads
- Time: At least 13 hours, with about 30 minutes of active work

Wedding zwieback are smaller and sweeter than everyday zwieback. Judy makes and bakes her rolls on the same day, usually Sundays she says, but I like the flavor and schedule better if I refrigerate the dough for up to two days.

These rolls are meant to be sturdy so that they hold their shape well, and the dough is a stiff one. (It actually makes perfect pan bread, the dense, fine-grained kind you can't buy anywhere that is so great for sandwiches, toast, croutons, and canapés.) For richer and much lighter rolls, add the eggs.

RECIPE SYNOPSIS Mix the dough and refrigerate it for at least 8 hours, then let it warm to room temperature, about 2 hours. Shape the dough and let it proof for 2 hours before baking about 30 minutes.

	Dough	volume	weight	metric	baker's percentages
UP TO 2 DAYS BEFORE BAKING OR EARLY ON BAKE DAY MIXING THE DOUGH	Milk, any kind	2 cups	17.4 ounces	475 grams	58%
	Instant yeast	1¾ teaspoons	0.1 ounce	6 grams	0.7%
	Unbleached all-purpose flour	5½ cups	30 ounces	825 grams	100%
	Granulated sugar	¼ cup	2.1 ounces	55 grams	7%
	Salt	2¼ teaspoons	0.5 ounce	12 grams	1.5%
	Unsalted butter, softened	6 tablespoons	3 ounces	85 grams	10%
	Eggs, optional	2 large			12%

Microwave the milk on high power or heat in a small saucepan on top of the stove until bubbles form around the edge, steam rises, and the milk smells cooked. Let it cool to 105° to 115°F, about the temperature of a comfortably hot bath. To cool the milk faster, pour it into a heavy crockery bowl. (Scalding the milk denatures a protein in the milk that attacks gluten; if this step is skipped, the bread's texture will be coarser and denser.) Sprinkle the yeast over the warm milk, stir it in, and let stand for 5 to 10 minutes.

by hand: Combine the flour, sugar, and salt in a large bowl, then add the milk mixture, butter, and the eggs, if using. With a wooden spoon or your hand, mix the dough just until well combined. Turn the dough out of the bowl and, without using any extra flour, knead until it is smooth and strong, 5 to 10 minutes.

continued

by stand mixer: Combine the flour, sugar, and salt in the mixing bowl, then add the milk mixture, butter, and the eggs, if using. With a wooden spoon or your hand, mix the dough just until well combined. Using the dough hook, mix the dough, starting on low speed and increasing to medium, until it is smooth and strong, about 5 minutes.

by food processor: Follow the instructions for mixing the dough by hand up to kneading the dough. Divide the dough in half and process half at a time in the food processor fitted with the steel blade. Process the dough for 15 to 30 seconds, remove it from the workbowl, and knead it by hand to cool it down and redistribute the heat. Repeat this procedure twice (a total of 3 times for each half). The dough should be very smooth and strong.

This will be a stiff dough unless you have added the eggs, in which case it will be soft and sticky.

REFRIGERATING AND FERMENTING THE DOUGH

Place the dough in a container at least 3 times its size and cover it tightly with plastic wrap. Refrigerate it for at least 8 hours or up to 2 days. About 2 hours before shaping the dough, remove it from the refrigerator to warm up and finish fermenting.

BAKE DAY SHAPING AND PROOFING THE ZWIEBACK

Line 2 half-sheet pans or 4 jelly-roll pans with aluminum foil and lightly oil the foil. Butter your hands well.

To shape these rolls as Judy does, grab the dough between your hands and squeeze off 2 tablespoons of dough, as if you were squeezing toothpaste from a tube. Put the dough on one of the foil-lined baking sheets and continue to squeeze out a total of 35 rounds, spacing them evenly on the lined baking sheets. Dip your index finger in water, then push the center of each round into a thin well. Now use the remaining dough to squeeze off 35 little rounds of dough, about 1½ teaspoons each. Push each little round firmly into the well of one of the larger rounds.

For those less skilled than Judy and her daughters, there is an easier method: Cut three quarters of the dough into thirty-five 1-ounce (30-gram) pieces; weigh them if you want. Cut the remaining quarter of the dough into thirty-five 4-ounce (10-gram) pieces. Smoothly round the larger pieces (page 35), then round the tiny pieces. Evenly space the larger rounds on the lined baking sheets. Dip your index finger in water, push the center of each large round into a thin well, and then push one tiny round into the well.

Cover the finished rolls with plastic wrap and let proof until fully expanded (the impression remains when the dough is lightly pressed), about 2 hours.

PREHEATING THE OVEN

About 30 minutes before the breads are fully proofed, arrange a rack on the oven's middle shelf for the zwieback. Clear away any racks above the one being used. Preheat the oven to 350°F (180°C).

BAKING THE BREAD

Slide an extra baking pan, if you have one, under each pan of rolls to prevent scorching and bake the rolls until well browned all around, 25 to 30 minutes. Serve the rolls immediately.

TO SHAPE AND PROOF
THE PAN BREAD

Butter two 9 x 5-inch baking pans. Divide the dough in half. Using a rolling pin, gently flatten 1 piece out into a thin sheet about ¼ inch thick, pressing out all the bubbles (photograph 1). Fold the sides of the dough into the center, letting them overlap by 1 inch or so (photograph 2). Roll out the dough again so that it is as wide from folded side to folded side as your baking pan. Moisten your hands with water and lightly pat the dough so that it is just slightly tacky. Now roll the dough up like a carpet, keeping the folded ends on either side (photograph 3). Pinch the seam to seal it and lay the cylinder seam side down in one of the prepared pans. The cylinder should fit lengthwise but should not touch the sides of the pan (photograph 4). Repeat with the other piece of dough. Cover the pans with plastic wrap and let proof until the dough has risen 1 inch above the pans, about 2 hours (photograph 5).

About 30 minutes before the breads are fully proofed, arrange the bottom shelf for the loaves. Clear away any racks above. Preheat the oven to 350°F (180°C).

Bake the loaves until dark brown all around, 45 to 50 minutes, rotating the pans halfway into the bake. Remove the loaves from the pans and let them cool completely on a rack before slicing.

STONE GRINDING

GRAY'S GRIST MILL

ADAMSVILLE, RHODE ISLAND

THE MILL'S FLOOR VIBRATED AS THE WATER RUSHED UNDERNEATH US, its low rumbling audible testimony to its power. We were standing in Gray's Grist Mill in Adamsville, Rhode Island, with René Becker, baker and owner of Hi-Rise Bread Company, and his muse, miller Tim McTague. For the grand finale to an afternoon spent showing us his mill and the art of making Rhode Island jonnycakes, Tim opened the proverbial floodgates, or, more precisely, the gate under the mill that controls the mill pond's holding tank. That venerable gesture was once the "on" button for this three-hundred-year-old mill, turning the pond's potential energy into kinetic energy—enough to turn the reaction wheel that turned the wheel shaft that turned the main shaft that turned the stone shaft that turned the mace that turned the stone that ground the corn the farmers grew.

Upon our arrival, the mill was in full swing grinding René's whole-wheat flour. Tim, white with flour dust down to the roots of his eyelashes, stood in a well below the stones, monitoring the grinding and filling bags with the freshly milled flour. Everything everywhere in the old room was white with flour dust, from the rafters to the sacks of dried corncobs stored in the corner. René had come to pick up the stone-milled corn, rye, and whole wheat that Tim mills for him, but he had also brought with him some visitors and a bottle of excellent Normandy cider to share. You can take the boy out of France, but . . .

Conversation is difficult above the rhythmic racket of the mill, so René showed me around the outside of the old mill building. Originally a water-powered system using a fanlike device called a reaction wheel, a precursor of the turbine, the mill was converted to mechanical power years ago when miller emeritus John Allen Hart applied some proverbial Yankee ingenuity by attaching a belt from the mill's main shaft to the engine of a Waterloo Boy, a now-antique tractor. John was frustrated by the mill pond's irregularity, which depended on sufficient rainfall and the watershed to stay full. Several vehicles later (including an old Buick and a 1946 Dodge

OPPOSITE: The bottom stone of a demonstration mill showing wheat kernels in mid-grind. Grain enters the stones through a hole in the center of the top stone and is guided toward the edge by grooves cut into the stone. The closer to the edge the grain gets, the more pulverized. ABOVE: Tim McTague weighing out small bags of cornmeal in his weighing room.

truck), the mill is now powered by an International Harvester tractor model M, which somehow doesn't look incongruous standing behind the mill, tethered to it by an extra-long belt, like an old-fashioned pull toy.

René and I slipped underneath the mill to get a closer look at the revolving gears and main shaft. The millstream flows below, underneath the mill room, and the original opening for the reaction wheel hadn't yet been boarded up. The stone foundation damming the pond channel's holding tank seeps water, creating a cool and peaceful place, a perfect hideaway on a hot summer day.

Back inside, I found Tim raking his hands through the dwindling wheat in the hopper. He explained that one of the cardinal rules of milling is to never let the stones grind empty, for then they would heat up and possibly even spark, burning the mill down. A hopper funnels the grain into a shoe, an open-ended wooden box whose angle Tim can adjust. The shoe empties directly into an opening in the top stone's center, the grain flow slowed or speeded by its tilt.

Both the revolving top stone and the stationary bottom stone are dressed, or cut, with grooves in a pattern called English quarter dress, those classic markings of a millstone. Counterintuitively, the grooves in the top and bottom stones run in the same, rather than opposing, direction. Yet, when the top stone turns, the grooves act like scissors, cutting and crushing the grain while simultaneously pushing the grist away from the center.

The top stone is slightly concave, giving the grain room to enter the stone's center, and narrowing toward the perimeter. As the grain makes its way from between the stones, it gradually gets reduced into finer and finer particles because of the ever-narrowing space. If Tim sets the stones close enough, the grain will be utterly powdered by the time it clears the stones.

A wooden enclosure, or tun, closely surrounds the stones, covering them and containing the falling flour. A small arm on the outside of the revolving upper stone keeps the flour moving, so it will eventually fall through the tun's chute and into an agitating window screen—another of John's inventions—for a coarse bolting. Tim monitors the grain in the shoe carefully and, when it is empty, darts out of the mill and shuts off the tractor, halting the mill.

Tim learned his trade from John, whose father, Roland, was the miller at Gray's before him. John had been running the mill since 1916, and by the time Tim began in 1982, John was "getting tired." John had a hard time accepting Tim at first, but Tim's devotion and hard work won him over. Tim apprenticed with him for about five years, virtually rebuilding the neglected mill in the process, before he took over entirely. Tim says of John, "He knew a lot, but he also knew what he didn't know, and he wasn't afraid to tell you that either. He taught me how to do stuff right."

Today, the restored mill is still well known for grinding Rhode Island flint corn, which Tim describes as a very old, pearly white variety and a direct descendant of the corn grown and developed by the Narragansett Indians. Very few people grow this old variety because its yield per acre is so humble, but an old farmer named Abe Quick still grows it for Tim, as he has for years. Rhode Islanders consider its flavor to be superior, and the best corn for making their beloved jonnycakes. Flint corn is very hard and mills into a flaky granular meal, while dent corn, the most common type and a much newer hybrid, is much softer and mills into fine flour. (Trivia: Dent corn is so named because of the way it shrinks as it dries, forming that eponymous dent.)

René loves the flavor of flint corn as well as what it represents. "Before I opened [Hi-Rise Bread Company], I started working with Tim's flour, and I knew that I really wanted to use Tim's mill as much as possible, because I really do believe in the ideas of regional and seasonal. First of all, he is grinding it to order, especially when it comes to something like corn. There is a really discernible difference in flavor. And I happen to really like that, even with my whole wheat I like that there is a certain grassy quality. I think it adds a dimension to the bread, a certain sweetness. It's a sweet hay or sweet grass flavor. At times when Tim's mill has broken down or the tractor isn't working or the bearings go out or whatever, and I have to use somebody

OPPOSITE, CLOCKWISE FROM TOP LEFT: Gray's Grist Mill; rounded flint corn in the lower hand and shriveled dent corn in the upper; under the mill, the belt of the main shaft being powered by the tractor; miller Tim McTague on the International Harvester that is the engine of the mill.

else's whole wheat, customers really notice. They say 'What's going on? This batch wasn't as good.'"

René, a former journalist and restaurant critic for *Boston Magazine*, had been operating his Cambridge, Massachusetts, bakery-café for just a year and a half before I visited. It is a beautiful place, one of the prettiest bakeries I have seen, and everything is delicious and tastes homemade. Large windows flood his production area with light, and café patrons can view the making of their bread as they eat their sandwiches.

René is truly inspired by Tim's mill products, and they continually put their heads together to come up with new breads. But as René expands, Tim's old mill is being worked far beyond its intended capacity, and Tim worries about the strain. The mill has two sets of millstones, one for cornmeal and flour and the other for animal feed. The second set is inoperable, and Tim explained that with all the original gears lost, it would be prohibitively expensive to restore. They are now working on a plan for expansion that would preserve the integrity of the process.

Once René's wheat was ground, Tim could turn his attention to making jonnycakes. Jonnycakes, Tim explains, were the bread staple in this part of New England, much the same as tortillas are the staple in Mexico. Jonnycakes were once eaten with every meal, and there are a few old-timers who continue to do that. Tim heats his electric griddle and mixes up the jonnycake batter. He likes his jonnycakes very thin, feeling that the corn flavor comes through much clearer than with the stodgier thick ones; he mixes the cornmeal with just enough water to make a thick paste, then thins the paste with milk. He pours spoonfuls of batter onto the hot greased griddle and the batter sizzles. Tim lets the cakes take their time, letting them get really brown before he flips them. This, he says, is one of the tricks. A few minutes later, Tim eases the thin golden disks off the griddle and hands them to us. We salt, fold, and devour them, then chase them with René's wonderful cider. The corn flavor is vibrant and toasty in the ephemerally soft-crisp cakes. Tim tops the next batch with smoked salmon, slivered red onion, capers, and crème frâiche, and as these go down just as quickly, I imagine a few flinty New Englanders turning in their graves at the sight of our decadence.

HURRICANE GLORIA AND THE EMPTY POND

Tim McTague, miller of Gray's Grist Mill, relates this tale of the perils of stone milling:

"I'm an unofficial pond warden. When I feel like we are going to get a lot of water, I'll take a board out of the pond, lower the level a little and let the water go out and then put the board back and then the water will come back to where it ought to be. It's sort of just a low-level management thing. And when Hurricane Gloria came, they told us about torrential rains, how it was going to flood on the coast. And actually the '46 Dodge wound up under water in the Hurricane of '54.

"So I hear all these stories and I hear about all this torrential rain coming and everything, so what I did was, I opened the gate and I took some of the boards out, basically draining the entire pond. And Hurricane Gloria went by and didn't drop any rain at all! 'Pond's, empty. Sorry. Look like a little bit of an idiot, don't I?' People just don't like to see a dry pond. Everybody goes [Tim speaks in a nasal voice], 'Where's the pond? Where're the little duckies?'"

René Becker, baker and owner of Hi-Rise Bread Company, shouldering a sack of flour. FOLLOWING PAGES: Corn Breads (page 64) stacked behind the counter at Hi-Rise.

Hi-Rise's Corn Bread

- Makes two 9 x 5-inch pan breads
- Time: About 7 hours, with 15 minutes of active work

A yellow pan bread replete with fresh corn kernels and cornmeal, this bread is perfect for toast, which brings out the corn flavor, and sandwiches. The key to really good bread, René says, is in the freshness of the cornmeal and kernels of corn. His cornmeal comes from Gray's, of course, which you can mail-order (see Sources, page 222).

RECIPE SYNOPSIS Mix the poolish and let it ferment for 2 hours; then mix the dough and let it ferment for 1½ hours. Shape the bread, let it proof for 2 hours, and then bake the bread for about 1 hour.

	Poolish	volume	weight	metric	baker's percentages
BAKE DAY **MAKING** **THE POOLISH**	**Unbleached bread flour**	1¼ cups	6.6 ounces	190 grams	100%
	Instant yeast	1½ teaspoons			2.5%
	Water, lukewarm	¾ cup	6.6 ounces	190 grams	100%

Combine the flour and yeast in a large bowl, then beat in the water. This will be a gloppy batter. Cover the poolish tightly with plastic wrap and let it ferment until it is very bubbly and well risen, about 2 hours.

	Dough	volume	weight	metric	baker's percentages
MIXING **THE DOUGH**	**Water, lukewarm**	⅔ cup	5.6 ounces	160 grams	31%
	Fermented poolish				75%
	Unbleached bread flour	2½ cups	13.2 ounces	375 grams	73%
	Stone-ground white cornmeal	1 cup plus 2 tablespoons	5 ounces	140 grams	27%
	Fresh corn kernels (1 large ear)	about ¾ cup	about 4 ounces	about 115 grams	22%
	Eggs	2 large (plus 1 for the glaze)			19%
	Honey	2 tablespoons	1.4 ounces	40 grams	8%
	Vegetable oil (René uses olive oil)	1½ tablespoons	0.7 ounce	20 grams	4%
	Salt	1 tablespoon	0.5 ounce	14 grams	2.7%

Add the water to the poolish and stir to loosen it from the container.

by hand: Combine the flour, cornmeal, and corn in a large bowl. Add the watered poolish, 2 of the eggs, the honey, and oil. Stir the mixture with your hand until it forms a rough dough. Turn it out onto your work surface and knead it, without adding flour and using a dough scraper to help (you are crushing the corn kernels into the dough as you knead). When the dough is soft and sticky, add the salt. Knead until the salt is dissolved and the dough is tighter and very smooth, about 2 minutes.

by stand mixer: Combine the flour, cornmeal, and corn in the mixing bowl. Add the watered poolish, 2 of the eggs, the honey, and oil. Stir the dough with your hand or a wooden spoon until roughly combined. Using the dough hook, mix the dough on low to medium speed until it is very smooth, about 5 minutes (the kernels will get crushed during kneading). Add the salt and knead until the salt is dissolved and the dough is very smooth, about 3 minutes.

by food processor: Combine the flour, cornmeal, corn, and salt in the workbowl fitted with the steel blade. Pulse the mixture a few times to combine (the corn will get processed into the dough). Add the watered poolish, 2 of the eggs, the honey, and oil. Process the dough until the workbowl fogs, about 30 seconds. Remove the dough from the bowl and hand knead it for a few turns to cool it and redistribute the heat. Return the dough to the workbowl and process it for 3 or 4 more 30-second intervals, hand kneading it between intervals, until it is very smooth and drier.

This is a soft and sticky dough.

FERMENTING THE DOUGH

Place the dough in a container at least 3 times its size and cover it tightly with plastic wrap. Let the dough ferment until it is light, well expanded, and doubled in bulk, about 1½ hours.

SHAPING AND PROOFING THE DOUGH

Generously butter two 9 x 5-inch baking pans. Cut the fermented dough in half. Using a rolling pin and plenty of extra flour for dusting this sticky dough, gently roll out one piece about ¼ inch thick, pressing out all bubbles. Fold the sides of the dough into the center, letting them overlap by 1 inch or so. Roll out the dough again so that it is as wide from folded edge to folded edge as your baking pan. Moisten your hands with water and lightly pat the dough so that it is just slightly tacky. Now roll the dough up like a carpet, keeping the folded ends on either side. Pinch the seam to seal it and lay the cylinder seam side down in one of the prepared pans. The cylinder should fit lengthwise but should not touch the sides of the pan. Repeat with the other piece of dough. Cover the loaves tightly with plastic wrap and let them proof until risen 1 inch above the pans, about 2 hours.

PREHEATING THE OVEN

About 30 minutes before the breads are fully proofed, arrange a rack on the oven's bottom shelf and clear away all racks above the one being used. Preheat the oven to 350°F (180°C).

BAKING THE BREAD

Beat the remaining egg until blended and brush the tops of the loaves with it. Bake the breads until well browned, 50 to 60 minutes, rotating them halfway into the bake. Remove the breads from the pans and let them cool on a rack.

Hi-Rise's Boston Brown Bread

- Makes 2 cylindrical loaves
- Time: About 1¾ hours, with 10 minutes of active work

René has discovered that he likes his Boston Brown Bread best when baked instead of steamed, saying it's not only less of a hassle, but the bread also has better texture—crispy instead of soggy (he loves the occasional crispy overflow on the sides of the can). The dried blueberries are his nod to New England, but currants or raisins can be substituted. This moist quick bread is great with good Cheddar cheese or cream cheese, but to be really traditional, it should be served on Friday with good homemade baked beans.

RECIPE SYNOPSIS Mix the batter and bake the bread for 1½ hours.

	Batter	volume	weight	metric	baker's percentages
BAKE DAY **PREHEATING** **THE OVEN AND** **PREPARING** **THE CANS**	Unsalted butter, softened, for buttering the cans				
	Unbleached all-purpose flour	1½ cups	8 ounces	230 grams	32%
	Stone-ground white cornmeal	⅔ cup	4 ounces	115 grams	15%
	Whole-rye flour	2 cups	8 ounces	230 grams	32%
	Whole-wheat flour	1 cup	5.3 ounces	150 grams	21%
	Baking powder	1½ teaspoons	0.3 ounce	7 grams	1%
	Baking soda	1 tablespoon	0.5 ounce	15 grams	2%
	Salt	1¼ teaspoon	0.2 ounce	6 grams	0.8%
	Light molasses	½ cup	5.7 ounces	165 grams	23%
	Milk, any kind	2 cups	17.6 ounces	500 grams	69%
	Dried blueberries, currants, or raisins	1 cup	4 ounces	115 grams	16%

Arrange a rack on the oven's bottom shelf and clear away all racks above the one being used. Preheat the oven to 300°F (150°C). Generously butter 2 clean 14- to 16-ounce coffee cans, or use cylindrical containers about 4 inches in diameter and 5½ inches high.

MIXING THE BATTER

Combine the dry ingredients in a large bowl. In a pitcher, combine the molasses and milk. Stir enough of the milk mixture into the dry ingredients to form a thick paste, then beat until the batter is smooth. Stir in the remaining milk mixture, then fold in the dried fruit. Spoon the batter into the prepared coffee cans; it should fill three quarters of each can.

BAKING THE BREAD

Put the breads immediately in the oven. Bake for 1½ hours, rotating them halfway into the bake. The breads should be well domed, browned, and crusty. Remove the breads from the cans while they are still warm and let them cool on a rack.

Gray's Grist Mill Thin Jonnycakes

- Makes 20 to 25 small jonnycakes
- Time: About 30 minutes

This is the thin version of the Rhode Island staple that some still eat as an accompaniment to breakfast, lunch, and dinner. These are wonderful plain with salt right off the griddle but can be gussied up however you like, although many Rhode Islanders cringe at the thought of a maple syrup glaze.

RECIPE SYNOPSIS Mix the batter and fry on a well-greased griddle.

	Batter	volume	weight	metric	baker's percentages
BAKE DAY **PREHEATING** **THE GRIDDLE**	**Stone-ground white cornmeal, preferably jonnycake (flint corn) meal**	2 cups	11 ounces	315 grams	100%
	Salt	½ teaspoon	0.1 ounce	3 grams	1%
	Water, cold	¾ cup	6 ounces	175 grams	56%
	Milk, any kind	1½ cups	12 ounces	345 grams	110%
	Vegetable oil, for frying				

Heat a griddle or a cast-iron skillet over medium heat.

MIXING THE BATTER

Combine the cornmeal and salt in a mixing bowl. Add the cold water and stir until smooth. Stir in the milk, adding more if needed to achieve a thin, pourable batter.

BAKING THE JONNYCAKES

Lightly oil the griddle. Stir the batter—it tends to settle—then spoon out 1 tablespoon of the batter for each cake onto the griddle. The batter should "dance" out into a thin disk. If it seems too thin, add 1 teaspoon of cornmeal to the batter. If the cake sits too high, thin out the batter with a little milk. Let the cakes bake on the griddle until the underside is deep brown, about 5 minutes. Tim says, "You wait, and then you wait some more." Flip them with a metal spatula, being careful, as they are fragile and tend to stick, and fry the second side just until spotted brown, about 1 minute. Serve them immediately. Lightly oil the griddle and stir the batter between batches.

ROLLER MILLING

ROCKY MOUNTAIN FLOUR MILLING

PLATTEVILLE, COLORADO

AS PICTURESQUE AND APPEALING AS STONE-MILLED FLOUR IS, it is roller-milled flour that is the mainstay of bread baking in this country. Few if any stone mills still bolt their whole-wheat flour to make white flour, the key ingredient of most artisan breads, so white-flour production is, by default, the domain of roller mills. Neglected in most baking books, probably because of its inherently industrial and complex nature, roller milling deserves to be better understood.

I can't think of a better place to start than in Lisa and Steve Curran's organic roller mill in Platteville, Colorado: Rocky Mountain Flour Milling L.L.C., better known as RMFM. Steve, a former milling professor of eighteen years at Kansas State University, and his wife, Lisa, a cereal chemist also at KSU, decided to harvest their knowledge and experience and build the mill of their dreams, combining their love of Colorado and support of organic farming. Steve cut his tether to the university, then fortuitously met a representative of a farming cooperative looking to build a mill in Colorado as an investment. They meshed plans and recruited three other investing groups, a farming co-op and two grain elevator co-ops, and constructed a mill according to Steve's specifications.

I visited when the mill had been in operation for only one year. We met in the mill's offices, which also house Lisa's wheat-quality laboratory, and Steve patiently answered all my questions before giving us a tour.

The purpose of milling is to separate the wheat kernel into its components—bran, the kernel's red or white seed coat; germ, the oil-rich embryo of the kernel; and endosperm, the starchy white center of the kernel—and then reduce the endosperm into the very fine particles called flour. RMFM uses an atypically short milling process developed by Steve, and my tour revealed a neat distillation of the ordinarily very lengthy process of extracting flour from wheat.

We started off at the loading area where the wheat first arrives. RMFM buys its wheat directly from the farmers, after Lisa has run tests on a sample and approved it. The wheat is

OPPOSITE: Steel rollers removed from the mill for repair. ABOVE: Steve and Lisa Curran.

trucked in directly from the organic farms, then quickly tested to confirm that the sample wheat corresponds to the wheat in the truck. The wheat is moved into one of six 60,000-bushel storage tanks, where it is held until it is milled.

We then walked to the cleaning building, which is separated from the mill itself to prevent contamination. The wheat comes into the mill very dirty—mixed with chaff, weed seeds, beans, and various foreign objects, collectively called dockage. Removing this debris is surprisingly laborious, each different contaminant requiring a separate procedure to remove it. No water is used, to leave the wheat as dry as possible for storage.

The wheat is funneled from the storage tanks to the third floor of the cleaning building, undergoing a series of cleaning operations as it makes its way down the floors. One machine removes stones, another removes light and heavy materials such as wheat hulls and beans, several machines remove various foreign grains, and one removes pieces of metal. When all the dockage is removed, the wheat is scoured and polished to remove its dust and dirt, then moved to separate clean storage tanks to await blending and tempering.

The mill building, where the tempering and milling occurs, is large and noisy, and hot in the summer. No air conditioning is needed, because no one works in there for too long; instead, computers monitor and regulate the flow. After Lisa has designated the blend of wheats to be used, wheat from the various bins moves from the storage tanks into the tempering mixer next to the mill. Water is added to the wheat to bring it up to a uniform moisture level, typically 15% to 16.5% moisture for hard wheat. Then the wheat rests for a minimum of ten to twelve hours to allow the water to penetrate the kernel. This tempering helps to moisten the bran so that it releases in big flakes rather than tiny dry particles, and it also mellows or softens the endosperm; so that it will reduce to flour-sized particles easily.

Once tempered, the wheat is ready to be milled. Wheat goes through multiple milling steps on its way to becoming white flour. Each step either grinds the stock, as the wheat is called once it enters the mill, or separates it into flour, bran, shorts, and overtails or "overs," these last two terms designating the stock that needs further processing.

At RMFM, the first set of rollers the tempered wheat encounters is called the prebreak rolls, two very heavy composite-iron rolls, both nine inches in diameter and several feet long. The rolls squash the wheat kernel into a flat flake, which helps the bran and germ to separate more cleanly and allows more flour to be released in the upcoming break rolls, just as rolling a lemon on the counter before squeezing it yields more juice.

The next set of rollers in the flow is called breaking rolls, and these are the same as the prebreak rolls but with a finely corrugated surface. The corrugation on the rolls actually has a grain to it, as I found by sliding my hands over an unused set. The breaking rolls are so called because they break the wheat up into large pieces, shearing away large flakes of bran while reducing the endosperm into chunks.

Steve opened the door covering the first set of rollers and stuck his metal slick, a type of metal spatula, against the rapidly spinning roll (the rolls rotate at 400 to 500 rpm). The stock he pulled out was coarse and just slightly warm, about 85°F. This stock is on its way to its first sifting. What passes through the sifter is flour; what remains, the overs, goes into the next set of breaking rolls. Steve likes the stock at this point to contain plenty of bran to "cushion" the endosperm chunks and prevent them from getting beaten up by the next and last set of breaking rolls. Then the stock gets sifted again, after which all the large bran flakes and most of the flour will have been extracted.

Steve explained that the best-quality flour produced in his mill, the flour coming from the center of the wheat kernel, is released at these breaking rolls. The remaining stock also produces flour, but it is brannier and contains more damaged starch, an indication of poor quality. To extract this last bit of flour, the stock passes through two sets of reduction rolls, so called because their original purpose was to reduce the cleaned endosperm into flour. The rolls are the same as the breaking rolls, but their surface is smooth, not corrugated. After each pass through the rolls, the stock is sifted again to separate a lightly tan flour. What cannot pass through the final sifter, mainly very finely ground bran called shorts, RMFM mixes with the bran to sell as organic mill feed for livestock.

At the end of this whole milling process, four different streams of flour will have been produced. The first two are the whitest, coming from the two breaking rolls, and the last two are the darkest, coming from the two reduction rolls. RMFM combines all these mill streams to make what is called a straight-grade flour. Larger mills with more elaborate flows separate the whiter grades, called patent flours, and charge a premium for them. The remaining darker grades of flour, called clear flours, are often used in rye and wheat breads.

At RMFM, the finished flour is pumped into the storage warehouse, where it is sifted once more, then bagged and stored before being shipped. Flour fresh from the mill is "hot" or "green," and cannot be baked immediately into high-quality bread. The flour needs to oxidize, a process most mills induce artificially with ADA or potassium bromate, both potential carcinogens, or leave to the baker to worry about. RMFM is one of the few mills to oxidize its flour naturally, which it does in a warehouse for ten days. The sight of pallets of freshly milled flour is impressive—all that lovingly milled flour just waiting to be baked into wholesome breads.

Note: Since my visit, Bay State Mills has partially bought out RMFM and become its managing partner. Steve and Lisa Curran have decided not to stay on, and both have accepted positions with General Mills.

An open bag of Rocky Mountain Flour Mill's Alpine flour

INVENTING THE KICE MILL

As a milling professor at Kansas State University, the only university in the world with a complete milling and cereal chemistry department, Steve Curran would get requests for help constantly. Petitioners from developing nations brought especially challenging problems, reflecting their countries' scarce resources. Steve came to realize that the advice he gave to millers here or from developed countries was wrong for millers from developing nations, who were just trying to produce enough flour to "feed the people," the whiteness and quality being secondary at best.

While tinkering in his experimental mill with the prebreak process, a preliminary milling step, Steve discovered a method that he believed could ulti-

mately benefit these millers. In an ordinary prebreak passage, wheat kernels are very lightly flattened between two smooth rollers before entering the break rolls. The wheat kernel is barely altered by the process, but its crease does get pushed out. When Steve tried narrowing the prebreak rollers to flatten the kernels rather than to gently press them, he found that the balance of all subsequent milling steps was altered. This single step somehow profoundly changed the kernel's structure.

Steve believed that he was on to something and decided to try to patent it. Remembering that Jack Kice, one of the founding brothers of the equipment company Kice Industries, had spoken of his dream to build a more practical mill for developing nations, he approached Tom Kice, the current president of Kice

Industries and Jack's nephew, with his results. With his discovery, he believed it would be possible to build a much simpler mill, requiring fewer passages and thus much less equipment and power than a typical flour mill. Kice responded enthusiastically and agreed to fund more research.

Steve went back to his lab and designed a small prototype mill. He first flaked the grain in the prebreak rolls, then ran it through just two sets of breaking rollers, instead of the usual five, skipped the purifiers—machines normally used to blow out the bran—and, finally, reduced all the overs on two sets of reduction rolls, down from the typical seven to ten. He expected to produce a very poor quality, if inexpensive, flour. Instead the mill's first run resulted in surprisingly decent flour. Kice enthusi-

astically funded a full-scale prototype, which produced even better flour. It seemed that the larger the prototype, the better the results. Steve was utterly confounded. According to the prevailing milling wisdom, you cannot eliminate that many steps and still get good results. How could this be?

Going back to the research, Steve was able to piece together a better explanation of why flour milled on his mill was "as good or better than flour milled on conventional flows." It seems that 65% to 70% of the flour produced was being generated in the breaking section! In traditional long-flow roller milling, very little if any flour is produced there; instead the endosperm is intentionally left in large chunks. The first flour released from the wheat is always the purest and least

damaged, since it is subjected to the least amount of processing and is most likely coming from the center of the wheat kernel. Most of the damage to the flour is inflicted during the reduction-roll phase of milling, which, in long-flow milling, is also where most of the flour is released. In the Kice Mill, most of the flour is released very early in the milling process, before the overs meet the reduction rollers. You could say that the Kice Mill is gentler on wheat.

Steve's mill exceeded everybody's expectations, so Kice leased the technology from Kansas State University and entered the milling market. Today, there are twenty-one Kice mills in countries all over the world, including the new one at Rocky Mountain Flour Milling in Platteville, Colorado (pages 71–73).

OPPOSITE, LEFT TO RIGHT: Storage tanks that hold unprocessed wheat; Steve Curran holding stock from the breaking rollers; Steve checking stock flow into vibrating sifters. ABOVE, LEFT TO RIGHT: Flour aging in the warehouse for over a week before being shipped out; the Kice Mill.

Steve Curran pushing his slick against a spinning roller to remove a wheat sample from the first set of breaking rolls

EXTRACTION RATES

An important concept in roller milling is extraction rate, which describes the amount of flour extracted from the wheat. Typically, millers can extract 72% of the wheat kernel into white flour; this is 72% extraction flour. Whole-wheat flour, which has nothing removed, is 100% extraction flour. Artisan bakers often prefer flours with higher extraction rates—with more of the bran and germ —for their darker color and wheatier flavor. An 85% extraction flour has a warm golden color and rich flavor, while a 95% extraction has just the least bit of bran removed and is almost as dark as whole-wheat flour. Baker Thom Leonard (see page 129) loves the 95% flour for its sweet robustness but lack of tannic astringency that comes from the outer- most layers of bran.

Essential's Sweet Perrin (Pear Bread)

- Makes two 17-ounce (500-gram) loaves
- Time: About 18 hours, with 30 minutes of active work

The Essential Baking Company is a certified organic bakery in Seattle, strictly wholesale, which I visited during one night shift. Founder and head baker George DePasquale apprenticed with Glenn Mitchell at Grace Baking in Albany, California, and then moved to the growing Seattle market to start this specialty bakery. George loaded me down with samples of all their breads, and the two given here were my favorites.

Sweet Perrin, named after a partner's daughter, was designed to look like a Christmas gift and is cleverly tied up in raffia twine. Fresh pears, figs, and hazelnuts are loaded into a complex dough made with a pre-ferment, rye, and two kinds of flour.

RECIPE SYNOPSIS **THE EVENING BEFORE BAKING:** Mix the pre-ferment and soak the cracked rye. Let it stand for 12 hours. **THE NEXT MORNING:** Mix the dough and let it ferment for 3 hours. Shape the dough, let it proof for about 1 hour, and then bake the bread for about 40 minutes.

	Pre-ferment	volume	weight	metric	baker's percentages
THE EVENING BEFORE BAKING **MAKING** **THE PRE-FERMENT**	**Instant yeast**	¼ teaspoon			(eventually 0.06%)
	Water, 110° to 115°F	1 cup			
	Unbleached bread flour, preferably organic	1 cup plus 3 tablespoons	6.2 ounces	175 grams	100%
	Water, lukewarm	¾ cup	6.2 ounces	175 grams	(eventually 117%)

Sprinkle the yeast over the warm water, stir, and let it stand for 5 to 10 minutes. Add the flour to a bowl. Measure 2 tablespoons yeasted water into the flour (throw the rest away), then mix in the lukewarm water. Cover this gloppy dough tightly with plastic wrap and let it ferment overnight until its surface is wrinkled and foamy, about 12 hours.

	Soaked Rye	volume	weight	metric	baker's percentages
SOAKING THE RYE	**Cracked rye**	1 tablespoon plus 1 teaspoon	0.6 ounce	17 grams	100%
	Water	2 tablespoons plus 1 teaspoon	0.6 ounce	17 grams	100%

Combine the rye and water in a bowl, stir until well combined, cover well with plastic wrap, and let soak overnight for 12 hours.

continued

Dough	volume	weight	metric	baker's percentages
Organic high-extraction flour or unbleached bread flour	2 cups	10.5 ounces	300 grams	88%
Whole-wheat flour	¼ cup	1.5 ounces	40 grams	12%
Instant yeast	¼ teaspoon			0.2%
Pre-ferment				112%
Soaked rye				10%
Water, lukewarm	½ cup	4.2 ounces	120 grams	35%
Pear baby food*	⅓ cup	2.8 ounces	80 grams	23%
Salt	2¼ teaspoons	0.4 ounce	12 grams	3.5%
Cinnamon	½ teaspoon			0.5%
Allspice	½ teaspoon			0.5%
Very hard, crisp pear, such as Bosc or Anjou, peeled, cored, and cut into ½-inch cubes	¾ cup	4 ounces	115 grams	33%
Dried Calimyrna figs, stemmed and cut into ½-inch pieces	½ cup	2 ounces	60 grams	17%
Hazelnuts, lightly toasted and skinned†	6 tablespoons	2 ounces	60 grams	17%
Untreated raffia twine to use as decoration				

*Essential uses pear concentrate, which I couldn't find, so I substituted the baby food with a good result.

†Toast the hazelnuts in a small baking pan in a 350°F oven until lightly browned and fragrant. Rub the warm nuts in a tea towel to remove the skins.

by hand: Combine the flours and yeast in a large bowl. Add the pre-ferment, soaked rye, water, and pear baby food and mix just until the dough is smooth. Cover the bowl with plastic wrap and let rest (autolyse) for 20 to 30 minutes.

Turn the dough out onto your work surface, add the salt and spices, and knead the dough until it is smooth and soft but not too sticky. The dough will feel drier when fully kneaded. Knead in the pear, figs, and hazelnuts just until evenly distributed.

by stand mixer: Combine the flours and yeast in the mixing bowl. Add the pre-ferment, soaked rye, water, and pear baby food and mix just until the dough is smooth. Cover the bowl with plastic wrap and let rest (autolyse) for 20 to 30 minutes.

Add the salt and spices to the dough. Using the dough hook, knead it on medium speed until it is very smooth, about 5 minutes. Remove the dough from the bowl and knead in the pears, figs, and hazelnuts by hand just until they are evenly distributed.

by food processor: Add the flours, yeast, salt, and spices to the workbowl of the food processor fitted with the steel blade and pulse the dry ingredients a few times to mix them. Add the preferment, soaked rye, water, and pear baby food to the dry ingredients. Processs the dough until the workbowl fogs, about 30 seconds. Remove the dough and knead it briefly to cool it. Process it again until the workbowl fogs, about 30 seconds, then knead again by hand to cool it. Continue processing and kneading the dough in intervals until it feels smooth, strong, and somewhat dry to the touch. Knead in the pears, figs, and hazelnuts by hand.

This is a soft dough.

FERMENTING THE DOUGH

Place the dough in a container at least 3 times its size and cover it tightly with plastic wrap. Let it ferment until it is airy and well expanded but not yet doubled in bulk, about 3 hours.

While the dough is fermenting, soak several long lengths of the twine in water.

ROUNDING AND RESTING THE DOUGH

Flour the surface of the dough and your work surface and turn the dough out. Cut the dough in half; each piece should weigh 20 ounces (565 grams). Lightly round the pieces (page 17), cover them loosely with plastic wrap, and let rest until well relaxed, 10 to 15 minutes.

SHAPING AND PROOFING THE DOUGH

Shape the dough pieces into tight round loaves. Seal the bottom seams tightly and place the loaves seal side down on 2 small sheets of parchment paper on a peel or cookie sheet. Loosely tie the soaked twine around each round to form a cross (like a present); allow enough room under the twine to slip in a few fingers. Cover the loaves well with plastic wrap and proof the breads until they are well expanded, but still spring back when gently pressed with a finger, about 1½ hours.

PREHEATING THE OVEN

At least 45 minutes before the dough is fully proofed, arrange a rack on the oven's second-to-top shelf and place a baking stone on it. Clear away all racks above the one being used. Preheat the oven to 375°F (190°C).

BAKING THE BREAD

If desired, just before baking, fill the oven with steam (page 18). Slide the breads, still on the paper, onto the hot stone and quickly spray them with a mister or a pressurized garden sprayer filled with water. Bake until the breads are dark and evenly browned all around, about 40 minutes, rotating them halfway into the bake. Let the breads cool on a rack.

LEFT: Essential's Columbia (page 82). ABOVE: Essential's Sweet
Perrin (page 77).

Essential's Columbia (Country French-Style Bread)

- Makes 2 long 22-ounce (625-gram) loaves
- Time: About 24 hours, with about 20 minutes of active work

George DePasquale of Seattle's Essential Baking Company has added a smattering of whole-wheat flour, whole-rye flour, barley malt, and wheat germ for the warm colors and flavors they provide in this simple and versatile country-style bread. The bread forms a rich brown crust, thanks to the malt, and a beautifully open-textured crumb. The bread is named for the Columbia River, which forms the border between Washington and Oregon.

RECIPE SYNOPSIS **THE EVENING BEFORE BAKING:** Eight to 12 hours before mixing the dough, mix the levain and let it ferment. **THE NEXT MORNING:** Mix the dough, and let it ferment for 4 to 6 hours. Shape the dough, let it proof for 3½ to 4½ hours, then bake the bread for about 40 minutes.

	Levain	volume	weight	metric	baker's percentages
THE EVENING BEFORE BAKING MAKING THE LEVAIN	**Fermented firm sourdough starter (pages 91–94), refreshed 8 to 12 hours before**	2 tablespoons plus 1 teaspoon	1 ounce	30 grams	20%
	Water, lukewarm	7 tablespoons	3.3 ounces	95 grams	63%
	Unbleached bread flour, preferably organic	1 cup	5.3 ounces	150 grams	100%

Dissolve the sourdough in the water in a bowl. Add the flour and knead this very stiff dough until it is smooth. It will be very hard at first but it will smooth out. Place the levain in a covered container and let it ferment until it is fully risen and deflates when pressed, 8 to 12 hours.

	Scrap Dough	volume	weight	metric	baker's percentages
BAKE DAY MIXING THE DOUGH	**Unbleached bread flour, preferably organic**	2 cups	10.6 ounces	300 grams	45%
	Unbleached all-purpose flour, preferably organic	2 cups	10.6 ounces	300 grams	45%
	Whole-wheat flour, finely ground	⅓ cup	1.9 ounces	55 grams	8%
	Whole-rye flour, finely ground	3 tablespoons	0.5 ounce	15 grams	2%
	Wheat germ, toasted	3 tablespoons	0.7 ounce	20 grams	3%
	Barley malt (non-diastatic malt syrup)	1 tablespoon	0.7 ounce	20 grams	3%
	Water, warm	2 cups	16 ounces	450 grams	67%
	Fermented levain				41%
	Salt	1 tablespoon plus ¼ teaspoon	0.5 ounce	16 grams	2.4%

by hand: Combine all 4 flours and the wheat germ in a large bowl. Measure the malt in an oiled tablespoon and dissolve it in the water. Pour the malted water over the flour mixture and mix with your hands or a wooden spoon just until the dough is combined. Cover the bowl with plastic wrap and let rest (autolyse) for 20 to 30 minutes.

Turn the dough out onto your work surface, add the levain and salt, and knead the dough until it is very smooth, about 10 minutes.

by stand mixer: Combine all 4 flours and the wheat germ in the mixing bowl. Measure the malt in an oiled tablespoon and dissolve it in the water. Pour the malted water over the flour mixture and mix the dough with your hands or a wooden spoon just until it is combined. Cover the bowl with a plate and let rest (autolyse) for 20 to 30 minutes.

Add the levain and salt to the dough. Using the dough hook, knead it on medium speed until it is very smooth, about 5 minutes.

by food processor: The dough can be mixed in a food processor if it is divided in half. Combine all the dry ingredients including the salt in a bowl. Measure the malt in an oiled tablespoon and dissolve it in the water. Pour the malted water over the dry ingredients, add the levain, and mix the dough with your hands or a wooden spoon just until the dough is combined. There is no need for a resting period.

Divide the dough in half and add half the dough to the workbowl fitted with the steel blade. Process the dough until the workbowl fogs, about 30 seconds. Remove this dough and knead it briefly to cool it. Process the second half of the dough the same way and knead it. Repeat this process until the dough is smooth and strong. Knead the 2 pieces together by hand just to combine them.

The dough should feel smooth, dry, and firm at the end of the kneading.

FERMENTING AND TURNING THE DOUGH

Place the dough in a container at least 3 times its size and cover it tightly with plastic wrap. Let it ferment for 1 hour. Turn the dough once (page 16), then continue to let it ferment until light and well expanded but not yet doubled in bulk, 3 to 5 hours more.

ROUNDING AND RESTING THE DOUGH

Flour the surface of the dough and your work surface and turn the dough out. Cut the dough in half; each piece should weigh about 24 ounces (690 grams). Lightly round the pieces (page 17), cover them loosely with plastic wrap, and let rest until well relaxed, 10 to 15 minutes.

SHAPING AND PROOFING THE DOUGH

Shape the dough into bâtards (page 35) about 10 inches long. Set them seam side down in a couche or lined banneton to proof. Cover the loaves well with plastic wrap and let the breads proof until well expanded but still springy when lightly pressed with a finger, 3½ to 4½ hours.

PREHEATING THE OVEN

At least 45 minutes before the dough is fully proofed, arrange a rack on the oven's second-to-top shelf and place a baking stone on it. Clear away all racks above the one being used. Preheat the oven to 425°F (220°C).

BAKING THE BREAD

Gently place the breads on a sheet of parchment paper, as far apart as your stone will allow (breads that are close together will "burst," that is, crack open at the sides instead of expanding at the slash). Slash each bread 5 times, beginning each slash at the middle of the last one, forming a grapevine pattern. Slide the breads on the paper onto the hot stone and quickly spray them with water from a plant mister or a pressurized garden sprayer filled with water. To create extra steam, crack open the oven door, insert the nozzle of the pressurized garden sprayer, and fill the oven with water mist for a minute. Bake the breads for 35 to 40 minutes, rotating them around halfway into the bake. The breads are finished baking when they are dark and evenly browned all around. Let the breads cool on a rack.

CRAFTING

BREAD

UNRAVELING SOURDOUGH

PEARL BAKERY

PORTLAND, OREGON

GREG MISTELL IS AN EXTRAORDINARILY SUCCESSFUL PORTLAND BAKER who purposely took a step backward in his career. After getting Delphina's Bakery in shape to hand over to his children, just the last of a long line of higher-volume artisan-style bakeries with which he has been involved, he opened a small, intimate neighborhood bakery with an emphasis on good bread. Pearl, named for the historic Portland district in which it is located, really is a jewel.

I visited on a Monday morning. Greg worked the oven just behind a pastry-filled case, while I chatted and helped him a bit, putting baskets away, finding his lost razor, and checking the breads. He even let me cut a few of his baguettes. Later that day, I watched Pearl bakers mixing Walnut Levain, Pane coi Santi, and Fig-Anise Panini, three of the delicious pains au levain offered at Pearl.

As we worked, the tables out front were continually refilled with customers, friends, and colleagues. One customer even stepped behind the counter to complain about the "lack of chairs"; it seems there were rarely two free when she comes in for morning coffee and pastry.

Greg and his original partner restored the former printing shop themselves, preserving its thick ceiling beams and huge wood-framed windows. They painted the walls deep eggplant and khaki green and strung brightly colored glass light fixtures to brighten the high-ceilinged room. Greg got a large baking space in the back with a superb climate-control system.

I first met Greg in 1993 at Professor Raymond Calvel's seminar hosted by the Bread Bakers Guild of America at the Culinary Institute of America in Hyde Park, New York. I was there to learn from the master himself how to conquer that trickiest of French breads, pain au levain. Greg loves to travel and learn, and was there just for the fun of it. A few years later, we found ourselves together again, this time for a seminar at the Ecole Française de Boulangerie d'Aurillac, a French baking school, also hosted by the Bread Bakers Guild of America. Walking along an old country lane, Greg told me that, despite all his accomplishments, what he really wanted to do was to open up a "jewel-box" bakery. It would seem that he accomplished exactly that at Pearl.

OPPOSITE: An invitation to lunch—a tray of sandwiches at Pearl Bakery. ABOVE: Pearl founder Greg Mistell.

SOURDOUGH BREADS

In all of baking, no method seems to capture people's imaginations and curiosity like sourdough. Little mysterious organisms, coming from who knows where, eating and reproducing in a jar on your countertop—what could be more intriguing? Even after the initial fascination wears off, bakers cherish their sourdough starters (sometimes for decades) for the superb baked goods that they leaven and imbue with their inimitable flavor.

Sourdough starters are colonies with three distinct populations: lactic-acid-forming bacteria, lactic-and-acetic-acid-forming bacteria, and sourdough yeasts. Learning to artfully balance the requirements of these three groups will empower your bread making, enabling you to master that best of all possible breads.

Sourdough starter is a batter or a dough that has been colonized by sourdough yeasts and bacteria, collectively called microflora. Its hallmark is its acidity. Its pH is considerably lower than that of a yeast-raised batter or dough because of the bacteria found there. The most important sourdough bacteria belong to a group called *Lactobacilli,* although other types have been identified as well. *Lactobacilli* ferment select simple sugars and excrete primarily acids as waste products. Some *Lactobacilli* excrete lactic acid almost exclusively, while others excrete lactic acid and a small amount of acetic acid (or vinegar). The acetic acid/lactic acid ratio plus the overall concentration of acidity determines the fundamental flavor of the sourdough product.

Controlling the bread's acidity *and* acetic acid/lactic acid ratio is a large part of the art of sourdough-bread making. French sourdough bread, called *pain au levain,* is one of the world's great breads and a source of great inspiration to American artisan bakers. Correctly made, pain au levain is moderately sour with a complex but well-rounded flavor that is less intense than our San Francisco sourdough bread. To find out more about the bacteriology of pain au levain, I spoke with Dr. Richard-Molard, a French microbiologist and a cereal chemist with the INRA (the French equivalent of the USDA) and one of France's foremost experts on bread flavor.

He explained that to achieve a well-balanced sourdough flavor it is necessary to have both acetic and lactic acid present in the bread. German bakers insist on a one-to-four ratio of acetic acid to lactic acid, but the French are not quite that precise, only insisting that some acetic acid be present. If only acetic acid is present, the bread will taste very sharp and vinegary, but if only lactic acid is present, the bread "will have no special taste," because lactic acid is much milder and less discernible. The true and correct sourdough flavor is achieved only when the two acids are present and balanced in the bread.

Interestingly, different conditions favor the production of different acids. Temperatures in the range of 95° to 104°F and wet batterlike starters favor the *Lactobacilli* that excrete lactic acid. Temperatures around 68°F and stiff doughlike starters favor the *Lactobacilli* that excrete both acetic and lactic acids.

Dr. Richard-Molard also pointed out that acetic acid takes a relatively long time to form in a starter or dough. Lactic acid is produced in much greater quantities, and so builds up more quickly in the dough. Many bakers, aiming for a more pronounced sour flavor, will refrigerate, or "retard," their doughs overnight for the extra time and cool temperatures to increase the acetic acid content of the dough. Bakers looking for a more mild effect use liquid starters and avoid the retarder, baking the bread the same day it is mixed.

All yeasts are sensitive to acidity and will not ferment well when their environment becomes too acidic. But each type of yeast has its own tolerance to acid, so some are able to flourish in a sourdough starter. Many different types of yeast have been identified in starter around the world but, surprisingly, the most common sourdough yeast is *Saccharomyces cerevisiae,* the same species, if not the same strain, found in commercial yeast preparations.

Some starters house only one type of yeast and one or two bacteria, while others have many. The most famous American starter, the San Francisco sourdough starter, has one type of yeast, now classified as *Candida milleri* (it was originally classified as *Torulopsis holmii,* a species of *Saccharomyces exiguus*), and one bacteria, *Lactobacillus sanfrancisco.* In most starters, the yeast and bacteria compete for the available carbohydrates, but in the San Francisco sourdough starter, the yeast eat a normal range of yeast sugars except for maltose, while the bacteria eat only maltose. This unique sharing of the food supply is believed to contribute to its stability.

The most baffling aspect of sourdough starters for home and professional bakers seems to be the origin of the yeast and bacteria. While many writers reflexively point to the air in the kitchen as the source, they are missing the gold mine under their noses: the flour or the fruit with which the starter was begun.

Sourdough microflora naturally grow on the grains and skins of fruits out in the field or orchard. Probably flying and crawling insects inoculate the crop with the microflora, since the microflora originates in the soil. Of course, every crop and every growing region will have a different mixture of bacteria and yeast, leading to the unique compositions of sourdough starters found around the world. In France, it is very common to start sourdough starters from raisins or apples, or whatever fruit is available and inexpensive. Some American bakers start sourdough starters with grapes. Realize, however, that by the time the starter is ready to inoculate a batch of bread, very little, if any, of the fruit flavor will remain.

Professor Calvel, the French baking expert, prefers to begin sourdough starter ferments for pain au levain with grains rather than fruit, reasoning that its microflora are already well adapted to doughs and will produce flavors more natural to bread. The best grain with which to start a sourdough starter is rye, as the Germans have known for centuries. Rye naturally is richly coated with the ideal types of yeast for sourdoughs, including *Candida crusei, Pichia saitoi, Torulopsis holmii* and, of course, *Saccaromyces cerevisiae.* Because these organisms always grow on the outside of a fruit or grain, whole-grain flours containing the bran will have a much higher microflora count than will white flours, which have very little bran. That is not to say that white flour is sterile, it just has fewer microflora, meaning that a sourdough starter made with white flour will be slower to develop than would one made with whole-grain flour.

. Spare Levain.
when you change.
this, keep 1 lb. of
it, add 1 lb. of
& 1 lb. Flour. Let sit
out for a few hours
before you put it away.

French-Style Sourdough Starter

- Makes 4 ounces (100 grams) sourdough starter
- Time: 7 to 14 days, with about 10 minutes of active work

This recipe produces a firm, French-style sourdough starter (called a *chef* in France), which is used to make pain au levain, French sourdough bread, but can be used in any sourdough recipe. It starts out very stiff, like a piece of modeling clay, and gets softer and stickier as it ferments. I think it is a better sourdough starter for home bakers than the typical batter-type one because it is very easy to tell if it is active enough to use: When ready, it will *quadruple in volume in 8 hours or less*. This means that ¼ cup starter should rise to fill 1 cup in 8 hours or less. If it is only doubling or tripling, that is, going to ½ cup or ¾ cup, it needs more refreshments.

Rye flour is used to start it, because rye naturally contains an ample population of sourdough yeasts and bacteria. The basic idea is to culture the yeasts and bacteria—microflora—in the rye flour until a high enough concentration is achieved. Typically, the first dough will ferment for 3 days, the next for 2 days, then 2 days again, then 1 day, then 18 hours, then 12 hours, and then, finally, 8 hours (added up, this is 10 days in total). In other words, the time between refreshments becomes progressively smaller until the starter's microflora population is large enough.

What nobody can predict for you is the time needed between successive refreshments or how many refreshments you will need before your starter is fully active. I have found that it can take anywhere from 7 to 14 days for the starter to become fully active. In the winter especially, when kitchens are colder, you will probably need up to 2 weeks of refreshments before the starter is ready to raise bread dough.

Finally, you will notice that very little sourdough starter is being made. This is because the formula produces such a strong and active starter that very little of it is needed.

continued

First Starter	volume	weight	metric	baker's percentages
Water, lukewarm	½ cup	3.5 ounces	100 grams	100%
Whole-rye flour	¾ cup	3.5 ounces	100 grams	100%

THE FIRST DAY
MIXING THE FIRST STARTER

Mix the water and rye in a nonreactive bowl and tightly cover it with plastic wrap, or transfer it to a sealed glass or plastic jar. Let stand for about 2 days. It should bubble up, smell and look awful, and then subside. At this point it is ready to refresh.

Second Starter	volume	weight	metric	baker's percentages
Unbleached all-purpose flour	⅔ cup	3.5 ounces	100 grams	100%
Fermented first starter				200%

THE THIRD DAY
MIXING THE SECOND STARTER

Mix the flour into the first starter, forming a firm dough, and transfer it to a clean nonreactive container. Cover it tightly with plastic wrap and let it ferment for 1 or 2 days. When it is very sticky and riddled with tiny bubbles, it is ready to refresh. It will have very little aroma and will not rise very much, if at all.

Third Starter	volume	weight	metric	baker's percentages
Fermented starter	¼ cup	2 ounces	60 grams	66%
Water, lukewarm	3 tablespoons	1.5 ounces	45 grams	50%
Unbleached bread flour	⅔ cup	3 ounces	90 grams	100%

THE FIFTH DAY
MIXING THE THIRD STARTER

Measure the amount of fermented starter you need and discard the rest. Dissolve it in the water, then add the flour and mix into a fairly firm dough. Tightly cover with plastic wrap and let the dough ferment until it is sticky and slightly expanded, 1 to 2 days.

After a day, the starter will appear not to be fermenting at all. But if you smell it, it will smell very sour, and if you pull it open with floured fingers, it will be very gooey, extensible, and riddled with tiny air bubbles.

THE SIXTH OR SEVENTH DAY

Make a fourth starter exactly as the third was made. Cover tightly with plastic wrap and let the dough ferment until it has risen slightly, is full of tiny holes, and has become very gooey, 18 to 24 hours. This starter will look as unpromising as the third.

THE REMAINING DAYS

Continue refreshing the sourdough starter as directed for the third and fourth starters, always waiting until it has risen fully and is starting to fall, until the starter is able to quadruple in 8 hours or less and has a sharp and very pleasant smell. This may take 3 or 4 more refreshments, each in a little less time than the last. At this point the sourdough starter is ready to use. It can be kept and refreshed indefinitely, using the instructions on page 93 for a completed sourdough starter.

TO REFRESH A COMPLETED SOURDOUGH STARTER

Completed Dough	volume	weight	metric	baker's percentages
Fermented sourdough starter	1½ teaspoons	0.4 ounce	10 grams	10%
Water, lukewarm	1 tablespoon plus 2 teaspoons	0.9 ounce	25 grams	60%
Unbleached bread flour	⅓ cup	1.6 ounces	45 grams	100%

Measure the starter you need and discard the rest, or save it to flavor another dough. Dissolve the starter in the water, then add the flour and mix it into a fairly firm dough. Cover tightly with plastic wrap and let the dough ferment for 8 to 12 hours. This will make about ⅓ cup (2.9 ounces, 80 grams) dough. It should rise to 1⅓ cups (at least its crown will) in 8 hours or less.

Use this refreshment formula to make a sourdough starter that only needs to be refreshed every 12 hours (professionals refresh their sourdough starters every 8 hours). The final starter should be very firm, to buffer its pH, preventing it from dropping too low, and to give it enough fuel to last until the next refreshment.

The sourdough starter can be stored in the refrigerator almost indefinitely. I have kept mine in there a good 4 months and have then been able to revive it to its full strength. (My tester, Rita Yeazel, has revived one to full strength after 18 months in the refrigerator!) Old sourdough starter will turn gray and exude a clear liquid (a.k.a. hooch), but that is normal. To get it back into working order, refresh the sourdough starter as directed above every 12 hours 3 or 4 times (over 1½ to 2 days), until it is again quadrupling in volume in 8 hours or less. It is then ready to use.

TO CONVERT A BATTER-TYPE SOURDOUGH STARTER INTO A FIRM STARTER

Many bakers already have liquid sourdough starters going and will want to convert them into firm starters to use in these recipes. Here is a simple way to proceed.

Firm Starter	volume	weight	metric	baker's percentages
Fermented liquid sourdough starter	1 tablespoon	0.5 ounce	15 grams	30%
Water, lukewarm	1 tablespoon	0.5 ounce	15 grams	30%
Unbleached bread flour	⅓ cup	1.8 ounces	50 grams	100%

Dissolve the liquid sourdough starter in the water, add the flour, and knead together this very firm dough. Cover tightly with plastic wrap and let the dough ferment for 8 to 12 hours. This will make about ⅓ cup (2.9 ounces, 80 grams) dough. It should rise to 1⅓ cups (at least its crown will) in 8 hours or less. If it does not, your starter could be weak and need several more refreshments to achieve full strength. Just follow the instructions for refreshing a completed sourdough starter to continue refreshments.

continued

TO CONVERT A SOURDOUGH RECIPE INTO A COMMERCIAL YEAST RECIPE

Many home bakers are intimidated or overwhelmed by the idea of starting, maintaining, and using sourdough starter. If that is you, take heart. *Any* sourdough-based recipe can be converted into a yeast-based recipe. The bread will not have the complex flavor, moist crumb, and long-keeping qualities of a true sourdough, but it will still be a very fine loaf.

To convert a recipe from sourdough to commercial yeast, you will just use a small amount of yeast in the levain and omit the sourdough starter. Use ⅛ teaspoon yeast per cup (150 grams, 5.3 ounces) flour *in the levain,* not the final dough (this is 0.3% yeast). Or, dissolve ¼ teaspoon yeast in ¼ cup warm water and use 2 tablespoons of the yeasted water per cup (150 grams, 5.3 ounces) flour. For example, for a levain calling for ½ cup flour, use 1 tablespoon yeasted water (measuring ¹⁄₁₆ teaspoon yeast). Be sure to reduce the water measure in the levain by the same amount as the added yeasted water.

Let the levain, which is now technically a pre-ferment, ferment for 2 to 3 hours, or until it has risen to about half again its original volume, then refrigerate it overnight until ready to use. Let it come to room temperature before adding it to the final dough. Continue with the recipe as directed—there is no need to add more yeast. The fermenting and proofing times for the yeasted version of the dough might be slightly faster than specified.

If you are unsure of how this method works, see Royal Crown's Tortano on page 203, which also uses this procedure.

The Pearl's Walnut Levain

- Makes two 19-ounce (500-gram) loaves
- Time: At least 21 hours, with about 20 minutes of active work

This is a simple pain au levain with the addition of walnuts. Pearl mixes stiffer doughs than others in this book, so expect a bread with a tighter grain and a tauter shape. They use an 11.5% protein flour, the same as King Arthur all-purpose. I have substituted a mixture of bread flour and all-purpose flour, the most commonly available, but if you have the King Arthur flour, just use that for the two white flours.

RECIPE SYNOPSIS **THE MORNING OF THE DAY BEFORE BAKING:** Refresh your sourdough starter. (If it has been stored in the refrigerator, start refreshing it 2 days before baking with it, for at least 3 times). **THAT EVENING:** Mix the levain and let it ferment overnight. **THE NEXT MORNING:** Mix the dough and let it ferment for 4 hours. Shape the dough, then let it proof for about 3 hours. Bake the bread for about 45 minutes.

	Levain	volume	weight	metric	baker's percentages
THE EVENING BEFORE BAKING **MAKING** **THE LEVAIN**	**Fermented firm sourdough starter (pages 91–94), refreshed 8 hours before**	1 tablespoon	0.5 ounce	15 grams	20%
	Water, lukewarm	3 tablespoons	1.6 ounces	45 grams	60%
	Unbleached bread flour	½ cup	2.6 ounces	75 grams	100%

Dissolve the sourdough starter in the water. Add the flour and knead this very stiff dough until it is fairly smooth. Place it in a covered container and let it ferment overnight until quadrupled in bulk and deflating if lightly pressed, about 12 hours.

	Dough	volume	weight	metric	baker's percentages
BAKE DAY **MIXING** **THE DOUGH**	**Unbleached bread flour**	2 cups	10.6 ounces	300 grams	43%
	Unbleached all-purpose flour	2 cups	10.6 ounces	300 grams	43%
	Medium rye flour	½ cup	1.8 ounces	50 grams	7%
	Whole-wheat flour	⅓ cup	1.8 ounces	50 grams	7%
	Water, lukewarm	2 cups	16.1 ounces	455 grams	65%
	Salt	1 tablespoon plus ¼ teaspoon	0.6 ounce	16 grams	2.3%
	Fermented levain				20%
	English walnut halves, lightly toasted	1 cup plus 3 tablespoons	4.2 ounces	120 grams	17%

continued

by hand: Combine the flours in a large bowl and mix in the water. When the dough is well combined, cover it tightly with plastic wrap and let rest (autolyse) for 10 to 30 minutes.

Add the salt and levain and knead the dough until it is smooth, about 10 minutes. Knead in the walnuts just until they are evenly distributed.

by stand mixer: Combine the flours in the mixing bowl and add the water. Using the dough hook, mix on low speed just until the dough is combined and wrapped around the dough hook, about 3 minutes. Cover the bowl with a plate and let rest (autolyse) for 10 to 30 minutes.

Add the salt and levain and mix the dough on medium speed just until it is smooth, about 4 minutes. Remove the dough from the bowl and knead in the walnuts by hand until they are evenly distributed.

by food processor: The dough can be mixed in a food processor if it is divided in half. Combine all the dry ingredients including the salt (but not the walnuts) in a bowl. Break up the levain in the water, then pour the mixture into the dry ingredients. Mix the dough with your hands or a wooden spoon just until the dough is combined. There is no need for a resting period.

Divide the dough in half and add half the dough to the workbowl fitted with the steel blade. Process the dough until the workbowl fogs, about 30 seconds. Remove this dough and knead it briefly to cool it. Process the second half of the dough the same way and knead it. Continue processing the 2 halves of the dough in 30-second intervals until they are smooth and strong. Knead them together by hand just to combine them. Knead in the walnuts by hand until they are evenly distributed.

This dough is firm, dry, and smooth. Add a tablespoon or two of water only if the dough seems excessively stiff.

FERMENTING AND TURNING THE DOUGH

Place the dough in a container at least 3 times its size and cover it tightly with plastic wrap. Let it ferment until it is airy and well expanded but not yet doubled in bulk, 4 to 5 hours. Turn the dough once (page 16) after 2 hours of fermenting, then leave the dough undisturbed for the remaining time.

ROUNDING AND RESTING THE DOUGH

Flour the surface of the dough and your work surface, then turn the dough out. Cut the dough in half; each piece should weigh 22 ounces (630 grams). Lightly round the pieces (page 17) and cover them loosely with plastic wrap. Let rest until well relaxed, 15 to 20 minutes.

SHAPING AND PROOFING THE DOUGH

Shape the dough into even and tight round loaves without deflating them. Place the shaped dough smooth side down in linen-lined baskets or large colanders. Lightly sprinkle them with flour and cover them well with plastic wrap. Proof the dough until it is well expanded and springs back slowly when gently pressed with a floured finger, about 3 hours.

PREHEATING THE OVEN

At least 45 minutes before the dough is fully proofed, arrange a rack on the oven's second-to-top shelf and place a baking stone on it. Clear away all racks above the one being used. Preheat the oven to 425°F (220°C).

BAKING THE BREAD

Turn the loaves out onto a sheet of parchment paper or a floured peel and slash a large and deep X into the top of each. In the center of each quarter, slash a small dash, dividing the surface into 8 wedges. If desired, just before baking, fill the oven with steam (page 18). Slide the breads onto the hot stone and quickly spray them with water from a plant mister or pressurized garden sprayer. Bake the breads, until they are dark and evenly browned all around and sound hollow when thumped on the bottom, 40 to 45 minutes, rotating them halfway into the bake. Let the breads cool on a rack.

The Pearl's Walnut Levain, LEFT, Fig-Anise Panini, CENTER, and Pane coi Santi, RIGHT

The Pearl's Pane coi Santi or Fig-Anise Panini

- Makes two 24-ounce (680-gram) pane or ten 4-ounce (115-gram) panini
- Time: At least 20 hours, with about 20 minutes of active work

Pane coi Santi, meaning "bread with saints" in Italian, is so called because of all the fruit and nuts in the dough, which are meant to symbolize saints. (Pearl's formula was loosely inspired by Michele Scicolone's recipe in *La Dolce Vita,* Morrow, 1993.)

RECIPE SYNOPSIS THE MORNING OF THE DAY BEFORE BAKING: Refresh your sourdough starter (if it has been stored in the refrigerator, start refreshing it 2 days before baking with it, for at least 3 times). **THAT EVENING:** Mix the levain and let it ferment overnight. **THE NEXT MORNING:** Mix the dough and let it ferment for 4 hours. Shape the dough, then let it proof for about 3 hours. Bake the pane for about 45 minutes; the panini for about 30 minutes.

	Levain	volume	weight	metric	baker's percentages
THE EVENING BEFORE BAKING MAKING THE LEVAIN	**Fermented firm sourdough starter (pages 91–94), refreshed 8 hours before**	1 tablespoon	0.5 ounce	15 grams	20%
	Water, lukewarm	1 tablespoon plus 2 teaspoons	1.6 ounces	45 grams	60%
	Unbleached bread flour	½ cup	2.6 ounces	75 grams	100%

Dissolve the sourdough starter in the water. Add the flour and knead this very stiff dough until it is fairly smooth. Place it in a covered container and let it ferment overnight for 8 hours, or until it has quadrupled in bulk and deflates if lightly pressed.

	Dough	volume	weight	metric	baker's percentages
BAKE DAY MIXING THE DOUGH	**Unbleached bread flour**	1⅔ cups	8.8 ounces	250 grams	42%
	Unbleached all-purpose flour	1⅔ cups	8.8 ounces	250 grams	42%
	Medium rye flour	½ cup	1.7 ounces	50 grams	8%
	Whole-wheat flour	⅓ cup	1.7 ounces	50 grams	8%
	Water, lukewarm	1¾ cups	13.8 ounces	390 grams	65%
	Salt	1 tablespoon	0.5 ounce	14 grams	2.3%
	Fermented levain				22%
	English walnut halves, lightly toasted, for the pane	1¼ cups	4.7 ounces	135 grams	22%
	Dark raisins, for the pane	1¾ cups	9.3 ounces	265 grams	44%
	Dried Calimyrna figs, for the panini	1¼ cups	7.4 ounces	210 grams	35%
	Anise seeds, for the panini	1 tablespoon plus 1 teaspoon	0.2 ounce	5 grams	0.9%

by hand: Combine the flours in a large bowl and mix in the water. When the dough is well combined, cover it tightly with plastic wrap and let rest (autolyse) for 10 to 30 minutes.

Add the salt and levain and knead the dough until it is smooth. Knead in until evenly distributed either the walnuts and raisins for the pane, or the figs and anise for the panini.

by stand mixer: Combine the flours in the mixing bowl and mix in the water. Using the dough hook, mix on low speed just until the dough is combined and wrapped around the dough hook, about 3 minutes. Cover the bowl with a plate and let rest (autolyse) for 10 to 30 minutes.

Add the salt and levain and mix the dough on medium speed just until it is smooth, about 4 minutes. Remove the dough from the bowl and knead in the walnuts and raisins for the pane, or figs and anise for the panini, by hand until they are evenly distributed.

by food processor: The dough can be mixed in a food processor exactly as instructed on page 96. After you have kneaded the 2 halves to combine, knead in the walnuts and raisins for the pane, or figs and anise for the panini, by hand until they are evenly distributed.

This dough is fairly firm, dry, and smooth. Add a tablespoon or two of water only if the dough seems excessively stiff.

FERMENTING AND TURNING THE DOUGH

Place the dough in a container at least 3 times its size and cover it tightly with plastic wrap. Let it ferment until it is airy and well expanded but not yet doubled in bulk, 4 to 5 hours. Turn the dough once (page 16) after 1 hour of fermenting, then leave the dough undisturbed for the remaining time.

ROUNDING AND RESTING THE PANE

Flour the surface of the dough and your work surface, then turn the dough out. Cut the dough in half. Lightly round the pieces (page 17), then nudge them into log shapes by pushing them across the work surface with your fingers. Cover them loosely with plastic wrap and let rest until well relaxed, 15 to 20 minutes.

SHAPING AND PROOFING THE PANE

Shape the dough into two 10-inch-long bâtards (page 35). Place the loaves seam side down in linen-lined baskets or in the folds of a raw-linen couche. Cover with plastic wrap and let proof until they are about doubled and spring back very slowly when lightly presssed with a floured finger, about 3 hours.

PROOFING THE PANINI

Flip the dough skin side up onto a lightly floured work surface and pat it into a block that is several inches thick. Transfer it to a couche, cover it, and let proof until the dough is airy but still bouncy when lightly pressed with a floured finger, about 2 hours.

CUTTING AND PROOFING THE PANINI

Cut the dough into 10 square chunks with a dough scraper or a kitchen knife; ideally, each should weigh about 4.2 ounces (120 grams), but they need not be perfect. Space the chunks about 2 inches apart on a sheet of parchment paper, cover them loosely with plastic wrap, and let proof until the dough is well expanded and only slowly springs back when pressed with a floured finger, about 1 hour.

PREHEATING THE OVEN

At least 45 minutes before the dough is fully proofed, arrange a rack on the oven's second-to-top shelf and place a baking stone on it. Clear away all racks above the one being used. Preheat the oven to 425°F (220°C) for the pane or 450°F (230°C) for the panini.

BAKING THE BREAD

Turn the pane out onto a sheet of parchment paper or a floured peel and slash shallow, parallel diagonal cuts about 1 inch apart on the tops (this cut is called a sausage cut or *coupe saucisson*).

If desired, just before baking, fill the oven with steam (page 18). Slide the pane or panini, still on the paper, onto the hot stone, using a peel or baking sheet to help you. Quickly spray the breads with water from a plant mister or pressurized garden sprayer. Bake the pane for 40 to 45 minutes, the panini for 25 to 30 minutes, rotating them halfway into the bake. The breads are finished baking when dark and evenly browned all around and they sound hollow when thumped on the bottom. Let cool on a rack.

IN PRAISE OF PRE-FERMENTS

ARTISAN BAKERS

SONOMA, CALIFORNIA

ON THE FLIGHT BACK FROM SAN FRANCISCO, I FOUND MYSELF SITTING NEXT TO the owner of a bakery equipment company. He told me about an olive bread that he had just eaten in Australia, "The best bread I ever had." This statement qualified him as a bread lover and thus worthy of my trove. We had just been served the pasty stale lumps that airline commissaries call dinner rolls, and I was longing for the real thing.

I asked this aisle-side gentleman to fetch my duffel bag, and I dug out one of the wrapped loaves. With as much drama as I could deliver, I held the loaf high and peeled away its bag. The huge golden ciabatta emerged. My seatmate and I sighed together—the loaf was exceedingly beautiful and obviously crafted by a master. I broke off two hunks for us, and we savored the full wheat flavor of the bread and marveled at its moistness and texture. The smell and sight of the bread proved too much for the passengers across the aisle, and they only half-jokingly asked for a taste. I broke off three more chunks and passed them around, showering the fuselage with crumbs. Happiness at ten thousand feet!

The baker of this fantastic bread, Craig Ponsford, had spent the previous afternoon with me in his bakery, Artisan Bakers in Sonoma, California, teaching me about yeast pre-ferments through the example of this beautiful ciabatta. Yeast pre-ferments are similar to sourdough starters, but they contain commercial yeast instead of sourdough yeasts (see page 11).

Yeast pre-ferments have gained popularity among American artisan bakers not only because of their flavor-enhancing qualities, but also because of the improving effect they have on the dough. While wholesale bakers add oxidizers, yeast foods, and other additives to allow their doughs to be shaped without ripping, to keep the breads from collapsing as they are proofing, to achieve better texture, and to lengthen shelf life, artisan bakers must rely on natural methods. Pre-ferments are a wonderful way to achieve all of these results without resorting to additives or masking the bread's wheaty flavor with heavy acidity, as a sourdough pre-ferment would do.

OPPOSITE: Ciabatta (page 104) cooling. ABOVE: Artisan Bakers' owner, Craig Ponsford.

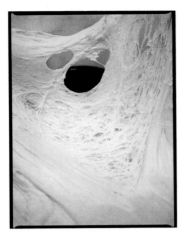  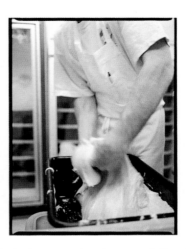 

LEFT TO RIGHT: The webbing of a fully fermented biga for ciabatta; Craig demonstrating the extensibility of this soupy dough; turning the dough in its tub; shaping the dough into loose folds.

Fortunately for me, Craig is as gifted a teacher as he is a baker. He would have to be: After representing the 1996 Baking Team USA in their first prize–winning specialty-breads category (he made baguettes, corn bread, beer bread, ciabatta, and a sourdough rye with sunflower seeds), he has been in great demand to give seminars around the world.

Craig told me about being shocked by the weak state of the French flour he used during the Coupe du Monde competitions. Accustomed to American flours that can withstand any kind of punishment, he was unused to handling doughs delicately, as French flours dictate. Without a pre-ferment, the dough would just shred when he tried to form it into baguettes, a very demanding shape. But with a pre-ferment in the dough, its extensibility was restored, and he was able to make competition-perfect baguettes. Craig has been enamored of pre-ferments ever since.

The first time I toured Craig's bakery, I was impressed by the wide variety of pre-ferments he uses in production every day. Craig is keenly aware of all the flavor nuances imparted by different pre-ferments and likes to take full advantage of them. When I returned to his bakery, he took a day off to give me a short but intensive course. We examined each one, tasting, touching and smelling them, then finally using one in that ambrosial ciabatta.

Craig enjoys pushing his pre-ferments to give their maximum to the dough. He often adds variety flours, such as whole wheat, cracked wheat, rye, or barley, for different levels of flavors and textures. He also stretches out the fermentations for a more intense flavor and longer shelf life by reducing the yeast and "retarding," or cooling, them, for a while. And he plays with amounts, fermenting more of the total flour in the pre-ferment for a more intense flavor.

Didier Rosada, a French master baker and teacher at the National Baking Center in Minneapolis, Minnesota, explains that a pre-ferment's flavor and performance in a dough will change depending on how much water is used in its manufacture and at what temperature it is fermented. Warmer, wetter pre-ferments containing no salt will give better extensibility to a dough because the enzymes that help to break down the gluten are more active (see autolyse, page 12, for a further explanation of this enzyme reaction). Cooler fermenting temperatures give a fruitier, sharper acidity because more acetic, rather than the milder lactic, acid is produced.

Overfermentation is the biggest pitfall to avoid when using pre-ferments, Craig emphasized. Doughs made with overfermented pre-ferments tend to tear during shaping, deflate while proofing, and bake up into smaller, less-open breads. Worst of all, beery and unpleasantly yeasty notes will mar the bread's flavor. Be sure to use the pre-ferment at its peak of readiness and discard it if it's past its prime.

FIVE TRADITIONAL YEAST PRE-FERMENTS

As artisan baking becomes increasingly professional, there has been an attempt to standardize terminology. As Didier Rosada says, "Traditionally, there are some names associated with specific characteristics of the pre-ferments." With that said, here are the classic yeast pre-ferments used by American artisan bakers with their traditional definitions and monikers.

Poolish

Of Polish origin, hence the name, this starter was brought to prominence by Viennese bakers in the nineteenth century (it is also called poolish in French and Italian). It always consists of an equal weight of flour and water, with a varying amount of yeast, depending on the length of fermentation desired (from 3 to 15 hours). Its high water content makes the starter very fluid, like a batter. If a flour is very strong, a poolish's water content can be increased to loosen the consistency.

In traditional French baking, a poolish is described in terms of how much water it contains, anywhere from one-third to four-fifths of the total water used in the dough.

About its flavor, Craig Ponsford says, "Poolish is almost the purest [starter], if you do it right. You get a very nice, sweet, flavorful wheat fermentation, and you taste wheat."

The key is to do it just right. When it is fully fermented and ready to use, the top of the starter will be very slightly pulled in and wrinkled. Both Didier and Craig warn that if a lot of yeast is used for a quick fermentation, the poolish may reach its peak in 10 minutes and steeply decline in quality after that. However, long, slow, cool overnight fermentations using small amounts of yeast are much more forgiving, and their peak of use lasts for 1 to 2 hours.

Scrap dough, a.k.a. old dough, pre-fermented dough, or *pâte fermentée*

This starter always contains all the ingredients found in a final dough, usually in the same proportion as the final dough, meaning that it has plenty of yeast and always contains salt. Professor Calvel invented this starter (he, of course, calls it *pâte fermentée*) to give bakers an easy way to use a pre-ferment without having to mix a separate preparation in advance. His idea was to mix extra dough with the regular batch, then hold the extra portion for the next day's dough. In practice, careful bakers usually mix up a separate batch and monitor its fermentation very carefully. While the salt in this starter helps to slow its fermentation somewhat, Craig warned that the larger amount of yeast means that this starter can easily become excessively acidic and alcoholic if it is not kept cool.

Biga

The term is used in Italy as a generic term for pre-ferment; however, a traditional biga is a very stiff pre-ferment, using about 50% to 60% water based on the flour weight, and 1% compressed yeast (or ⅓% to ½% instant yeast). It is given a long, cool fermentation at 65°F and delivers ample acetic acid. This pre-ferment was developed to bolster extremely weak Italian flours and is still used to strengthen a dough via the acetic acid, which reinforces the gluten.

Sponge, a.k.a. *levain-levure*

This is probably the easiest and most common starter. It contains only flour, yeast, and water and traditionally is very firm. It is always fermented at room temperature. According to Didier, the amount of yeast can vary depending on the desired fermentation time. For a very slow fermentation, very little yeast is used. Didier pointed out that while this starter is very easy to handle and remains at its peak of use for several hours, it does not contribute much extensibility to a dough because of its stiffer consistency, making it less appealing.

Mixed starter, a.k.a. *levain de pâte, travail sur rafraîchi, or travail mixte*

This is an easy way to mimic a sourdough or levain. Flour, water, and sometimes salt are "seeded" or "built" with a small piece of old dough and given a slow fermentation at room temperature, from 6 to 15 hours. The "chef" (or starter) that seeds the pre-ferment can be from 5% to 30% of the pre-ferment's flour weight, depending on desired fermentation. Breads tend to be full flavored and fairly acidic but lack the deep acidity, moistness, and long shelf life of true sourdough.

Craig Ponsford's Ciabatta

- Makes two 1-pound (500-gram) ciabatte
- Time: About 30 hours, with 15 minutes of active work

This is a large, dramatic bread full of huge holes and beautifully striped with flour. *Ciabatta* means "old shoe" or "slipper" (as in Grandpa's, not Cinderella's) in Italian, and refers to this bread's rough appearance and irregular shape. It goes beautifully with salads and sauced foods like pasta and can be split horizontally and cut into squares for sandwiches.

Craig used some unusual techniques when he made this bread for me. He hardly mixes the dough at all, bragging that his dough is actually lumpy when it comes out of the mixer (not really). But he does mix his doughs very little, and turns or folds the dough as it is fermenting to develop the gluten. He believes that minimizing the dough's exposure to the air allows the bread to retain its creamy color and wheaty aroma and flavor. He also likes to give his dough a loose letter fold, instead of leaving it as it is cut.

Because of this bread's high water content, Craig emphasized, it is especially important not to underbake it if you want a crisp crust and full flavor.

RECIPE SYNOPSIS THE MORNING OF THE DAY BEFORE BAKING: Mix the biga and let it ferment for 24 hours. THE NEXT MORNING: Mix the dough and let it ferment for 3 hours. Shape the bread, let it proof for 45 minutes and then bake for 40 minutes.

	Biga	volume	weight	metric	baker's percentages
THE MORNING OF THE DAY BEFORE BAKING **MAKING THE BIGA**	**Active dry yeast***	¼ teaspoon			(eventually 0.002%)
	Water, 110° to 115°F	1 cup			
	Unbleached bread flour	1⅓ cups	7.1 ounces	200 grams	67%
	Unbleached all-purpose flour	⅔ cup	3.5 ounces	100 grams	33%
	Whole-wheat flour, preferably coarsely ground	2 tablespoons	0.5 ounce	15 grams	5%
	Whole-rye flour, preferably coarsely ground	2 tablespoons	0.5 ounce	15 grams	5%
	Water (see method for temperature)	¾ cup	6.5 ounces	185 grams	61%

*Or use instant yeast if that is all you have. The active dry yeast gives a slightly slower fermentation, desirable here but not absolutely necessary.

Sprinkle the yeast over the warm water, stir, and let it stand for 5 to 10 minutes. Mix the flours in a bowl. Measure ½ teaspoon of the yeasted water into the flour mixture (throw the rest away; the point of this step is not to proof the yeast but to measure $1/_{384}$ teaspoon yeast). Then add the ¾ cup water, using ice water in the summer and warm water in the winter. This biga is incredibly stiff and will resist kneading, but persevere: It has a very long fermentation and will soften considerably. Knead in a tablespoon of water or two if you absolutely must. Cover it tightly with plastic wrap and let it ferment for 24 hours, in a cool spot in the summer or a warm one in the winter. Don't be alarmed if it does nothing for at least 10 hours; this is correct. The biga is ready when it has tripled in volume, smells aromatic, and is well expanded.

	Dough	volume	weight	metric	baker's percentages
BAKE DAY **MIXING** **THE DOUGH**	**Unbleached all-purpose flour**	2 cups plus 3 tablespoons	11.5 ounces	325 grams	100%
	Instant yeast	1 teaspoon	0.1 ounce	3 grams	1%
	Salt	2¾ teaspoons	0.5 ounce	13 grams	4%
	Water, lukewarm	1½ cups	12.1 ounces	342 grams	105%
	Fermented biga				158%

by hand: Combine the flour, yeast, and salt in a large bowl. Add the water and biga and stir the dough with your hand until it has formed a rough dough. Turn it out onto the work surface and knead it for 5 minutes. It should be gooey, more like a batter than a dough. If this is too intimidating, you can knead it in the bowl. Use a dough scraper or a spatula to help you, but do not add extra flour.

If you are a very talented kneader, your dough will look smooth after about 5 minutes of kneading; if you're not, it may look like the same mess you started with. Don't worry about it, for this will be corrected during the fermentation.

by stand mixer: Combine the flour, yeast, and salt in the mixing bowl. Add the water and biga and mix the dough on low speed with the paddle until it forms a rough dough. Continue to mix the dough on medium speed or until it is fairly smooth, about 5 minutes. If your dough appears very firm, add extra water.

This is a very soft dough. If your dough is not really gloppy, add extra water until the dough is soft enough to spread (your flour might be old or absorbing more water for a variety of reasons).

FERMENTING AND TURNING THE DOUGH

Scrape the dough into a container at least 3 times its size and cover it tightly with plastic wrap. Let it ferment until light, well expanded, and about doubled in bulk, 2½ to 3 hours. Turn the dough (page 16), using plenty of flour for dusting 3 or 4 times in 20-minute intervals, that is, after 20, 40, 60, and 80 minutes of fermenting, then leave the dough undisturbed for the remaining time. You will be amazed at how the dough firms up during the turning.

CUTTING, SHAPING, AND PROOFING THE DOUGH

Lightly but thoroughly flour a couche or heavily flour 2 tea towels. Flour the top of the dough and the work surface, then turn the dough out. With a dough scraper, cut the dough approximately in half. Gently stretch the pieces out and fold them loosely into thirds, like a business letter, arranging the folds so the last seam is slightly off center. Try to handle the dough as little as possible to avoid deflating it. Place the loaves seam side down on the floured cloth and sprinkle more flour over the top. Cover them with folds of the couche or more tea towels. Let them proof until they are very soft, well expanded, and barely spring back when gently pressed, about 45 minutes.

PREHEATING THE OVEN

Immediately after shaping the dough, arrange a rack on the oven's second-to-top shelf and place a baking stone on it. Clear away all racks above the one being used. Preheat the oven to 450°F (230°C).

BAKING THE BREAD

When the ciabatte are ready to bake, place a sheet of parchment paper on a peel. Gently flip the loaves onto it so that they are seam side up and stretch them very slightly to make them vaguely rectangular. Don't be afraid to handle the dough; the breads will recover in the oven as long as you are gentle. Dimple the dough all over with your fingertips, pressing down to the paper without breaking through the dough. Slide the breads on the parchment paper onto the baking stone. Bake the breads until very, very dark brown all around, for 35 to 40 minutes, rotating them halfway into the bake. Let cool on a rack.

FOLLOWING PAGES: Dough proofing in couches at Della Fattoria

A VERY SMALL ARTISAN BAKERY

DELLA FATTORIA

PETALUMA, CALIFORNIA

KATHLEEN WEBER HAD ALWAYS DREAMED OF HAVING HER OWN BAKERY, but she'd never believed she could do it.

On impulse one weekend, she, her husband, some friends, and brick oven–builder Alan Scott constructed a wood-burning brick oven in the backyard of her rural Petaluma, California, home. Kathleen imagined that with this marvelous oven in her backyard, they would have barbecues and cookouts and that neighbors from all around would "bring their little pots-au-feus over." While that scenario never transpired, Kathleen did find herself indulging her passion for baking bread. She was heavily inspired by Carol Field's *The Italian Baker* and basically taught herself to bake using that book.

In 1994, while her son, Aaron, was a chef at the Sonoma Mission Inn and Spa, Kathleen got to know Aaron's executive chef, bread lover Mark Vann. Whenever she had extra loaves, Kathleen would take a few in to Mark, who would always offer his encouragement and criticism. When Mark needed bread for an olive oil tasting, he asked Kathleen if she could bake enough for two days of tastings. She delivered the bread to the tasting and an hour later got a phone call from Mark. The bread had already run out. Could she possibly bake some more? "People just went nuts," she recalls.

Soon Mark offered Kathleen the restaurant's account, even though, she says, "He knew how rustic we were. We weren't set up to do anything professional." Kathleen took on the challenge and went from baking forty loaves three times a week (for pleasure) to sixty to one hundred loaves every day.

At first, Kathleen did all the baking herself, but the workload quickly became overwhelming. Now, production at Della Fattoria has settled into a comfortable twenty-four-hour routine, with husband, Ed, and son, Aaron, each attending different "shifts." The cycle begins when Aaron, as one of his last duties, mixes up the starter for the next day's bake at around 2 P.M. At around 5:30, Ed stokes the oven with wood and fires it up for the next morning's bake, letting

OPPOSITE, COUNTER-CLOCKWISE FROM TOP LEFT: Rounds of dough resting on a shaping table; dough rounds for Rustic Roasted Garlic Bread (page 113) being swabbed with garlic puree and sprinkled with cheese; creating a neat pocket of dough; round garnished with garlic clove and dampened cilantro sprig; Aaron Weber loading proofed rounds into the oven for baking. ABOVE: Kathleen Weber with some of her breads.

the wood burn the night through. In the early evening, Kathleen prints out the spreadsheet that tells her how much of each dough she will need to mix for the next day—customers have the luxury of being able to change orders up to the day before.

After just a few hours of sleep, Kathleen gets up at midnight and goes into the "shaping room" behind her kitchen to begin mixing her doughs. This former play-room has been transformed into a bright and cheerful bakeshop, small but efficiently laid out, anchored by a large wooden baker's table at its center. She drinks her coffee—a necessity after three hours of sleep—consults her spread-sheet, and then prepares all the ingredients, "toasting the seeds and getting the currants soaking in their brandy."

Kathleen uses an electronic scale on her baker's table to weigh the ingredients, then transfers them to the workbowl of a small but very cute spiral mixer. Water she gets from the tap. Batches are small, since she can mix no more than seventy pounds of dough at a time in the lit-tle mixer. When a dough is finished mixing, she drops it into a covered bin, then slides it onto a wheeled rack. Kathleen mixes from nine to thirteen doughs a night, for up to three hundred loaves: three levains, five compagna, a baguette, a polenta, a seeded wheat, and a currant. By 4 A.M. the doughs are mixed and beginning to ferment, the little shaping room is tidy, and Kathleen goes back to bed to finish her night's sleep.

We came to the bakery just before dawn, "the magic hour" as Kathleen calls it, when her work was finished and Aaron's was just beginning. Aaron spends most of his time in the high-ceilinged skylit shed that shelters the oven. The morning's first task is to clean out the oven, sweeping the wood and ashes into a wheelbarrow to be dumped in the back pasture. In between shaping doughs, he thoroughly cleans the oven with an earsplitting industrial vacuum. This oven is direct fired, meaning that it is fired in the baking chamber itself, and so must be scrupulously cleaned to avoid having ash or bits of coal adhere to the bread.

As the first dawn light just starts to beam through the bakery's east windows, Aaron overturns a tub of fermented dough onto the floured baker's table. He cuts and weighs the dough into correctly sized pieces, which he then gently rounds and leaves to rest. Della Fattoria's breads are known for their unique flavors and frankly labor-intensive shapes. To mold the Rustic Roasted Garlic Bread, Aaron flips over a piece of well-relaxed dough, smears on roasted garlic purée, and sprinkles on a dusting of grated dry Jack cheese. He folds up the dough and eases it over to round it more tightly, being careful to keep the flavors in the center. As a final touch, he makes a small incision, twists a clove of unpeeled garlic, or even a whole tiny head, into the gash, then pats a garland of wetted fresh cilantro around it. Plunking it face down into a flour-dusted plastic chips basket (see page 10), he slides the shaped and decorated dough back onto a rack to proof.

As their baking routine evolved, the Webers faced problems that could arise only in a backyard bakery. Even the simple act of loading the oven had to be rethought. Ordinarily, a single baker loads the oven, propping his peel on two sawhorses, easing on the proofed breads, slashing them, and sliding them onto the hearth. But Della Fattoria's original oven was out-doors, and given Sonoma's frequent winter rains, the Webers needed a different system. Standing in front of the oven, Aaron swings the long peel into the shaping room onto the baker's table, where Ed or Kathleen fills it and slashes the dough. Aaron swings the peel back around to the mouth of the oven and peels in the bread. Unloading is simpler, with Aaron just shoving the breads onto the peel and lifting them onto cooling racks on the shed's far wall.

After cooling, Ed and Aaron sort the breads into baskets for delivery. Each account has two baskets, so as Ed delivers a full basket, he brings home with him the empty one, to be filled with the next day's assortment of Della Fattoria's meticulous home-baked breads.

Della Fattoria's shed bakeshop aglow in the early morning

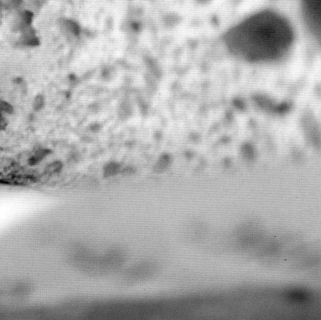

Della Fattoria's Rustic Roasted Garlic Bread

- Makes two 1-pound (500-gram) loaves
- Time: At least 30 hours, with about 45 minutes of active work

One of Della Fattoria's most popular varieties, this must be the ultimate garlic bread. A round of sourdough bread seasoned with a sprinkling of whole wheat surrounds a layer of grated cheese and roasted garlic purée. The bread is beautifully decorated with an unpeeled clove of roasted garlic for one lucky person to squeeze out and an herb wreath protected from the fire by a coating of flour.

The dough is too soft to be mixed in a processor, and it requires a lot of mixing before it is fully developed, making hand mixing nearly impossible; using the stand mixer is the only option for this recipe.

continued

THE MORNING OF THE DAY BEFORE BAKING: Refresh your sourdough starter. (If it has been stored in the refrigerator, start refreshing it 2 days before baking with it, for at least 3 times.) **THAT EVENING:** Mix the levain and let it ferment overnight. **THE NEXT MORNING:** Mix the dough and let it ferment for 4 hours. Shape and decorate the dough, then let it proof for about 4 hours. Bake the bread for about 40 minutes.

	Levain	volume	weight	metric	baker's percentages
THE EVENING BEFORE BAKING **MAKING** **THE LEVAIN**	**Fermented firm sourdough starter (pages 91–94), refreshed 8 hours before**	1 tablespoon plus 1 teaspoon	0.6 ounce	18 grams	30%
	Water, lukewarm	2 tablespoons plus 1 teaspoon	1.2 ounces	35 grams	58%
	Unbleached bread flour, preferably organic	3 tablespoons	1 ounce	30 grams	50%
	Whole-wheat flour	3 tablespoons	1 ounce	30 grams	50%

Dissolve the sourdough starter in the water in a small bowl. Add the flours and knead until a very firm dough forms. Place it in a covered container and let it ferment overnight for 8 hours, or until fully risen and just slightly deflated.

	Roasted Garlic Purée	volume	weight	metric	baker's percentages
MAKING **THE GARLIC** **PURÉE**	**Garlic heads**	3 whole			
	Extra virgin olive oil	2 to 3 tablespoons			
	Salt and freshly ground pepper	to taste			

(This purée can also be made while the dough is fermenting the next day, if it is more convenient.) Cut the whole heads of garlic in half to expose the cloves, drizzle with some of the olive oil, wrap in aluminum foil and bake in a 350°F oven until the garlic is very soft, about 1 hour. It can also be baked while something else is in the oven, adjusting the baking time to reflect that temperature. (If you enjoy roasted garlic, you might as well bake a few extra heads.) Let the garlic cool.

Squeeze the garlic cloves out of their skins into a small bowl. Mash them with a fork, then blend in about 2 tablespoons olive oil. Season the spread with salt and pepper to taste. Scrape it into a container, cover it, and store it in the refrigerator.

	Dough	volume	weight	metric	baker's percentages
BAKE DAY **MIXING** **THE DOUGH**	**Fermented levain**				23%
	Water, warm	1¾ cups	14 ounces	390 grams	78%
	Unbleached bread flour, preferably organic	3⅓ cups	18 ounces	500 grams	100%
	Salt	1 tablespoon	0.5 ounce	15 grams	3%

Dissolve the fermented levain in the water in the bowl of a stand mixer. Add the flour. Using the dough hook, mix on low speed until the dough comes together on the hook. Increase the speed to medium and mix until the dough is very silky, 25 to 30 minutes. When the dough is sufficiently mixed, it will briefly wrap around the hook and clean the bowl, then splatter back around the bowl. If your mixer is rocking too much, reduce the speed a notch or two. Add the salt and mix until the dough tightens and totally cleans the bowl, about 5 minutes more.

This dough is very soft. If it does not splatter back around the pan, add 1 to 2 tablespoons more water.

FERMENTING AND TURNING THE DOUGH

Place the dough in a container at least 3 times its size and cover it tightly with plastic wrap. Let it ferment, preferably at 70° to 75°F, until it is airy and well expanded but not yet doubled in bulk, about 4 hours. Turn the dough (page 16) 3 times at 30-minute intervals, that is, after 30, 60, and 90 minutes of fermenting, then leave the dough undisturbed for the remaining time.

ROUNDING AND RESTING THE DOUGH

Flour the dough and work surface and turn the dough out. Cut the dough in half; each piece should weigh about 18 ounces (500 grams). Lightly round the pieces (page 17) and cover loosely with plastic wrap. Let rest until very relaxed and starting to expand again, 15 to 20 minutes.

Garnish	volume	weight	metric	baker's percentages
Roasted garlic purée	3 tablespoons			
Dry Jack or Asiago cheese, grated	1 cup loosely packed	2 ounces	60 grams	12%
Garlic cloves, unpeeled	2			
Beautiful sprigs flat-leaf parsley or cilantro	6 to 8			

SHAPING AND GARNISHING THE DOUGH

On a lightly floured surface, place one of the dough rounds skin side down and flatten it a little, keeping the middle very thick. Smear half the garlic purée in the center of the dough, then sprinkle with half the cheese. Pull the dough up around the filling to form a sort of pleated pouch. Turn the dough over and round it tightly but not too strenuously, trying to keep the filling in the center of the dough (if you round it too much, the filling will rise to the top and explode out during baking). With a sharp knife, make a small cut in the center of the top of the dough; twist 1 garlic clove into the cut until it is about one third of the way into the dough. Wet 3 or 4 sprigs of parsley or cilantro and pat them in a wreath around the garlic. Repeat with the other dough round. Sift some flour over the shaped breads to cover the decorations.

PROOFING THE DOUGH

Place the loaves, decorated side down, in heavily floured linen-lined baskets or plastic chips baskets (see page 10). Cover well and proof the breads until they are well expanded, about 4 hours.

PREHEATING THE OVEN

At least 45 minutes before the dough is fully proofed, arrange a rack on the oven's second-to-top shelf and place a baking stone on it. Clear away all racks above the one being used. Preheat the oven to 425°F (220°C).

BAKING THE BREAD

If desired, just before baking, fill the oven with steam (page 18). Turn the breads out onto a sheet of parchment paper or a floured peel. Slash the top of each loaf by cutting a large circle about 1 inch from the bread's perimeter. Slide the breads, still on the paper, onto the hot stone. Bake the breads until dark and evenly browned all around, 35 to 40 minutes, rotating them halfway into the bake. Let the breads cool on a rack.

Della Fattoria's Polenta Bread

- Makes two 21-ounce (600-gram) loaves
- Time: At least 28 hours, with about 30 minutes of active work

This beautiful polenta-encrusted sourdough is a bit tricky to mix, and is not for the inexperienced baker. The dough is mixed in several stages to allow it a full development before cooked and cooled polenta is added. This long and involved mixing process yields a high-rising bread with a lacy crumb.

The dough is too soft to be mixed in a food processor, and it requires a lot of mixing before it is fully developed, making hand mixing nearly impossible; using the stand mixer is the only option for this recipe.

RECIPE SYNOPSIS THE MORNING OF THE DAY BEFORE BAKING: Refresh your sourdough starter. (If it has been stored in the refrigerator, start refreshing it 2 days before baking with it, for at least 3 times.) **THAT EVENING:** Mix the levain and let it ferment overnight. **THE NEXT MORNING:** Make the polenta and let it cool. Mix the dough and let it ferment for 3½ hours. Shape the dough, then let it proof for about 2½ hours. Bake the bread for about 45 minutes.

	Levain	volume	weight	metric	baker's percentages
THE EVENING BEFORE BAKING **MAKING THE LEVAIN**	**Fermented firm sourdough starter (pages 91–94), refreshed 8 hours before**	1 tablespoon plus 1 teaspoon	0.7 ounce	20 grams	20%
	Water, lukewarm	¼ cup	2.1 ounces	60 grams	60%
	Unbleached bread flour	⅔ cup	3.5 ounces	100 grams	100%

Dissolve the sourdough starter in the water in a small bowl. Add the flour and knead the dough until it is very smooth. Place it in a covered container and let ferment overnight for 8 hours, or until it has quadrupled in bulk and deflates when lightly pressed.

	Polenta	volume	weight	metric	baker's percentages
BAKE DAY **COOKING THE POLENTA**	**Coarse polenta***	3 tablespoons	1.2 ounces	35 grams	100%
	Cold water	¾ cup	6.2 ounces	175 grams	500%

*Yellow corn grits work well if you cannot find polenta.

Mix the polenta and water in a microwavable container and microwave on high power for 4 minutes. Stir and microwave for 2 minutes more. The mixture should be very thick. (Alternatively, cook the polenta and water in a small heavy pan, stirring constantly, until the mixture is very thick, about 5 minutes.) Spread it out on a plate to cool to room temperature, about 20 minutes.

Preceding pages: Della Fattoria's Polenta Bread

Dough	volume	weight	metric	baker's percentages
MIXING THE DOUGH **Water, cold**	1¾ cups	13.8 ounces	390 grams	65%
Unbleached bread flour, preferably organic with 11.5% to 12% protein*	1¾ cups	9.3 ounces	265 grams	44%
Unbleached high-gluten flour, preferably organic with 13% to 14% protein*	2¼ cups	11.8 ounces	335 grams	56%
Fermented levain				30%
Salt	1 tablespoon plus ¾ teaspoon	0.6 ounce	18 grams	3%
Cooled polenta				35%
Coarse polenta (or yellow corn grits), for coating the dough				

*You can substitute the flour Kathleen uses, Rocky Mountain Flour Milling's Columbine, for both flours (see Sources, page 222).

Measure the cold water into the mixing bowl, add the flours, and stir with your hands or a wooden spoon just until a rough dough forms. Let the dough rest (autolyse) for about 15 minutes.

Using the dough hook, mix on medium speed until the dough is very smooth, about 15 minutes. Add the levain and salt and mix until the dough is firm and smooth. Add the cooked polenta in bits and mix until it is fully incorporated. The dough will become very wet, like porridge.

FERMENTING AND TURNING THE DOUGH

Place the dough in a container at least 3 times its size and cover it tightly with plastic wrap. Let it ferment until it is airy and well expanded but not yet doubled in bulk, about 3½ hours. Turn the dough (page 16) 3 times at 30-minute intervals, that is, after 30, 60, and 90 minutes of fermenting, then leave the dough undisturbed for the remaining time. The dough will firm up considerably after the turns.

ROUNDING AND RESTING THE DOUGH

Flour the surface of the dough and your work surface and turn the dough out. Cut the dough in half; each piece should weigh 23 ounces (650 grams). Lightly round the pieces (page 17) and cover loosely with plastic wrap. Let rest for 15 minutes.

SHAPING AND PROOFING THE DOUGH

Pour some coarse polenta into a large pie plate. Shape the dough pieces into even and tight round loaves without deflating them. Spray their tops with water, then roll them in the polenta to coat them. Place each shaped loaf coated side down in an unlined tightly woven basket, plastic chips basket (see page 10), or large colander. Cover them well with plastic wrap and proof the dough until it is well expanded, about 2 to 2½ hours.

PREHEATING THE OVEN

At least 45 minutes before the dough is fully proofed, arrange a rack on the oven's second-to-top shelf and place a baking stone on it. Clear away all racks above the one being used. Preheat the oven to 425°F (220°C).

BAKING THE BREAD

If desired, just before baking the bread, fill the oven with steam (page 18). Turn the breads out onto separate sheets of parchment paper. In one continuous motion, slash a spiral on the top of each bread: Begin at the bread's center and, holding the razor almost horizontally, turn the bread on its paper while you cut the spiral. Slide the breads, still on the paper, onto the hot stone. Bake the loaves until dark and evenly browned all around, 40 to 45 minutes, rotating them halfway into the bake. Let the breads cool on a rack.

A VERY BIG ARTISAN BAKERY

TOM CAT BAKERY

LONG ISLAND CITY, NEW YORK

DELLA FATTORIA (SEE PAGE 109) MAKES THREE HUNDRED LOAVES A DAY. Tom Cat makes a repertoire of three hundred *shapes* into about ten thousand loaves a day, from more than six thousand pounds of flour; yet Tom Cat started out almost as cozily as Della Fattoria. While a chef at New York's Quilted Giraffe restaurant, president Noel Comess figured out that his was not the only restaurant whose need for high-quality bread was not being met. So he quit his job as a chef and waited tables for a year as he developed his business plan, raised money, and searched for used bakery equipment. Tom Cat Bakery was born in Long Island City, New York, in a garage with "one oven, two fork mixers, a baguette molder, a divider, two tables, one truck, one desk, six hands, and two chairs." Two moves and more than ten years later, Tom Cat leads the way in bakery design, and Noel is in frequent demand as a speaker.

James Rath, Tom Cat's vice-president of production, walked us through the bakery, showing us how Tom Cat's aromatic Semolina Filone is born. We started off in a large, sealed, temperature-controlled room where mixing, makeup, and oven preparation all have their own areas. Mixing goes on in a corner almost as filled with keypads as with mixers.

The most frequently used flour is kept in a two-tank silo, with one tank for aging the flour and the other in current use. Silos are extremely unusual in artisan bakeries but very practical, because it means Tom Cat can buy flour in entire truckloads, eliminating the expense of paper bags. Also, with two tanks, the flour can be aged for ten to twelve days before going into production, which is important in this day when few mills age their own flour and artisan bakers refuse to use chemically aged flour. Noel explains that when the flour arrives at the bakery, it is "still warm from the friction of the milling process, so it's completely green." Because green, or unaged, flour is very weak, this natural aging makes a huge difference in the quality of the bread.

The baker checks the board to see which silo is currently in use, then enters the amount of flour needed on the silo computer. The flour moves pneumatically through pipes in the bakery,

OPPOSITE: A bowl lifter tipping over a batch of just-mixed dough; in the foreground, an information sheet used to track the dough. ABOVE: Tom Cat's mascot, adopted after the fact.

LEFT TO RIGHT: Adding flour to the workbowl directly from the silo as water is metered in at the correct temperature; hand-scaling dough for Tom Cat's premium breads; adjusting rolls on the automatic oven loader. OPPOSITE: James Roth explaining Tom Cat's tracking system to the author.

entering the mixing bowl through a scale hopper in the center of the mixing area.

After the remaining ingredients have been added, the baker then enters the mixing time required on the mixer's computer and lets the mixer complete the dough. Tom Cat has several mixers, the largest of which mixes up to 450 pounds of dough. Despite the automation, the baker makes adjustments, adding more flour or water to correct the consistency, and monitors the dough carefully. When the dough is fully mixed, the baker will cut the dough out of the bowl and add it to plastic tubs to ferment. If the large mixer was used, an impressive piece of equipment called a bowl lift tilts the contents of the bowl onto a table where it can be cut into twenty-kilo pieces and placed in the bins. Back strain caused by lifting heavy mixing bowls is one of the most frequent bakery injuries, so this piece of equipment is a real godsend for the workers. The filled bins are then stacked near the shaping area to ferment.

At this point, the mixer or supervisor must complete some paperwork. He fills out a form listing his name, the time the dough finished mixing, its temperature, the age of the pre-ferment, its consistency, whether or not extra flour or water was added, and notes for the shapers. James explains that with this

paper trail, problems are easily tracked and remedied.

After the dough has fermented, it gets passed to a team of shapers for cutting, weighing, shaping, and oven preparation. While rolls and some baguettes are molded by machine, the "big breads," of which James is particularly proud, get shaped by hand. Shapers overturn the bins of dough onto the table, cut the dough with a dough knife, and weigh it into correctly sized pieces. Machines exist to tackle this chore, but they pummel all the gas out of the dough. The shaped doughs are then loaded onto flour- or linen-lined wooden proofing boards and stacked on wheeled racks.

Rolls and other machine-molded breads get wheeled into a proofer, which is simply a room with controlled temperature and humidity. The proofers straddle the shaping area and the baking area, so shaped breads get wheeled in on the shaping side and wheeled out on the oven side. A more "rustic" look is sought for the big breads, so they are allowed to proof out in the open on racks at room temperature.

Tom Cat's enormous Spanish oven has eighteen hearths and an automatic loader with eighteen stacked canvas belts to fill them all simultaneously. The oven operator loads the proofed breads while still on their proofing boards onto a metal setter. This setter is

TEMPERATURE CONTROL

Dough temperature is critical in large, precisely scheduled bakeries. A cool dough ferments slowly and may not be fully proofed when it is scheduled to be baked. If it is held back, the batches following it will be delayed as well. On the other hand, a warm dough ferments fast and may be overproofed by the time the oven is free. To keep things moving on schedule, dough temperatures must be spot on. (At home, dough temperatures are much less important, because batches are small and we do not have a production schedule to meet.)

Generally, Tom Cat likes to keep its dough—and the room temperature—around 75° to 77°F. The temperature of the pre-ferment, which might be chilled, the flour, the water, the room, and the heat of friction from the action of the mixer all contribute to the temperature of the dough at the end of mixing, the "arrival temperature." Bakers have found that the simplest method to achieve a desired arrival temperature is to control the temperature of the water. The basic theory depends on balance: If a dough contains a large portion of chilled pre-ferment, warm water is added; if a dough is mixed for a long time, adding frictional heat, chilled water is used. A formula called "base temperature calculation" has been devised to determine the exact water temperature needed to achieve the desired arrival temperature.

At Tom Cat, this calculation is made for the baker by a computerized water meter. The baker simply enters the amount of water needed and the dough's arrival temperature, and the computer automatically meters out the desired amount of water at the calculated temperature. "It's one of the best pieces of equipment we ever bought," Noel concludes.

wheeled behind the loader, and the proofed breads, minus their boards, are deposited onto all eighteen canvas belts. The loader is then pushed into the oven, where it automatically drops the breads onto the oven's deck. Finished breads are unloaded in the same manner, but in reverse: The loader scoops the breads onto the canvas belt as it is pushed into the oven. A setter fitted with cooling racks retrieves the baked breads from the wheeled-out loader, which is then wheeled into the packaging area where the breads are allowed to cool.

After cooling, the breads are packaged and sorted for delivery. "We have three deliveries a day, so we can give people the freshest bread." At best, the breads are at their final destination—groceries or restaurants—just four hours after they are baked.

When I questioned Noel about the extraordinary size of Tom Cat, he replied, "Certainly having a plant that is a size that allows you to work properly, I think that is really critical. The workers work more efficiently; it allows them to control the process more effectively; our quality is higher than it ever was before. We are very clear as to what it is about the handmade process that makes the product better, and what there is about the process that has no significance to the product whatsoever." It seems that their assiduous thoughtfulness has paid off. Their bread is superb.

Tom Cat's Semolina Filone

- Makes one 1½ pound (750-gram) loaf
- Time: At least 13 hours, with about 15 minutes of active work

This bread (Tom Cat pronounces it fi-LONE-ee) is an upscale version of the well-known Italian American seeded semolina. A huge beautiful loaf scored with a single cut, it is rolled in sesame seeds and baked to a deep brown. Its crumb is open golden lace, and the durum flour's sweet, rich flavor is underlined by a poolish (see Five Traditional Yeast Pre-ferments, page 103, for more information about poolishes).

I have mixed all-purpose and bread flours to achieve 11.5% protein. If you are using King Arthur all-purpose or another 11.5% protein flour, just substitute it for both flours.

James likes to give this dough a very long rest period (autolyse), at least 15 minutes but preferably up to 1 hour, saying that they really get "better volume and sharper cuts" with the autolyse.

Finally, Tom Cat's filone weighs 1 kilo and is 28 inches long, but I have scaled this one down to fit easily into a home oven.

continued

RECIPE SYNOPSIS **THE EVENING BEFORE BAKING:** Make the poolish and let it ferment for 8 hours. **THE NEXT MORNING:** Mix the dough, and let it ferment for 3 hours. Shape it, let it proof for 1 hour, and bake it for about 55 minutes.

	Poolish	volume	weight	metric	baker's percentages
THE EVENING BEFORE BAKING **MAKING THE POOLISH**	**Instant yeast**	¼ teaspoon			(eventually 0.1%)
	Water, 110° to 115°F	1 cup			
	Unbleached bread flour	½ cup	2.6 ounces	75 grams	50%
	Unbleached all-purpose flour	½ cup	2.6 ounces	75 grams	50%
	Water (see method below for temperature)	½ cup plus 1 tablespoon	4.7 ounces	135 grams	(eventually 110%)

Sprinkle the yeast over the warm water in a glass measure, stir, and let stand for 5 to 10 minutes. Mix the flours in a bowl. Add ¼ cup of the yeasted water to measure 1/16 teaspoon yeast. Add the remaining water, using ice water in the summer and warm water in the winter. Mix this gloppy batter with a wooden spoon until it is smooth. Cover it tightly with plastic wrap and let it ferment overnight for about 8 hours, or until its surface bubbles are breaking and deep wrinkles are forming.

	Dough	volume	weight	metric	baker's percentages
BAKE DAY **MIXING THE DOUGH**	**Durum flour***	1⅔ cups	8.8 ounces	250 grams	83%
	Unbleached all-purpose flour	⅓ cup	1.8 ounces	50 grams	17%
	Water, lukewarm	¾ cup plus 3 tablespoons	7.5 ounces	205 grams	68%
	Instant yeast	¼ teaspoon			0.3%
	Fermented poolish				103%
	Salt	1½ teaspoons	0.3 ounce	9 grams	2.9%
	Sesame seeds	about 2 cups			

*Look for extremely fine, double-milled flour from durum wheat, which is sometimes called durum flour and sometimes extra fancy pasta or patent durum flour. Semolina, a more granular product, will not work here. (See Sources, page 222.)

by hand: Combine the flours and water and knead this stiff dough until fairly smooth. Cover with plastic wrap and let rest (autolyse) for at least 15 minutes but preferably up to 1 hour.

Sprinkle the yeast over the poolish, stir it in, and let it stand for 5 minutes. Add the poolish to the dough and knead the two together on an unfloured work surface until very smooth, about 10 minutes. Use a dough scraper to help you manipulate the dough. Sprinkle on the salt and continue kneading until the salt is dissolved.

by stand mixer: Combine the flours and water in the mixing bowl and mix this stiff dough with the dough hook on low speed until combined. Cover with plastic wrap and let rest (autolyse) for at least 15 minutes but preferably 1 hour.

Sprinkle the yeast over the poolish, stir it in, and let it stand for 5 minutes. Add the poolish to the dough and mix them together on low speed until the dough is very smooth and cleans the side of the bowl, about 5 minutes. Sprinkle on the salt and continue mixing until the salt is dissolved, about 2 minutes.

Add a tablespoon of water if the dough seems too dry or 2 to 4 tablespoons of all-purpose flour if the dough is too wet. The consistency of this dough can really vary depending on the freshness and fineness of the durum flour. This dough should be soft and tacky but not gloppy.

FERMENTING AND TURNING THE DOUGH

Place the dough in a container at least 3 times its size and cover tightly with plastic wrap. Let it ferment until it is light and bubbly and about doubled in bulk, about 3 hours. Turn the dough (page 16) 3 times at 20-minute intervals, that is, after 20, 40, and 60 minutes of fermenting, then leave the dough undisturbed for the remaining time.

RESTING THE DOUGH

Pour the sesame seeds onto a baking sheet. Make a trough in a couche for the dough to proof in. There is no need to flour the couche. Lightly flour the top of the dough and your work surface. Turn the dough out and lightly round it (page 17). Cover it and let rest for 20 to 30 minutes. It needs to be extremely relaxed.

PREHEATING THE OVEN

While the dough is resting, arrange a rack on the oven's second-to-top shelf and place a baking stone on it. Clear away all racks above the one being used. Preheat the oven to 400°F (205°C).

SHAPING AND SEEDING THE DOUGH

Place the skin side of the dough down on your lightly floured work surface. Fold the bottom edge of the dough up and lightly seal it with the palm of your hand, then repeat with the top edge (like a business letter). Try to handle the dough delicately to avoid popping its bubbles. Make a shallow trough in the center of the dough with the side of your hand and fold the top edge of the dough over all the way to the work surface, then push it back toward the dough with your thumbs, making a tight but still very airy cylinder. Seal the seam with the heel of your hand. Turn the dough seam side down and gently begin elongating it: Place your hands palms down in the center of the dough and lightly roll the dough back and forth, making sure the heels of your hands and the tips of your fingers remain in contact with the work surface. As the dough elongates, gradually move your hands apart without stretching the dough but letting it elongate itself. Continue elongating the dough until it is about 12 inches long; this will fit comfortably on a 16-inch-long baking stone (the dough will elongate more during proofing and handling).

Roll the shaped dough in the sesame seeds, coating it well on all sides. If your dough is moist enough, the seeds should stick; if necessary, paint or mist it with water first.

Place the dough seam side up in the couche (if you can still find the seam; if not, don't worry), cover it well with the couche, and let proof until it is very soft, well expanded, and slowly springs back when gently pressed with a finger, 30 to 60 minutes.

BAKING THE BREAD

If desired, just before baking, fill the oven with steam (page 18). Flip the bread onto a piece of parchment paper, so that the side resting on the couche is up, and straighten it. With a single-edged razor, make a single shallow cut down the length of the bread. Spray the bread well with water and slide it, still on the paper, onto the baking stone. Bake the bread until the edge of the cut is very dark brown and the entire loaf is golden brown; 45 to 55 minutes, rotating the bread halfway into the bake. Let the bread cool completely on a rack.

A BAKER'S WOOD-FIRED OVEN

WHEATFIELDS BAKERY/CAFÉ

LAWRENCE, KANSAS

THE NAVY NIGHT SKY IS FULL OF CONSTELLATIONS, its clarity one of the few blessings of this early hour. Fin-de-siècle apocalyptic ramblings on the radio's strongest signal keep us alert with wonderfully goofy paranoid prophecies. (Among other ghastly predicted events, noxious gases will seep out of a fissured Southwest, compelling local governments to place a permanent ban on outdoor barbecuing.)

Finally, the first sign to Lawrence, a small university town and bedroom community of Kansas City, Missouri, flashes in our headlights. We drive through the dark streets, easily finding WheatFields bakery/café on the main road into town.

A light shines in the bakeshop beyond the front counter. Thankfully we have been preceded by Thom Leonard, baker and WheatFields partner, who arrived a few minutes earlier, at 4 A.M. A devoted bicyclist, Thom normally cycles to work, but a crash with a car the previous month (he ran a stop sign) shattered his kneecap, knocking him out of commission. He is unable to work and unable to drive, and mighty miserable.

At 4:15 A.M. the thermometer on the outside of the Llopis, a circular twenty-five-ton Spanish oven, reads a reassuring 250°C, or about 480°F. Thom loves this oven and, like the captain of an old sailing ship, has had it beautifully adorned. Gratings were hand wrought by a local blacksmith, and sculpted tiles with designs of wheat, wheat kernels, and other earthy swirls replaced red brick on the oven's outer wall. Just over the firebox door is a name spelled out in tile letters—Fornax—Roman goddess of the oven and, Thom adds, "Latin, singular, feminine, nominative for oven."

The oven has cooled very little since its last stoking yesterday noon. Thom, a lean, intense man with a square face, closely cropped dark hair, and wide-open blue eyes, is sitting in a small well in front of the firebox door, his bad leg stiffly extended in front of him. Deep inside, a small pile of ashy gray coals smolders on the grate. "We try to have enough coals so that we

OPPOSITE, CLOCKWISE FROM LEFT: Thom Leonard scoring the dough; stoking the firebox before baking the first breads; Thom's silver-handled lame; sliding a peel of breads onto the hearth, his lame gripped in his teeth. ABOVE: The facade of WheatFields.

don't have to start a fire going from tinder and kindling every day." He adds a few more logs of wood from a stack neatly arranged an arm's length away under the pastry counter. This stack will slowly dwindle during the day's baking, as Thom or David Roller, his temporary replacement, feeds in more logs.

"It's remarkable how well you can control the oven. I think you have more control on this oven than you do with a gas-fired deck oven," Thom asserts.

"Where do you get the control from?"

"How much wood you put in, how much bread you put in, where the temperature is when you start. It's all in the baker's hand."

"What if the bread is ready to be baked and the temperature isn't where you want it to be?"

"It is. It just is."

Or maybe it just is for Thom. Having grown up in Kansas, where wheat futures are updated on the radio every fifteen minutes, he claims to have taken in baking bread almost osmotically. But his craftsmanship reaches a level beyond ordinary passion, integrating a profound understanding of wheat, wheat growing, and milling into what amounts to an encyclopedic knowledge of artisan baking.

His catholicity has been honestly earned. For the first year at his first bakery in Salina, Thom was baking breads from Turkey Red whole-wheat flour that he had grown organically, combined, cleaned, and stone-milled himself. (Turkey Red is that famous variety brought over by Mennonites, a wheat with ancient roots and clearly appealing to Thom's sense of purity. "It certainly isn't stamped with Chicago Board of Trade," he wryly remarks.) Not surprisingly, trying to farm, mill, and bake simultaneously proved unmanageable, yet Thom counts it as an invaluable lesson.

"I think it's important for a baker not necessarily to have done all of those things, but certainly to have observed and studied and understood what it takes to grow wheat, what it takes to mill wheat."

With the oven stoked and the baking chamber steamed with a tray of water-soaked towels, David is beginning to load the day's first breads. He has propped the peel between the mouth of the hearth and the shaping bench behind him. Breads made the day before and proofed overnight in the walk-in cooler are the first to bake. Dave makes precise incisions in the cool dough, his actions careful but cautious as Thom looks on. It is only his fourth day at WheatFields and he clearly wants to impress.

Dave loads just a few boards of breads before Thom must have a go. He ducks under the peel and grabs his silver-handled lame, or razor, from a magnetic holder on the oven's steel front. Rhythmically and quickly, he falls into his familiar routine, knocking the proofed breads from the basket onto the peel, slashing them rapidly, transferring to his mouth the lame, which he grips with clenched teeth, jerking the breads onto the hearth with both hands, then cranking the hearth around, rotating the breads to the back of the baking chamber. His movements are efficient, smooth, and well practiced. He is in his flow, and it is blindingly obvious how difficult it must be for him to be stuck on the sidelines, away from his crucible.

Once the overnight loaves are out of the oven, at 6:45 A.M., Dave stokes the oven and leaves it to lie fallow, rebuilding its heat reserve.

When he's not injured, much of Thom's working day is spent right here, at the oven's mouth, loading breads. He has studied the oven's idiosyncrasies thoroughly and learned how to get the best bake for each bread.

"You have to time each bread. We can't just decide that we are going to make baguettes first because we want to. We bake overnight breads first, then the retarded breads [breads kept in the cooler, or retarder, overnight]. Then we start our same-day baking. We do ciabatta first; they take less humidity in the oven and like a hot oven. We bake baguettes after that, in a slightly cooler oven, and they like lots of steam. The ciabatte take off the edge of the 250°C, bring it down a little bit, and put steam into the oven. Our mixing schedule is part of the baking schedule. It's not so much determined by when customers need things—it's when the oven is right for which bread."

Even the steam in this oven is extraordinary. Thom points out that the door to the hearth is small and lower than the ceiling of the baking chamber, preventing steam from rolling out when the door is opened. "The steam is not just water vapor. It's carrying all the volatiles out of the breads that are already baking in the oven, and that recondenses and affects the crusts. Every bread that's in the oven affects every other bread in the oven. The effect is subtle but profound."

Thom holding a split loaf of Country French Bread (page 133)

The oven is central to the bakery, so large in girth that it bursts out into the sidewalk. The oven costs just as much as a good imported gas deck oven and is trickier to use, but Thom would have it no other way. "I don't know where I picked up the pieces that convinced me that it had to be naturally leavened and a wood-fired brick oven, but somehow that is the element of bread that for me is really worth pursuing.

"Every fuel makes a subtle difference, even when it's completely indirect. The heat that comes off wood is different from what comes off coal, is different from what comes off gas. They may be equally good, but they are awfully different, in ways that nobody will tell by just eating the bread." Clearly Thom believes that

the heat generated in this oven is the best for his breads.

Dave unloads finished breads onto a rack. Their crusts are thick but not unyielding as Thom presses his thumb into a loaf, listening for its crackle and assessing its depth. The finish is more matte than shiny, with no trace of burn. The cuts splay wide open, revealing a craggy honey-colored grigne, or undercrust. I am learning that this is the crust of a bread perfectly baked in a wood-fired oven.

Note: Since my visit, Thom Leonard has moved from WheatFields and is now baking in his beloved Llopis oven at Farm to Market Bread Company, a wholesale bakery in Kansas City, Missouri.

Thom Leonard's Country French Bread

- Makes one 4-pound (1.8-kilo) loaf
- Time: At least 18 hours, with about 30 minutes of active work

Much of what makes this bread so special is the high-extraction flour used in it. This is a bolted whole-wheat flour much lighter in color and sweeter in flavor than a whole-wheat flour (at 100% extraction), but much darker and more flavorful than a white flour (at 72% extraction). Thom uses Rocky Mountain Flour Milling's Alpine flour (see Sources, page 222).

The method I give here for making your own high-extraction flour will work best on coarsely ground whole-wheat flour. If you already have a good high-extraction flour, substitute it for the whole-wheat and bread flour in the final recipe. Thom also includes a little of his sourdough rye starter in the dough, but it is such a small amount that I have bumped up the levain slightly and added rye flour to the final dough instead.

RECIPE SYNOPSIS THE MORNING OF THE DAY BEFORE BAKING: Refresh your active sourdough starter. (If it has been stored in the refrigerator, start refreshing it 2 days before baking with it, for at least 3 times.) **THAT EVENING:** Mix the levain and let it ferment overnight. **THE NEXT MORNING:** Mix the dough and let it ferment for 3 hours. Shape the dough, then let it proof for about 4 hours. Bake the bread for a little more than 1 hour.

	Levain	volume	weight	metric	baker's percentages
THE EVENING BEFORE BAKING MAKING THE LEVAIN	**Fermented firm sourdough starter (pages 91–94), refreshed 8 hours before**	1½ tablespoons	0.8 ounce	25 grams	17%
	Water, lukewarm	⅔ cup	4.9 ounces	140 grams	100%
	Unbleached bread flour	1 cup minus 1 tablespoon	4.9 ounces	140 grams	100%

Dissolve the sourdough starter in the water in a small bowl. Add the flour and beat this batterlike dough until very smooth. Place in a covered container and let it ferment overnight for 8 hours, or until fully risen and just starting to sink in the middle.

	Dough	volume	weight	metric	baker's percentages
BAKE DAY MIXING THE DOUGH	**Coarsely ground whole-wheat flour, preferably milled from an organic, hard winter wheat**	about 2½ cups	about 12 ounces	about 350 grams	(eventually 25%)
	Unbleached bread flour, preferably organic	5 cups	26.5 ounces	750 grams	75%
	Organic whole-rye flour	¼ cup	1 ounce	30 grams	3%
	Water	3 cups	24 ounces	660 grams	80%
	Fermented levain				30%
	Salt	1 tablespoon plus 1½ teaspoons	0.8 ounce	23 grams	2.3%

continued

PREPARING THE FLOUR	Sift the whole-wheat flour through your finest sieve or flour sifter. The large flakes of bran should be caught in the sieve (use them for flouring your peel or for muffins). Measure out 2 cups 3 tablespoons (8.8 ounces, 250 grams) sifted flour. Mix this dark flour with the bread flour and the rye flour in a large bowl or in the work bowl of your mixer.
	Add the water to the fermented levain to loosen it from the container.
MIXING THE DOUGH	*by hand:* Pour the watered levain into the flours and stir with your hands or a wooden spoon just until a rough dough forms. Turn the dough out onto the *unfloured* work surface and continue kneading until the dough is very smooth and shiny, about 10 minutes. This is a lot of dough and will take some muscle. Sprinkle on the salt and continue to knead the bread until the salt has fully dissolved and the dough is very smooth and shiny.
	by stand mixer: Add the watered levain to the flours in the work bowl and stir the dough together with a wooden spoon or your hand (this will make the mixing go more quickly). Using the dough hook, mix the dough on medium speed for about 10 to 15 minutes, or until the dough is very smooth and almost cleans the bowl. Add the salt and continue mixing until the dough is much tighter and cleans the bowl, about 5 more minutes.
	This should be a soft, sticky, and extensible dough.
FERMENTING AND TURNING THE DOUGH	Place the dough in a container at least 3 times its size and cover it tightly with plastic wrap. Let it ferment until it is airy and well expanded but not yet doubled in bulk, about 3 hours. Turn the dough (page 16) 3 times at 30-minute intervals, that is, after 30, 60, and 90 minutes of fermenting, then leave the dough undisturbed for the remaining time.
ROUNDING AND RESTING THE DOUGH	Flour the surface of the dough and your work surface and turn the dough out. Tuck the edges of the dough in to tighten it, round it (page 17), and cover it loosely with plastic wrap. Let it rest until well relaxed, 10 to 15 minutes. While the dough is resting, sift flour over a linen-lined basket or line a large colander with a well-floured tea towel.
SHAPING AND PROOFING THE DOUGH	Shape the dough into an even and tight round loaf without deflating it. Place the dough topside down in a linen-lined basket or large colander, lightly sprinkle it with flour, and cover it well with plastic wrap. Proof the dough until it is well expanded, about doubled in volume and remains indented when lightly pressed with a floured finger, after about 4 hours.
PREHEATING THE OVEN	At least 45 minutes before the dough is fully proofed, arrange a rack on the oven's second-to-top shelf and place a baking stone on it. Clear away all racks above the one being used. Preheat the oven to 450°F (230°C).
BAKING THE BREAD	If desired, just before baking the bread, fill the oven with steam (page 18). Turn the bread out onto a sheet of parchment paper or a floured peel and slash 3 to 4 diagonal slashes and 3 to 4 horizontal slashes into the top. It will look like a skewed grid with diamond-shaped openings. Slide the bread, still on the paper, onto the hot stone and bake until the bread is dark and evenly browned all around and sounds hollow when thumped on the bottom, 70 to 80 minutes, rotating it halfway into the bake. If the bread is browning too quickly, reduce the oven temperature to 400°F (205°C), but still bake the bread for at least 70 minutes. Let the bread cool on a rack.

Thom Leonard's Kalamata Olive Bread

- Makes two 1½-pound (750-gram) loaves
- Time: At least 27 hours, with about 20 minutes of active work

This has become an artisan-bakery classic, found in almost all bakeries and bread books, but I include it because Thom Leonard's version is by far the best I have ever tasted. Thom says it is so good because of the huge amount of almost whole, very ripe, black-purple Kalamatas he adds to the simple sourdough base. His olive source, Nicola, is strictly wholesale, but Zingerman's in Ann Arbor, Michigan, will send you olives of equal quality if you ask for the "bulk Kalamatas" (see Sources, page 222). Do not use the small, hard, pale purple Kalamatas you find at the grocery; the bread just won't be the same.

RECIPE SYNOPSIS THE MORNING OF THE DAY BEFORE BAKING: Refresh your active sourdough starter. (If it has been stored in the refrigerator, start refreshing it 2 days before baking with it, for at least 3 times.) **THAT EVENING:** Mix the levain and let it ferment overnight. **THE NEXT MORNING:** Mix the dough in the morning and let it ferment for 3½ hours. Shape the dough, then let it proof for about 2 hours. Bake the bread for about 45 minutes.

	Levain	volume	weight	metric	baker's percentages
THE EVENING BEFORE BAKING **MAKING THE LEVAIN**	**Fermented firm sourdough starter (pages 91–94), refreshed 8 hours before**	1½ tablespoons	0.8 ounce	25 grams	20%
	Water, lukewarm	½ cup	4 ounces	115 grams	100%
	Unbleached bread flour	¾ cup	4 ounces	115 grams	100%

Dissolve the sourdough in the water in a small bowl. Add the flour and beat this batterlike dough until very smooth. Place in a covered container and let it ferment overnight for 12 hours, or until fully risen and just starting to sink in the middle.

	Dough	volume	weight	metric	baker's percentages
BAKE DAY **MIXING THE DOUGH**	**Water, lukewarm**	1¼ cups plus 2 tablespoons	11.3 ounces	320 grams	63%
	Fermented levain				50%
	Unbleached bread flour, preferably organic*	1⅔ cups	9 ounces	250 grams	50%
	Unbleached all-purpose flour, preferably organic*	1⅔ cups	9 ounces	250 grams	50%
	Whole-rye flour, preferably organic	¼ cup	1.1 ounces	30 grams	6%
	Salt	1 tablespoon	0.5 ounce	14 grams	2.7%
	Very ripe and flavorful Kalamata olives	1¾ cups	10 ounces	285 grams (225 grams pitted)	45% (pitted olives)

*Or use 3¼ cups (17.6 ounces, 500 grams) King Arthur all-purpose for both flours.

continued

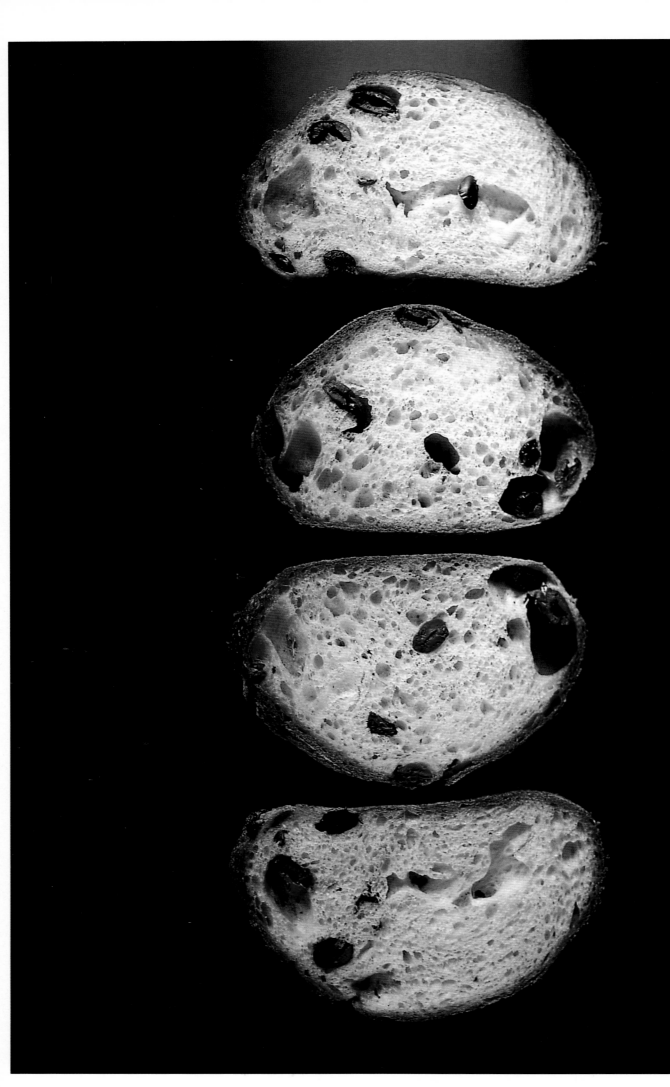

by hand: Add the water to the fermented levain to loosen it from the container. Combine the flours in a large bowl. Pour in the watered levain and stir with your hand or a wooden spoon just until a rough dough forms. Turn the dough out onto an unfloured work surface and knead, using a dough scraper to help, until the dough is very smooth and shiny, about 10 minutes. Sprinkle on the salt and continue to knead the bread until the salt has fully dissolved.

Pit the olives and gently knead them into the dough until evenly distributed. You want the bread marbled with purple, rather than completely purple.

by stand mixer: Add the water to the fermented levain to loosen it from the container. Add the flours to the mixing bowl and combine them quickly with your hand. Pour in the watered levain and stir with your hand or a wooden spoon just until a rough dough forms. Using the dough hook, mix the dough on medium speed until it is very smooth and shiny and cleans the bowl, about 15 minutes. Sprinkle on the salt and continue mixing until the salt is fully dissolved and the dough is much tighter, about 3 minutes. Remove the dough from the bowl and place it on an unfloured work surface.

Pit the olive. To pit them easily, lightly smash the olives with the side of a chef's knife, then pick out the pits with your fingers. Gently knead them into the dough by hand until evenly distributed. You want the bread marbled with purple, rather than completely purple.

The dough should be soft, sticky, and very extensible.

FERMENTING AND TURNING THE DOUGH

Place the dough in a container at least 3 times its size and cover it tightly with plastic wrap. Let it ferment, preferably at 75°F, until it is airy and well fermented but not yet doubled in bulk, about 3 hours. Turn the dough (page 16) 3 times at 20-minute intervals, that is, after 20, 40, and 60 minutes of fermenting, then leave the dough undisturbed for the remaining time.

ROUNDING AND RESTING THE DOUGH

Flour the surface of the dough and your work surface and turn the dough out. Cut the dough in half; each piece should weigh 24 ounces (680 grams). Gently round them (page 17) with more flour; cover them loosely with plastic wrap, and let them rest until well relaxed, 15 to 20 minutes.

SHAPING AND PROOFING THE DOUGH

Shape the dough into even and tight round loaves without deflating them. Place the dough topside down in linen-lined baskets, lightly sprinkle with flour, and cover well with plastic wrap. Proof the dough until it is well expanded, about 3 hours.

PREHEATING THE OVEN

At least 45 minutes before the dough is fully proofed, arrange a rack on the oven's second-to-top shelf and place a baking stone on it. Clear away all racks above the one being used. Preheat the oven to 425°F (220°C).

BAKING THE BREAD

If desired, just before baking the bread, fill the oven with steam (page 18). Turn the breads out onto a sheet of parchment paper or a floured peel and slash an off-center line across the top. Spray the breads lightly with water, then slide them, still on the paper, onto the hot stone. Bake the breads until dark and evenly browned all around, 40 to 45 minutes, rotating them halfway into the bake. Let the breads cool on a rack.

SPECIALTY

BREADS

Baker Biagio
Settepani sugaring
his statuesque
Pandoro (page 164)

OLD WORLD RYE BREADS

DUTCH REGALE BAKERY

DALLAS, TEXAS

IN THE STATES, FEW BAKERIES TACKLE RYE BREADS AND, OF THOSE THAT DO, most fake it and just add a little rye flour, caramel coloring, and caraway seeds to ordinary white-bread dough. But in Texas, George Eckrich, an American baker who has completed the German journeyman-level apprenticeship, and Carsten Kruse, a full-fledged German master baker, are baking some pretty wonderful rye breads at Dutch Regale Bakery, a large wholesale bakery that Mr. Eckrich founded with two partners (he has since bought out his partners and sold their part of the equity to the natural-foods supermarket chain Whole Foods).

One of their best breads is a very heavy, very grainy bread called Korn Bread—*korn* means seed or grain in German. Dutch Regale's version contains whole sunflower seeds, rye meal, and dark rye flour, but no wheat flour at all. It is singularly dense and, for rye lovers like my husband and me, manna. I spent an evening in Dallas, watching Eric Castel, Dutch Regale's night manager, mixing and baking a giant batch for their Dallas stores.

The evening before, Eric had prepared a cracked-rye sourdough starter and two rye "soakers," one of cracked rye and the other of whole rye kernels, for the next day's bake. Soaking the kernels and cracked rye ahead of time ensures that both will be fully hydrated by the time they are added to the dough, creating a moister bread. Eric added these preliminary preparations to a large T-mixer, a Dutch mixer designed for slowly mixing rye doughs, along with sunflower seeds, salt, yeast, and dark rye flour for the final dough. Mixing was completed when the initially granular dough became sticky and cohesive, after about an hour. The dough is not given a fermentation; bakery workers immediately weighed the dough out into huge six-pound pieces and fitted them into large oiled pans. After the dough rose to the top of the pans, it was put to bake in a fairly cool, steam-filled oven for more than three hours. This unique production yields a dark, moist bread with a pleasing, well-rounded flavor; it is best served in thin slices with marmalade or cheeses.

OPPOSITE: Korn Bread dough (page 143) proofing in strapped pans. ABOVE: A baker scaling Korn Bread dough at Dutch Regale Bakery.

SOURDOUGH AS NECESSITY

Study of sourdough-rye-bread production reveals an interesting synergy. While we appreciate the flavor, moistness, and keeping quality of rye breads made with a sourdough starter, for hundreds of years the sourdough method was a necessity, because it was the only way for rye flour to be baked into an edible loaf.

Rye is a very tolerant grain and can withstand great cold and poor soils. No other cereal is grown as far north. Rye fares best when grown under dry conditions, but summers in northern and central Europe, where rye is sometimes cultivated exclusively, are often cool and wet. This weather spurs the rye kernels to sprout or germinate prematurely, while heaped in a windrow in the field after harvesting or even while still on the stalk before the harvest. Sprout damage, or growth impairment as this defect is sometimes called, occurs to some degree at every harvest in some areas.

While sprout-damaged kernels do not necessarily show any external signs of change, inside many chemical changes have taken place to undermine their bread-making quality. The most important change is an increase in an enzyme called alpha amylase. Alpha amylase is critical to germinating plants, liquefying the starch in the endosperm by breaking it into smaller sugars, which the germinating sprout uses as an energy source. For the baker, however, excessive alpha amylase is a giant headache.

Sprout-damaged rye flour will bake into bread that is inedible—virtually unaerated, flat as a pancake, gummy, and inelastic—because too much of its starch was liquefied by the alpha amylase. The starch in rye bread is extremely important to the bread's texture, forming an integral part of the structure. Liquefying the starch utterly demolishes the bread's scaffolding, collapsing it. Yet, even in areas where sprout-damaged flour is the norm, good sourdough rye bread has been made for hundreds of years. How?

All enzymes have a pH range in which they work the best, called a pH optimum. The acids produced by fermenting sourdough lower the dough's pH. With the dough's pH lowered beyond the point where alpha amylase liquefies most efficiently, the enzyme's destructiveness is mollified and the bread is thereby saved.

American rye-bread bakers are not faced with this particular challenge since the rye available in our market is grown primarily in Canada, where growing conditions are much drier. They use sourdough instead for the complex, potent flavor, moist texture, and keeping quality it imparts. Eckrich also astutely observes that rye bread made without sourdough or caraway seeds has a weak, grassy flavor that is rather unpleasant.

Dutch Regale's Korn Bread sliced and served with a dollop of honey

Dutch Regale's Korn Bread

- Makes one 2-pound (900-gram) korn bread
- Time: At least 13 hours, with about 40 minutes of active work

If you love *very* heavy German rye bread, this recipe is for you. It might seem complicated on paper, but once you collect all the ingredients (and assuming you have an active sourdough starter), the bread is pretty simple to make. The bread can be stirred by hand or mixed in a stand mixer; either way, the mixing will take about a half hour (when mixing by hand, the dough is just stirred intermittently). This bread can even be started in the morning by fermenting the starter and soaking the rye, then baked that same evening. However, the bread must be aged before it is eaten—it will be gummy on the first day. It can then be kept in the refrigerator for several weeks or frozen almost indefinitely.

RECIPE SYNOPSIS **THE EVENING BEFORE BAKING:** Make a sourdough starter with rye meal, and soak the cracked rye and rye kernels separately. (If the starter has been stored in the refrigerator, start refreshing it 2 days before baking with it, for at least 3 times). **THE NEXT MORNING:** Mix the starter and the two ryes with the remaining ingredients for about 30 minutes, shape the dough immediately, and let it proof for about 1½ hours. Bake the bread for about 3 hours, let it cool, and serve it the next day.

	Cracked Rye Sourdough Starter	volume	weight	metric	baker's percentages
THE EVENING BEFORE BAKING MAKING THE CRACKED RYE SOURDOUGH STARTER	**Fermented firm sourdough starter,* refreshed 8 hours before**	3 tablespoons	1.8 ounces	50 grams	22%
	Water, lukewarm	1 cup	8 ounces	225 grams	100%
	Cracked rye	1¼ cups	8 ounces	225 grams	100%

*You do not need a special rye-flour starter, because you are making one now. Just use whatever starter you have; I use my firm white-flour starter (pages 91–94).

Dissolve the sourdough starter in the water, then stir in the cracked rye. Place it in a nonreactive container, cover it tightly with plastic wrap, and let it ferment for 8 to 12 hours.

	Soaked Rye Kernels	volume	weight	metric	baker's percentages
SOAKING THE RYE KERNELS	**Rye kernels**	⅓ cup	2.4 ounces	70 grams	100%
	Boiling water	½ cup plus 1 tablespoon	4.4 ounces	130 grams	184%

Stir together the rye kernels and boiling water. Place in a nonreactive container, cover it tightly with plastic wrap, and let soak for 8 to 12 hours.

continued

Soaked Cracked Rye	volume	weight	metric	baker's percentages
SOAKING THE CRACKED RYE				
Cracked rye	⅔ cup	3.7 ounces	105 grams	100%
Salt	2 teaspoons	0.4 ounce	11 grams	11%*
Water, room temperature	⅓ cup plus 1 tablespoon	3.7 ounces	105 grams	100%

*2.3% overall.

Stir together the cracked rye, salt, and water. Place in a nonreactive container, cover it tightly with plastic wrap, and let soak for 8 to 12 hours.

Dough	volume	weight	metric	baker's percentages
BAKE DAY MIXING THE DOUGH				
Soaked rye kernels				68%
Soaked cracked rye				78%
Rye-meal sourdough starter				175%
Water, lukewarm	¾ cup plus 2 tablespoons	6.9 ounces	195 grams	68%
Rye meal	1⅔ cups	9.2 ounces	260 grams	91%
Raw sunflower seeds	¼ cup	1.4 ounces	36 grams	14%
Medium or dark rye flour, plus extra for dusting	2 tablespoons	0.9 ounce	25 grams	9%
Instant yeast	1 teaspoon			1%

Drain any excess water from the rye kernels. Combine the rye kernels, soaked cracked rye, and sourdough starter with the water.

by hand: Mix the rye meal, sunflower seeds, rye flour, and yeast in a large mixing bowl. Add the starter mixture and mix this stiff, heavy dough for as long as you can with a wooden spoon. Cover the dough and let it rest for 15 minutes. Stir the dough again for as long as you can and let it rest again for 10 minutes. Stir the dough again for as long as you can. When the dough looks pasty and is quite sticky, the mixing is complete.

by stand mixer: Mix the rye meal, sunflower seeds, rye flour, and yeast in the mixing bowl. Add the starter mixture and begin mixing on the lowest speed with the paddle. Initially the dough will be like wet sand and very grainy, but as mixing progresses, the dough should become sticky, pasty, and more cohesive. The dough is fully mixed when it is very sticky and cohesive, after about 30 minutes of mixing.

SHAPING AND PROOFING THE DOUGH

Heavily oil a 9 x 5-inch loaf pan. Scrape the dough into the pan in a heap and pour some water into the now-empty mixing bowl. Wet your hands in the water and pat the dough flat in the pan, smoothing the top.

Cover the dough with plastic wrap and let it proof at room temperature until it rises to the top of the pan, 1 to 1½ hours.

PREHEATING THE OVEN

Immediately after shaping the loaf, arrange a rack on the oven's middle shelf and clear away all racks above the one being used. Preheat the oven to 400°F (205°C).

BAKING THE BREAD

When the bread is fully proofed, wet the top of the loaf heavily with water and place the pan in the oven. Close the door and immediately reduce the temperature to 300°F (150°C). Bake the bread for 2½ to 3 hours. When the loaf is slipped out of its pan, the side of the bread should bounce back when pressed. This bread will not brown very much at all. (Carsten told me that, in Germany, this bread is baked to an internal temperature of 207°F, then held at that temperature for 2 hours before the baking is considered complete.) Remove the bread from the oven, slide the loaf out of the pan onto a rack, and let it cool. When the bread is fully cool, store it in a plastic bag overnight before eating.

RYE DOUGH INELASTICITY AND STICKINESS

Those who have baked with rye flour know that compared with wheat it is a horse of a different color. The dough is incredibly sticky and lacks elasticity. Rye's peculiar behavior can be explained by its different constituents.

Gluten, the building material of wheat doughs, is absent in rye doughs, but not for want of protein. Rye flour contains gliadin, also found in wheat flour, and glutelin. When these two proteins are isolated from the rest of rye flour in a laboratory, they do combine to form gluten. However, rye flour is rich in pentosans, a type of gum found in much lesser quantity in wheat flour. Pentosans are believed to compete with the gluten-forming proteins for water, preventing the proteins from becoming fully hydrated. Other research indicates that the pentosans mingle with the proteins in some way, surrounding them or getting in between them to prevent the proteins from bonding. Rye flour's famous stickiness is also believed to be caused by this gum.

Dutch Regale's Finnish Rye Bread

- Makes one 2-pound (900-gram) bread
- Time: About 12½ hours, with about 15 minutes of active work

This flattish, round loaf is quite dense and branny, with a good amount of soaked rye meal and whole-wheat flour. It is wonderful for a Scandinavian-style breakfast or with cheese.

Mix it in a stand mixer, for it is way too sticky to be mixed by hand or in a food processor. A small amount of molasses is included, just enough to give it a mahogany color and touch it with its distinctive flavor. For an interesting texture (and if you are trying to increase your fiber intake), add the flax seeds in the recipe.

continued

RECIPE SYNOPSIS **THE EVENING BEFORE BAKING:** Soak the cracked rye, and flax seeds if using, and make a sourdough starter. (If it has been stored in the refrigerator, start refreshing it 2 days before baking with it, for at least 3 times.) **THE NEXT MORNING:** Mix the dough, give it a short rest, shape it, and let it ferment for 3 to 4 hours. Bake it for about 50 minutes.

	Soaked Cracked Rye	volume	weight	metric	baker's percentages
THE EVENING BEFORE BAKING SOAKING THE CRACKED RYE	**Cracked rye**	¾ cup plus 2 tablespoons	5 ounces	145 grams	100%
	Water, hot	⅔ cup	5 ounces	145 grams	100%

Stir together the cracked rye and hot water. Place in a nonreactive container, cover it tightly with plastic wrap, and let soak for 8 to 12 hours.

	Soaked Flax Seeds (optional)	volume	weight	metric	baker's percentages
SOAKING THE FLAX SEEDS	**Flax seeds**	⅓ cup	1.8 ounces	50 grams	100%
	Water, hot	½ cup	3.6 ounces	100 grams	200%

This step is optional: Stir together the flax seeds and hot water. Place in a nonreactive container, cover it tightly with plastic wrap, and let soak for 8 to 12 hours.

	Sourdough Starter	volume	weight	metric	baker's percentages
MAKING THE SOURDOUGH STARTER	**Fermented firm sourdough starter (pages 91–94), refreshed 8 hours before**	1 tablespoon plus 1 teaspoon	0.7 ounce	20 grams	20%
	Water, room temperature	¼ cup	2 ounces	60 grams	60%
	Unbleached bread flour	⅔ cup	3.5 ounces	100 grams	100%

Dissolve the sourdough starter in the water, mix in the flour, and knead the starter just until it begins to smooth out. Place it in a nonreactive container, cover it tightly with plastic wrap, and let ferment for 8 to 12 hours.

	Final Dough	volume	weight	metric	baker's percentages
BAKE DAY **MIXING** **THE DOUGH**	**Sourdough starter**				55%
	Soaked cracked rye				89%
	Soaked flax seeds (optional)				47%
	Water, lukewarm	1 cup minus 1 tablespoon	7.5 ounces	215 grams	67%
	Light molasses	3 tablespoons	2.1 ounces	60 grams	19%
	Salt	2 teaspoons	0.4 ounce	11 grams	3.4%
	Whole-wheat bread flour, preferably coarsely ground	1⅔ cups	8.7 ounces	250 grams	78%
	Medium or dark rye flour	½ cup	2.5 ounces	70 grams	22%

Combine the sourdough starter, soaked cracked rye, soaked flax seeds if using, the water, molasses, and salt in the bowl of a stand mixer. Add the whole-wheat and rye flours and begin mixing on the lowest speed with the paddle. Mix until the dough cleans the bowl and is somewhat elastic; about 5 minutes. This dough does not need much development.

RESTING THE DOUGH

Cover the dough in the bowl tightly with plastic wrap and let rest for 30 minutes.

SHAPING AND PROOFING THE DOUGH

Flour a linen-lined banneton, or heavily flour a tea towel and line a round basket, colander, or bowl with it. Shape the dough into a round loaf and place it seam side down in the banneton. Wrap loosely but well with plastic wrap. Let the dough proof until it is slightly expanded but still springs back when lightly pressed, 3 to 4 hours.

PREHEATING THE OVEN

About an hour before the dough is fully proofed, arrange a rack on the oven's second-to-top shelf and place a baking stone on it. Clear away all racks above the one being used. Preheat the oven to 475°F (240°C).

BAKING THE BREAD

Gently tip the proofed bread out of the banneton onto your hand and place it seam side up on a piece of parchment paper. Spray or paint it heavily with water and slide the dough, still on the paper, onto the hot baking stone. Close the oven door and immediately reduce the heat to 425°F (220°C). Bake the bread until it is richly browned and sounds hollow when it's thumped on the bottom, 45 to 50 minutes, rotating it halfway into the bake. Let the bread cool on a rack.

A NEAPOLITAN PIZZAIOLO

GEMELLI

NEW YORK, NEW YORK

NEAPOLITAN PIZZA IS EXTRAORDINARILY SIMPLE, ALMOST MINIMALISTIC, FOOD. While it differs from American pizzas in many ways, the most important deviation is that Neapolitans consider the toppings as mere embellishment to the crust, while Americans think of crust as simply the vehicle for the topping. To the Neapolitan way of thinking, crust is supreme, which brings pizza back into bread-making territory.

Late one afternoon at Tony May's restaurant Hosteria, in Port Chester, New York, I was treated to a private pizza-making lesson with pizzaiolo Emanuele Leonforte. When I first got there, the wood fire in the beehive-shaped oven had burned down to embers, but Emanuele quickly rekindled it with cardboard and then with more wood. With the oven heating to its requisite 800°F, he could start showing me how the dough is mixed. (The oven needs such intense heat to bake the pizza quickly—not more than four minutes. "Otherwise," Tony points out, "you get a biscuit.")

To begin with, Emanuele mixed about three parts American 14% protein flour with about one part Italian 00 flour, a soft-wheat flour. (The resulting mix ends up close to 12.5% protein bread flour, which substitutes very well.) He then dissolved compressed yeast and salt in water, and mixed the liquid into the flour. Mixing the dough in an oblique mixer until it was homogeneous but still quite rough, Emanuele stopped the mixing long before the dough could be stretched out into a gluten window. The dough was soft and just slightly sticky.

Emanuele carefully weighed the dough into seven-ounce pieces and rolled them into tight balls. This is a critical step; for the amount of dough per pizza must be correct. Too little dough and you have a cracker (popular now, but not very Neapolitan); too much and you have doughy pizza. The balls were then allowed to double in bulk, which could take anywhere from one to six hours, depending on the amount of yeast used. This dough is not given a fermentation, only a proof, which I discovered is also critical for the bubbly texture of the pizza. And

OPPOSITE: Pizzaiolo Emanuele Leonforte.
ABOVE: Sullivan Street's super-long pizza bianco.

Tony pointed out that the only way to achieve that sought-after high soft crust was for the dough to be well, but not over, risen.

With dough that had been fermenting all afternoon, Emanuele demonstrated two methods for shaping the perfectly round, quarter-inch-thick disks required, both of which relied solely on his hands. In the first, he flattened the dough on a floured work surface and then stretched it out using the edge of his hands. In the second, he tossed the dough back and forth between his hands to enlarge it and then threw it up in the air like a Frisbee in that classic pizzaiolo motion, the dough disk spinning, its shape perfected through centrifugal force. To be honest, both methods are awfully difficult and require a great deal of practice. Luckily, home bakers need not worry if their pizzas are not perfectly round—pizza looks rustically chic when slightly irregular.

But getting the sauce right is almost as important as the dough itself. The sauce used at Hosteria is brilliantly simple: crushed Italian tomatoes with basil, a scant sprinkling of dried oregano, one small minced clove of garlic, a little salt, extra virgin olive oil, and *basta*. The ingredients are just swished in and the sauce is left raw. How much easier can it get? In Italy, a special variety of partially air-dried tomatoes is used, but here, imported crushed tomatoes make a workable and very tasty substitute. The critical thing is that the sauce is left uncooked.

To finish the pizza, Emanuele spread a modest amount of sauce on the dough, sprinkled a few cubes of fresh mozzarella over it, and then peeled it into the oven a few feet away from the fire. A few minutes later, he peeled out the baked pizza onto a hand-painted, slightly oversize dinner plate. A drizzle of extra virgin olive oil, a scattering of fresh basil leaves, and *eccola!*, a fragrant masterpiece.

Note: Since my visit, Tony May has sold Hosteria, but he continues to offer authentic Neapolitan pizza at Gemelli, his Italian restaurant in the World Trade Center in Manhattan.

THE PIZZAIOLO'S TEN COMMANDMENTS

For a pizza maker to rightfully call his pizza Neapolitan, he must not deviate from these commandments.

The denomination of **VERA PIZZA NAPOLETANA** (True Neapolitan Pizza) is reserved exclusively to Pizza made according to the following rules:

1. It must be made only with flour, natural yeast or (baker's) yeast, salt to taste, and water as needed. All types of fat are absolutely forbidden from inclusion in the pizza dough.

2. The diameter of the Pizza should never exceed 30 centimeters (10 to 12 inches).

3. Dough must be kneaded by hand or by approved mixers that do not cause the dough to overheat. (If the dough overheats it speeds up the fermentation process.)

4. The Pizza dough must be punched down by hand and not by mechanical means (never use a rolling pin, etc.).

5. The cooking is done directly on the floor of the oven (the use of sheet pans or other pans is not allowed).

6. The oven must be made of brick and *materiale refrattario* (refractory material similar to volcanic stone) and must be fired with wood. (Operator's choice.)

7. The oven temperature must be at least 400°C or 750° to 800°F.

8. The classic Pizza ingredients are: MARINARA: tomato, oregano, garlic, olive oil, salt; MARGHERITA: tomato, mozzarella, olive oil, basil, salt; AL FORMAGGIO: grated Parmigiano, lard, garlic, basil, salt (tomato optional); CALZONE: stuffed with ricotta, salami, olive oil, salt.

9. Variations on the classics, which are inspired by tradition and fantasy, are accepted, provided they are not in conflict with the rules of good taste and culinary laws.

10. The Pizza must have the following characteristics: not crusty, well done, and fragrant, with the border (*cornicione*) high and soft.

The above rules are set by the Association of **VERA PIZZA NAPOLETANA**, which is part of the Association of Pizzaioli Europei and sustaining members.

Gemelli Pizza Margherita

- Makes 4 pizzas, to serve 4
- Time: About 6½ hours, with about 20 minutes of active work

The wonderful thing about this professional method of making pizza dough is that it is so flexible. You can make the dough in the morning, let it rise all day, and bake your pizzas in the evening. You can also mix the dough up to 36 hours in advance, shape it into balls, and refrigerate it. The next morning, put the tray of chilled dough on the kitchen counter to proof all day, and it will be ready to bake in the evening.

What makes this method different is that it is cut and rounded into individual balls immediately after kneading. The dough then proofs, essentially skipping fermentation, giving it hours instead of minutes to relax before being shaped. Thus, this dough stretches out gorgeously into thin, even disks, even though it contains no oil.

The keys to making great pizza are to shape the dough exactly when it's proofed enough and to bake it quickly at a high temperature, so the crust will be browned and well cooked but still flexible—it is not supposed to be crisp. Proofing enough but not too much is the essence of mastery. Well-proofed dough is light, extensible, and bubbly; overproofed dough collapses when it is handled. Ideally you would make your pizza as soon as your dough is well proofed, but if you are trying to time it for a dinner party, that can be hard. Consider that underproofed is better than overproofed.

The sauce recipe makes enough for 8 pizzas (crushed tomatoes are available only in 28-ounce cans), but the extra can be tossed with pasta for a delicious sauce.

To make pizza marinara, just omit the cheese and basil.

RECIPE SYNOPSIS Mix the dough for 10 minutes and let the dough proof for 5 to 6 hours. Shape and top the pizza, then bake the pizza for about 4 minutes.

	Dough	volume	weight	metric	baker's percentages
BAKE DAY **MIXING** **THE DOUGH**	**Unbleached bread flour**	3⅓ cups	17.6 ounces	500 grams	100%
	Instant yeast	¼ teaspoon			0.2%
	Salt	2 teaspoons	0.4 ounce	10 grams	2%
	Water, lukewarm	1½ cups	12 ounces	330 grams	66%

by hand: Mix the flour, yeast, and salt together in a large mixing bowl. Add the water and mix until the dough is shaggy and most of the water has been absorbed. Turn the dough out of the bowl and knead, without adding extra flour, until it is just blended but not too smooth. Cover the dough with a bowl and let it rest for 10 to 15 minutes to allow the yeast to fully hydrate. Knead the dough for 5 to 10 minutes, until it is fairly smooth, using a dough scraper if it is difficult to handle.

by stand mixer: Measure the flour, yeast, and salt together in the mixing bowl and stir them together by hand. Using the dough hook, mix on low speed while pouring in the water; continue to mix on low speed just until the dough gathers around the hook, about 3 minutes. Cover the bowl and let the dough rest for about 10 to 15 minutes to allow the yeast to fully hydrate. Mix the dough on medium speed for about 3 minutes, until the dough is fairly but not perfectly smooth.

continued

by food processor: Add the flour, yeast, and salt to the workbowl fitted with the steel blade. Process for a few seconds to mix the dry ingredients. With the machine running, pour in the water through the feed tube and process just until the dough forms a ball, about 30 seconds. Let the dough rest for about 10 to 15 minutes to allow the yeast to fully hydrate. Process the dough until the workbowl fogs, about 30 seconds. Remove it and hand knead it to cool it and redistribute the heat. Repeat this process 3 or 4 times, until the dough is fairly smooth.

This firm dough should feel sticky at first, and then soft but dry to the touch. Adjust the dough's consistency with extra water or flour only if it is excessively sticky (add 1 tablespoon flour at a time) or stiff (add 1 tablespoon water at a time).

DIVIDING THE DOUGH

On a lightly floured work surface, cut the dough into 4 equal pieces, each 7 ounces (200 grams). Shape each piece of dough into a tight ball: Roll the dough up like a carpet, turn the roll around, position it seam side up, and roll the cylinder up again. Roll the cylinder perpendicular to itself a third time. Turn the dough so that the seam is on the bottom and round the dough under your palm into a tight ball. Roll each rounded piece in flour and arrange each on a floured tray. Cover the tray tightly with plastic wrap.

FERMENTING THE DOUGH

Let the balls of dough proof at room temperature until they are soft and puffy but still springy, 5 to 6 hours. Or refrigerate the dough, after shaping it, for up to 36 hours. Remove it from the refrigerator and let it finish proofing at room temperature for 7 to 8 hours.

PREHEATING THE OVEN

One hour before baking the pizzas, arrange a rack on the oven's second-to-top shelf and place a baking stone on it. Clear away all racks above the one being used. Preheat the oven to its highest-possible temperature setting. Hopefully this will be between broil and clean—you are trying for 750°F (400°C), but 550°F (290°C) or even 500°F (250°C) will still work.

	Sauce	volume	weight	metric	baker's percentages
MAKING THE SAUCE	**Imported Italian crushed tomatoes with basil**		28 ounces	793 grams	
	Dried oregano	I teaspoon			
	Garlic, minced	I clove			
	Extra virgin olive oil	2 tablespoons			
	Salt	to taste			
	Fresh mozzarella,* cut into ½-inch dice		8 ounces	225 grams	
	Fresh basil leaves	I6			

*Alfonso Carusone, Gemelli's master pizzaiolo, advises using cow's-milk mozzarella, called *fior di latte*, not mozzarella di bufala, which he says is too watery. However, Marcella Hazan, in *Essentials of Italian Cooking*, says that the buffalo-milk mozzarella "is just too expensive . . . for commercial pizza, but it will immeasurably enhance homemade pizza," and I would have to agree.

While the oven is preheating, mix together the tomatoes, oregano, garlic, olive oil, and salt to taste. Set the sauce aside.

SHAPING THE DOUGH

Flour your work surface well and place a fully proofed dough ball on it. Flatten the ball with your hands and press it into a disk. The easiest way I have found to shape the dough is to just pull it out gently between your hands, rotating the disk as each side is pulled. To perfect the shape, place one hand on the center of the dough (to prevent it from getting too thin, which it has a tendency to do) and gently tug around the edges until the dough is about ⅛ inch thick in the center and about ¼ inch at the very edge. Keep a serving plate next to you and be sure not to stretch the dough larger than the plate's diameter.

**TOPPING
AND BAKING
THE PIZZA**

Place the shaped dough on a sheet of parchment paper or, if you are more confident, directly on a lightly floured peel, which could be any lightweight, rimless baking sheet. Spread about ¼ cup sauce on the dough and scatter with 2 ounces cheese. Peel the pizza onto the baking stone or slide it, still on the paper, onto the hot stone. Bake until the crust has colored slightly, burning in spots and staying pale in other areas, and the cheese has melted. The baking time should be around 4 minutes if your oven is hot enough, up to 6 if it is cooler. Do not overbake the pizza. To serve, drizzle on a little olive oil and arrange 4 basil leaves decoratively on top. Shape, top, and bake the remaining dough balls one at a time but eat the hot pizza right away.

LEFT TO RIGHT: Emanuele's shaping method, which is slightly different from the one in the recipe: After flattening the dough into a thin disk, press your cupped hands just up to the edge of the dough (this allows the edge to stay thicker). Next, spread your hands apart to stretch the dough. Finally, when fully shaped, the dough should be thin and round, the edge about ¼-inch thick.

Sullivan Street
Potato Pizza

- Makes two 13 x 9-inch pans or one half-sheet pan
- Time: About 6 hours, with 30 minutes of active work

Sullivan Street Bakery is named for its street in the SoHo section of New York City. The bakery has a very SoHo feeling to it, from the hip customers to the gritty beauty of the space itself. The bakeshop just behind the counter was converted from an old pushcart storage garage, and its ceiling rafters and white plaster walls lend it an urban rusticity. The bakery's product line is small, but each item is beautifully crafted and special. The bakery is well known for its pizza bianca, but my favorite is this potato pizza. It is very unlike a traditional pizza, more like a very thin-crusted tart heaped with golden waves of potatoes, onions, rosemary, and olive oil.

The dough is unusual but not difficult to make. It starts out as a batter but is beaten in a stand mixer into a very fluid dough, which bakes into a very thin and bubbly crust. I have mixed flours to achieve an 11.5% protein flour, but if you use King Arthur all-purpose flour, as Sullivan Street does, the entire amount of flour can be King Arthur.

continued

RECIPE SYNOPSIS Mix the dough for 20 minutes and let it ferment for 4 hours. Line the pan(s) with the dough, and proof for 1 hour, then top the pizza and bake for about 40 minutes.

	Dough	volume	weight	metric	baker's percentages
BAKE DAY **MIXING THE** **DOUGH**	**Unbleached bread flour***	¾ cup plus 2 tablespoons	4.6 ounces	130 grams	50%
	Unbleached all-purpose flour*	¾ cup plus 2 tablespoons	4.6 ounces	130 grams	50%
	Instant yeast	¼ teaspoon			0.3%
	Water, lukewarm	1¼ cups	10 ounces	285 grams	109%
	Granulated sugar	½ teaspoon			1%
	Salt	½ teaspoon			1%
	Extra virgin olive oil, for coating the pan				

*Or use 1¾ cups (9.2 ounces, 260 grams) King Arthur all-purpose flour.

Measure the flours and yeast into the mixing bowl and mix them together by hand. Using the paddle, mix on low speed while pouring in the water. Mix just until the batter comes together, about 3 minutes. Increase the speed to medium and beat this batter until it cleans the bowl and comes together into a smooth if very wet dough, about 20 minutes. Add the sugar and salt and mix until both are well dissolved, 2 to 3 minutes.

FERMENTING THE DOUGH

Cover the dough tightly with plastic wrap and let it ferment until it is very light, about 4 hours.

LINING THE PANS

Very generously coat two 13 x 9-inch baking pans or 1 half-sheet pan with olive oil. Pour the fermented dough directly into the pan(s). Coat your hands well with olive oil and spread the dough in a thin layer in the pan(s). Spread the dough as much as you can without ripping it, then let it rest for about 10 minutes. Spread the dough to the pans' (pan's) edges (you may need another 10-minute rest to stretch it out fully). Bubbles are desirable, so try not to pop them. Cover the pan(s) and let the dough proof until light and risen by about half, about 1 hour.

	Topping	volume	weight	metric	baker's percentages
PREPARING THE TOPPING	**Yukon Gold or other yellow-fleshed potatoes, peeled**	7 large	about 4 pounds	about 1800 grams	680%
	Coarse salt				
	Sweet or yellow onion, sliced into half-moons	1 large	about 10 ounces	about 280 grams	100%
	Fresh rosemary, chopped	2 tablespoons			2%
	Extra virgin olive oil				

While the dough is proofing, prepare the topping. Slice the potatoes into paper-thin rounds using the 2-millimeter blade of a food processor or a mandoline. Toss them with a sprinkling of salt and let them exude their liquid for about 15 minutes. Gently squeeze them dry in a colander to release most of their liquid (the slices will clump together). Toss the potato slices with the onion and rosemary.

PREHEATING THE OVEN

About 30 minutes before baking the pizza, arrange a rack on the oven's top shelf for the half-sheet pan, or the top and lower-third shelves for the 2 pans, and clear away all racks above the ones being used. Preheat the oven to 425°F (220°C).

TOPPING AND BAKING THE PIZZA

When the dough is proofed, spread on the topping. Brush it generously with olive oil and sprinkle with more salt. Bake the pizza until the potatoes are brown and crusty at the edges and easily pierced with the tip of a knife, about 40 minutes, rotating the pan(s) halfway into the bake. Serve the pizza hot or at room temperature.

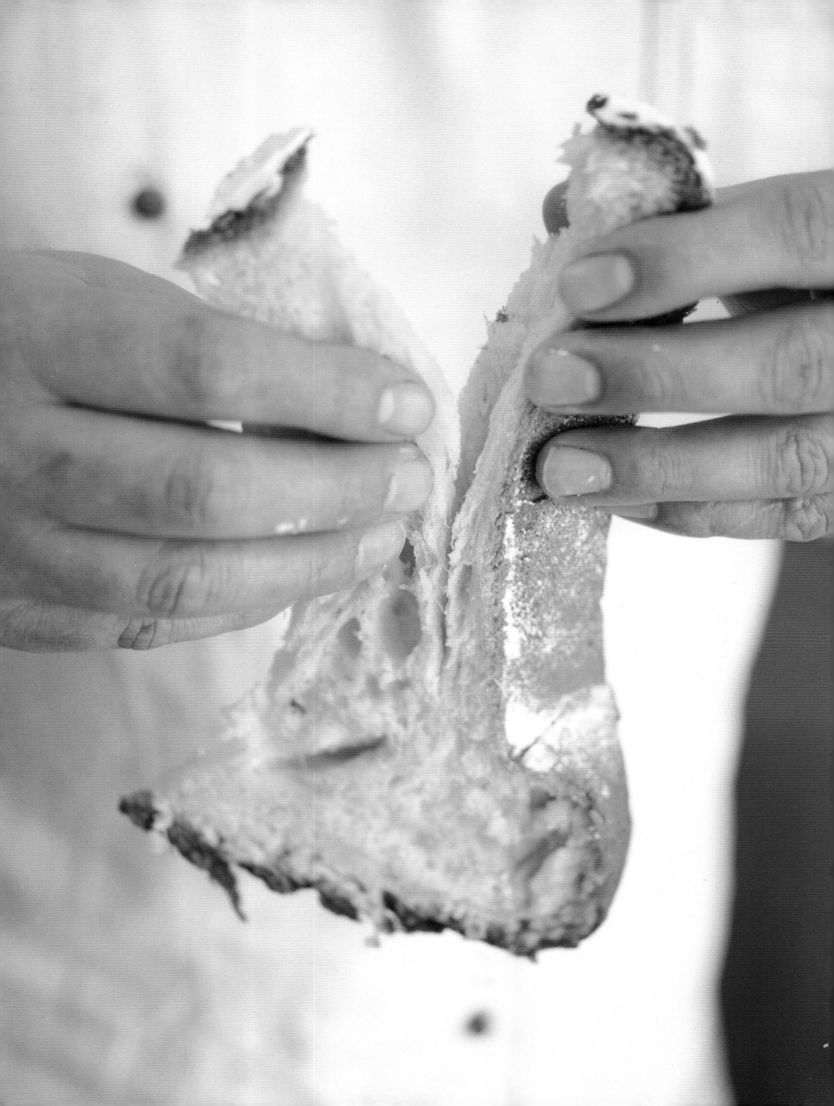

PANDORO: PATIENCE'S REWARD

BRUNO BAKERY

BROOKLYN, NEW YORK

BIAGIO SETTEPANI HAD WARNED ME, "FOR PANDORO, WHAT YOU NEED IS PATIENCE," but he didn't mean ordinary patience. He meant Pygmalion-like patience, the kind that would allow him to mix pandoro dough for over an hour and a half, while he slowly builds it with mere dribbles of eggs, egg yolks, sugar, and butter. Never does he foist too much ingredient on the budding dough. Instead he waits, biding his time, until the dough signals its readiness by gracefully lifting cleanly off the bowl and onto the mixer's arms. The reward for this restraint, his Galatea, is one of Italy's grandest celebration breads—pandoro.

I had tasted pandoro once years ago when I was in Italy during Christmastime and have never forgotten it. A tall star-shaped bread with a large cushion-shaped bottom, it is intensely fragrant, with a golden honeycombed interior. All that slow careful mixing makes the crumb light as spun gold, capable of being pulled away in long gossamer strands.

Biagio is sure that pandoro is related to brioche and was probably developed during the days when sourdough starter, called *la madre* in Italian, was the only leavener. Generations of Italian bakers have since tweaked the formula, and in its present incarnation, a small amount of yeast is used with the sourdough starter, allowing it to contain more sugar than any other bread in this book. When correctly made and stored, pandoro has a shelf life of at least a month, despite the absence of additives or preservatives.

Wholesale versions of the bread are imported from Italy at Christmastime, but, as far as I know, Biagio is the only American baker who is making it on an artisan scale. The owner and head baker of Bruno Bakery, Biagio is a medal-bedecked pastry chef, and his two stores in the New York City area have gained recognition for their wide variety of superb cakes, cookies, and rustic Italian breads. In addition to running the two stores, he is a wonderfully generous teacher, teaching at the New School, bringing groups from the local trade junior high into his bakery, and now serving on the board at the French Culinary Institute.

OPPOSITE: A perfectly crafted Pandoro (page 164) ripping into long strands. ABOVE: Biagio Settepani at his Greenpoint shop, Bruno Bakery. In his arms, his *madre,* or sourdough starter, which he bundled in cloth and tied in twine the traditional way.

Years ago, Biagio decided to sell the traditional Italian celebration breads panettone and pandoro at Christmas and colomba di pasqua ("Easter dove") at Easter. These sourdough-based breads require a high degree of technical mastery, but even after years of practice, Biagio's attempts still fell short of his expectations. Since these breads were available by import from large Italian wholesale bakeries, his would have to be even better to win customers and justify their expensive production. So he attended a seminar in Italy taught by master pastry chef Silvio Bessone; there he was able to fill in all his knowledge gaps and finally attain the perfection he sought.

When I went to see Biagio in his Greenpoint store, he already had his *impasto lievito* ("sourdough starter") going, having refreshed it that morning. As he was taught at the seminar, his starter is wrapped in the traditional Italian manner—first in a sheet of plastic, then in a muslin cloth, finally tied all around with twine. The starter begins as a soft flexible bundle and gradually gets harder—"stronger"—as it ferments and fermentation gases build up. When the starter becomes rigid enough to virtually bounce off the workbench, it is deemed really "strong" and ready to use.

We began by mixing the *secondo impasto,* the second dough. Biagio combined the fermented sourdough starter with high-gluten flour, fresh yeast, and half the eggs. When the dough became smoother, he slowly dribbled in more eggs and siftings of sugar. These additions alone took over an hour, but in the end the dough was very smooth and strong. He left this second dough to ferment for three to four hours.

While we were waiting for the dough to rise, an adorable little girl with ringlets wandered in. Biagio shouted, "Bilen," and scooped her up in a bear hug. Bilen was being baby-sat by her grandmother, Biagio's mother, Fina, when she asked to visit her uncle, who after all bakes some of the best cookies and cakes in town. Biagio ripped off a chunk of panettone and handed it to her. She took it, smiled adorably at him, and toddled off for a tour of the bakery, daintily nibbling her chunk of cake. Soon Biagio's wife, Pina, and youngest son, Joseph, showed up with some of the ribbons and fabric swatches Pina had found to decorate the Easter baskets and chocolates Biagio makes for Easter. "Easter is my favorite holiday," she told me with a gleam in her eye. "I put all my heart into it."

By early evening, after Biagio and I shared a pizza and Cokes, the second dough had risen to its requisite triple, and the *terzo impasto,* third dough, was ready to be mixed. This dough is mixed almost identically to the second but takes an hour longer. After the eggs and sugar are added, Biagio slowly spoons in butter whipped almost white with melted cocoa butter. At the end of mixing, this dough is so soft and fine that it feels like liquid silk. We gently rounded up the dough pieces and eased them into their star-shaped molds to rise overnight.

The next day, I came back in time to see that the dough had risen over the tops of the molds and was ready to go into the oven. After baking for an hour, the pandoros emerged hugely mushroomed over the edges of their molds. Biagio was thrilled with their stratospheric height but waited patiently for them to cool down before he cut into one. He held up a wedge and proudly showed me how the crumb could be pulled away in a long strip. Then we tasted it. The soft moist cake was so light that it almost dissolved in my mouth, its multiple flavors mingling in a heady perfume.

TOP, LEFT TO RIGHT: Adding sugar during mixing of pandoro dough; fully mixed dough, which will be very liquidy but will fall from the paddle in smooth sheets. BOTTOM, LEFT TO RIGHT: Shaped pandoro looking very scant for the size of the pan; baked pandoro in a traditional star-shaped mold and in a ring-shaped mold (the dough more than quadruples in height during proofing and baking).

Bruno's Pandoro

- Makes two 1-pound (450-gram) cakes
- Time: At least 33 hours, with about 1½ hours of active work

If you are an experienced sourdough baker looking for a worthy challenge, this cake is it. You will need a very good sourdough starter and lots of patience while you mix it, but otherwise the recipe is not that difficult to make.

Unlike the other recipes in the book, this one includes a schedule, which Biagio has been perfecting for years. It is such a comfortable, sensible schedule that it really is worth following.

This is a recipe that I have been working on for a long time, even before I watched Biagio. After many batches and Biagio's clarification, I have finally found success. What constantly stymied me was the yeast and flour. Neither active dry nor instant active dry yeast will work in this incredibly sweet dough unless an ungodly amount is used. You must use either fresh yeast or an osmotolerant yeast (see page 8), known as special instant active dry yeast, such as SAF Instant Gold. Because the latter is available to all (see Sources, page 222), I have converted the recipe's original compressed yeast to the special instant yeast, and added a tiny fraction of water to rehydrate it.

You will need to use high-gluten flour with a protein level of 14% if you want your cakes to be really light, for the high sugar, egg, and fat levels combined with enzymatically active sourdough-based dough strain this high-rising cake's structure to the maximum.

The only changes I have made to Biagio's original formula are to shorten and simplify his mixing procedure, which I haven't found to affect the quality at all, and to use special instant yeast instead of compressed. I worked on this recipe in the summer, when my kitchen hovered around 75°F. I used ¼ teaspoon SAF Instant Gold yeast, which gave me the timing I wanted. In the winter, when kitchen temperatures are more like 68° to 70°F, I believe that ½ teaspoon SAF Instant Gold yeast works better.

If this mixing procedure seems unduly elaborate, it is not without logic. Sugar and butter interfere with gluten formation—the sugar by competing with the gluten for water, the butter by surrounding the gluten and preventing it from bonding with itself, so the dough is first developed in their absence, and then each is added gradually so as not to swamp the dough. Biagio learned to whip the butter before adding it, and it does seem to incorporate into the dough better and probably contributes to the dough's light texture.

Pandoro makes a superb gift for sending because of its long shelf life, but it is easily crushed and should be double boxed before shipping. This recipe produces two 1-pound cakes, but you could increase it as needed, doubling the recipe to make four cakes or two 1-kilo cakes, if you can find the correct molds. I have not been able to locate the authentic Italian molds, but the more deeply pleated Portuguese molds that all the upscale kitchenware catalogs offer are a decent alternative.

RECIPE SYNOPSIS **THE EVENING BEFORE MIXING THE DOUGH:** Refresh a very active sourdough starter. **THE MORNING OF THE DAY BEFORE BAKING:** At 9 A.M., refresh the starter again. **AT 1 P.M:** Mix the first dough with the refreshed and fermented starter by hand. Let it ferment. **AT 4:45 P.M.:** Whip the butter with the melted cocoa butter and prepare the molds. **AT 5 P.M.:** The first dough should have tripled or even quadrupled and be ready to be mixed into the final dough. In the first stage of the mix, most of the eggs, flour, and first dough are mixed in a stand mixer with some flavorings. When that dough is smooth, the remaining eggs, yolks, and vanilla are slowly added. The sugar is added next, in two increments, and finally the whipped butter, also in two increments. The entire mixing procedure takes about an hour to complete. The dough is immediately shaped, put into the prepared molds, and allowed to proof at room temperature for 12 hours. **THE NEXT MORNING:** When the dough is well domed over the molds, the cakes are baked for about 35 minutes.

	Sourdough Starter	volume	weight	metric	baker's percentages
THE DAY BEFORE BAKING 9 A.M.: REFRESHING THE SOURDOUGH STARTER	**Very active, fully fermented firm sourdough starter (pages 91–94), refreshed 8 to 12 hours before**	¼ cup	2.1 ounces	60 grams	92%
	Water, lukewarm	2 tablespoons	1.1 ounce	30 grams	46%
	Unbleached high-gluten flour	7 tablespoons	2.3 ounces	65 grams	100%

Dissolve the sourdough starter in the water. Add the flour and knead this very stiff dough until it is smooth. It will be very hard at first but it will smooth out.

Place in a covered container and let it ferment until it is fully risen and deflates when pressed, about 4 hours. This starter is larger than needed so that some can be cut off for the next starter.

continued

Primo Impasto	volume	weight	metric	baker's percentages
1 P.M.: **MIXING THE PRIMO IMPASTO**				
Osmotolerant instant yeast, such as SAF Instant Gold	¼ to ½ teaspoon*			0.7 to 1.4%
Water, 105° to 115°F	1 tablespoon			13%
Fermented sourdough starter	7 tablespoons	3.7 ounces	105 grams	93%
Unbleached high-gluten flour	¾ cup	4 ounces	115 grams	100%
Egg	1 large			44%
Granulated sugar	2 tablespoons	1 ounce	30 grams	26%

*Use the larger amount of yeast if your kitchen is below 72°F and the lesser amount if it is above 72°F.

Stir the yeast into the water and let it stand for about 5 minutes. Measure the sourdough starter and reserve the remaining for your next baking project. Break up the starter into 5 chunks and add them to the flour in a mixing bowl. Add the yeast and egg and knead this incredibly stiff starter by hand until it smooths out. Add the sugar and continue kneading until the sugar dissolves and the dough softens and is very smooth. You might think this ropy starter will never come together, but if you put some muscle into it, it will eventually smooth out. Put it into a container at least 5 times its size and cover it tightly with plastic wrap. Let it ferment until it has tripled or quadrupled in bulk, 3 to 4 hours.

Secondo Impasto	volume	weight	metric	baker's percentages
5 P.M.: **MIXING THE SECONDO IMPASTO**				
Hard cocoa butter, crumbled*	about 1 tablespoon	0.3 ounce	10 grams	4%
Unsalted butter, preferably European style, at room temperature, plus about 3 tablespoons for buttering the molds	½ cup plus 5 tablespoons	7 ounces	200 grams	89%
Unbleached high-gluten flour	1½ cups	7.8 ounces	225 grams	100%
Salt	½ teaspoon	0.2 ounce	5 grams	2%
Primo impasto				143%
Honey	1 teaspoon	0.3 ounce	10 grams	4%
Eggs	4 large			88%
Pure vanilla extract	1 tablespoon	0.5 ounce	15 grams	7%
Egg yolks	2 large			13%
Granulated sugar	⅔ cup	4.7 ounces	135 grams	60%
Powdered sugar, for dusting the tops of the cakes				

*You can find pure cocoa butter at health food stores, often in the cosmetics department. As long as it contains no perfumes or preservatives, it is edible and fine to use.

Melt the cocoa butter in the microwave on high for 2½ to 3 minutes (it takes a long time to melt because of its lack of moisture) or in a small pan on the stove. Whip the unsalted butter with an electric mixer or with a balloon whisk while drizzling in the cocoa butter. Stop when the butter is whitish and about doubled in volume. Set aside.

Melt about 3 tablespoons unsalted butter and brush it very carefully into two 8-cup pandoro molds (you can use any mold with an 8-cup volume but taller molds work best). Dust the molds with flour and set them aside.

Mix the flour and salt in the bowl of a stand mixer, then add the primo impasto broken into 5 chunks, the honey, and 3 of the eggs. Using the dough hook, mix the dough on medium speed until it is smooth and cleans the bottom of the bowl. Turn the mixer off and switch to the paddle. On low speed, add the remaining egg and mix until the dough is smooth again, increasing the speed to medium when the egg is slightly absorbed (this prevents splashing). The dough will be very soft and will cling to the bowl. Repeat with the vanilla and 1 of the egg yolks. When the dough is smooth again, repeat with the last egg yolk.

Now reduce the mixer speed to low and begin adding half the granulated sugar in the same way, increasing the speed to medium as the sugar is absorbed. Repeat with the remaining granulated sugar. Once the sugar is dissolved in the dough, mix on medium speed until the dough is very smooth. Now add half the whipped butter in the same way, and when that is incorporated, add the last of the butter. You may need to stop the machine and push the dough from the paddle to get the butter evenly distributed. When the dough is smooth and silky, the mixing is complete.

SHAPING AND PROOFING THE DOUGH

Cut the dough in half; each piece should weigh 17.6 ounces (500 grams). Flour your work surface and place one piece of dough on it. Roll up the dough into a cylinder, then roll the cylinder onto itself into a ball. Round the dough into a smooth, tight ball and place it smooth side up in one of the molds. Repeat with the other piece. The dough will look very skimpy for the size of the molds. Cover the molds loosely with plastic wrap and let the dough proof at room temperature until well domed over the tops of the molds, about 12 hours.

BAKE DAY 6 A.M.: CHECKING THE CAKES AND PREHEATING THE OVEN

Check the cakes to see if they have fully risen; they should be well domed over the molds. If they are not yet fully risen, go back to bed. When they are ready, uncover them to let them form a light skin. Arrange a rack on the oven's bottom shelf and clear away all racks above the one being used. Preheat the oven to 350°F (180°C).

BAKING THE CAKES

Bake the cakes for 30 to 35 minutes, rotating them halfway into the bake. The cakes are done when well browned all over (look at the sides of the cakes touching the mold to see if they are brown yet). Let the cakes cool in the molds for 30 minutes, then remove them from the molds and let them finish cooling upside down on a rack. You will notice their bottoms flattening out; this is correct. When they are completely cool, store them in large plastic bags. If they are well wrapped, they will keep for at least 1 month, if not longer. Before serving them, dust them liberally with powdered sugar.

A NEW YORK BIALY

KOSSAR'S BIALYSTOKER KUCHEN

NEW YORK, NEW YORK

KOSSAR'S BIALYSTOKER KUCHEN IS A LIVELY OLD BIALY BAKERY where the spirit of old Jewish bakeries lingers. Under neon signs that don't even have to try to look retro, large plywood trays filled with onion pletzel, bialys and bulkas, hero bread, sesame sticks, and onion pockets beckon passersby. Customers pick up their bialys just a few yards away from the bakery's ever-turning heart, a revolving-shelf pizza oven. Long ago the baking would have been done by a lung-choking coal-fired brick oven in some basement tenement, but this more modern and health-ful replacement has good heavy hearths and does its job well.

Danny Scheinin, the retired owner and son-in-law of founder Morris Kossar, explains this bagel sibling's provenance. "Bialy is a short name for bialystoker kuchen [*kuchen* means "cake" in Yiddish]. Bialystok is the second largest city in Poland. That's where they originated. It was a Jewish bread. Bialystok had a very big Jewish population—before the war. And it was brought over here, as far as we know, around the turn of the century."

I visited early one weekday morning. At the back of the shop, Alan Klapman and Brian Gorman were cutting pieces of fermented dough on a huge table and pressing it out into 2½-ounce rounds using an ancient and noisy roll press. The two men work well together—with a *bissel* of humor. I asked their names. Alan told me his, then introduced me to his colleague.

"We call him 'Loch-in-Kopf' for short," Alan says to me.

"What do you call him?" I can't hear above the racket of the rounding machine.

"Loch-in-Kopf!" he shouts.

"Noodle-Head?" I am trying to remember my Yiddish.

"It means 'Hole in the Head.'"

"My Yiddish isn't so good." I apologize.

"Neither is his. He just found out what it means." We all laugh together, then Alan explains: "He got hit with a box years ago, and that's what we called him."

OPPOSITE: The perfect lox and bialy sandwich. ABOVE: The mandatory neon sign at Kossar's Bialystoker Kuchen.

ABOVE, LEFT TO RIGHT; Baker Brian Gorman operating the roll press; Brian smearing shaped bialys with a dash of ground onion; Alan Klapman and Brian filling the depressions of an oven full of bialies. OPPOSITE, LEFT TO RIGHT: Alan stretching out proofed rolls into bialy shapes; Alan peeling dozens of bialys into the oven.

"I got a hole in my head, so they called me that," Brian nods.

Alan, who has worked at Kossar's for more than twenty-five years, really loves to bake, and he told me that he even bakes when he goes home. He showed me just how sticky bialy dough is supposed to be. The dough is mixed in the same kind of old horizontal mixer I found at Royal Crown in Brooklyn (see page 197), which seems to excel at these soft doughs. This dough is too tacky to be run through the kind of high-volume machinery used in wholesale bagel production, a reassuring thought considering the bagel's fate. The bialy trade has always been and always will be strictly artisanal.

After watching Brian and Alan load round after round of dough onto floured wooden trays, then stacking the trays into tall columns around the shop to proof for an hour, we figured we had enough time to visit Russ & Daughters. This is another landmark Jewish food purveyor, an "appetizer store" owned by Mark Russ, the grandson of founder Joel Russ, which specializes in lox, smoked fish, and wonderful all-natural cream cheeses from Canada. What's a bialy without lox and cream cheese, after all? Russ & Daughters also carries superb caviar, homemade pickles and sauerkraut, salads, and sweets of all kinds, including that oriental splendor, chocolate-and-pistachio-studded halvah. This gleaming white store with polished-steel display cases is so clean, my grandmother, who washes garbage before throwing it away, would be impressed.

Herman Vargas, the store manager, made me a beautiful sandwich with a Kossar bialy and Russ & Daughters' Gaspé ("luxurious divine") smoked salmon and chive cream cheese. Clearly a conscientious man, Herman arranged the sandwich a little too perfectly for its photo opportunity, so I styled it a bit on the counter. This being New York, the shop's customers couldn't help commenting, "Why don't you stop messing with it and eat it already?" I will, I will, but we have to take a picture. "What are you, picky or something?" Another, after intently studying our tableau, suggested the addition of a parsley sprig. We compromised with a pickle. (I got to eat that sandwich and pickle later, and I can tell you it tasted even better than it looked.)

After all that, we hurried back to Kossar's and were happy to find Alan and Brian still in the midst of final shaping. Alan picked up a round and deftly stretched the center into a thin sheet, leaving a narrow rim of dough around the perimeter, almost like a pizza. Later Danny explained to me that when bialys originally were baked in the coal-fired ovens, the shaping technique was different. "They had a very little rolling pin with two ends and a little bump in the middle. That's how you would roll it out. When they came in with gas ovens, the heat was too strong, and they had to make the middle thinner, so that's when they started to pull it out by hand."

Stretching what looked like about six bialys a second, Alan flipped them onto the wooden peels lined up on a table. When all the peels were full—each holds three dozen bialys—Brian followed him with a tiny smear of ground fresh onion, just enough to give it a

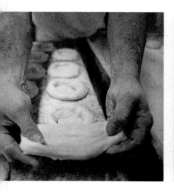

good flavor. Alan then opened the oven door and jerked in the entire peelful, adding peel after peel until the hearth was full. In the oven, five of these hinged hearths, called shelves, rotate Ferris-wheel fashion. The bialys baked for just a short time, only about 6 to 8 minutes or two to three revolutions, before Alan peeled them out to cool on racks.

What has always stumped amateur bialy bakers like myself is the onion filling, which lies in small brown bumps in the center. Why is that onion brown? Is it fried, dehydrated, or what? At Kossar's, I finally found out that the onion is actually fresh and raw, ground in an old-fashioned meat grinder. Sitting on a shelf in front of the hot oven all day, it begins to caramelize, changing to that characteristic brown color. Mystery solved!

Kossar's has passed out of family ownership for the first time since 1936, when Morris Kossar and his partner, Shorty Mirsky, bought it from the original owners. Danny inherited the bakery from his father-in-law, Morris Kossar. Now, Juda Englemayer and Danny Cohen, two brothers-in-law, have bought the bakery from Danny, but plan to keep it exactly the same except for the hours. The bakery used to be open twenty-four hours a day, seven days a week except for Rosh Hashanah and Passover, but it will now close for the Jewish Sabbath—from sundown Friday to sundown Saturday—so that the bakery can finally, after all these years, get its kosher certification. Could it be that these two energetic young men will even improve the old place?

WHAT IN THE WORLD IS A BIALY AND WHAT SHOULD A BAGEL BE?

Bialys are more closely related to English muffins than to bagels. Dusty with flour, they are made from a very stiff dough overmixed to stickiness and quickly baked on a hearth, leaving them soft, spotted brown, and in need of a preprandial toasting. Instead of a hole, they have a deep indentation at their center, which is filled with a smear of ground onion, infusing them with an oniony scent. They are much lighter and less caloric than bagels.

Traditional bagels are made from high-gluten flour mixed into an extraordinarily stiff dough. The bagels are shaped almost immediately, and the dough is given no fermentation, but chilled, or "retarded," for at least a day to proof slowly. They are shiny and heavy and undergo an unusual cooking process: first boiled, then baked briefly on wet canvas-covered planks, then finally flipped over onto a hot stone hearth to finish baking. Good bagels are slightly sweet and off-white from the addition of malt syrup, and they have a crisp, slightly blistered crust and a very dense, chewy texture. By definition, they must have a hole through their center, about the only real feature left in the counterfeits sold today.

The "bagels" most Americans are buying aren't even stepchildren to the original. The bagel chains sell a product made from frozen dough that is loaded with dough conditioners. Mixed and shaped in a central plant, the dough is frozen and then trucked to the "retail units," where the "bagels" are proofed and baked "fresh that day." Such travesties do not even deserve to be called bagels, more like circular buns for the additive-deprived.

GROWING UP WITH BIALYS

When I was growing up in Milwaukee, one was either a bagel or a bialy person; I was the latter. During the week, I loved toasted and well-buttered bialys for breakfast. I still remember my precise bialy-eating ritual: I would eat the thicker bottom half first, taking care to circumvent the oniony central crater. Then I would eat the thinner, bubblier top half, which often had some onion flavor carried over from the center. Finally I got to that crater where, if I was lucky, a pool of melted butter would remain. This last bit was thoroughly delicious, and its memory warmed me on the cold, dark bus ride to school.

Kossar's Bialys

- Makes twelve 2.5-ounce (75-gram) bialys
- Time: About 5 hours, with 20 minutes of active work

At Kossar's, a heavy-duty horizontal mixer beats the incredibly stiff bialy dough into a slack exten-sible mass (the effect of intentional overmixing). I have found this procedure impossible to replicate in our home kitchens—our equipment is just not strong enough. What I have settled on is mixing the very stiff dough until it is soft, smooth, and supple, yet still pretty stiff. The only machine that can manage this job is a food processor. Homemade bialys are harder to stretch out, but they end up looking and tasting pretty close to the originals, with the right tight-grained, properly chewy texture—thanks to high-gluten flour (see Sources, page 222).

Bialys have an unusual two-step shaping procedure. The dough is first cut and rounded, then allowed to proof. When the bialys are almost fully proofed, they are stretched out and smeared with their onion garnish. This procedure is the only way to get the authentic bialy look.

RECIPE SYNOPSIS Mix the dough and let it ferment for 2 hours. Prepare the onion while the dough is fermenting. Shape the dough into rounds, proof them for about 2½ hours, and then stretch them out and smear with the browned onion. Bake the bialys for about 7 minutes in a very hot oven.

	Dough Ingredients	volume	weight	metric	baker's percentages
BAKE DAY **MIXING** **THE DOUGH**	**Yellow onion, peeled and cut into chunks**	I medium			
	Unbleached high-gluten flour	4 cups	21.2 ounces	600 grams	100%
	Instant yeast	I teaspoon			0.5%
	Salt	2¼ teaspoons	0.4 ounce	12 grams	2%
	Water, cold	1¾ cups	13.8 ounces	390 grams	65%

Grind the onion to a purée in the food processor fitted with the steel blade. Remove the onion and reserve it. Without washing out the workbowl, add the flour, yeast, and salt and process them for a few seconds to combine them. With the machine running, pour the water through the feed tube. Process the dough until it is cohesive, soft, and probably hot, 2 to 3 minutes. Remove the dough and knead it on your work surface for a few seconds to redistribute the heat. The dough will feel very hot at first but will quckly cool, tightening into a very stiff dough as it does so. Process the dough for 1 minute, then knead it by hand to cool it down and redistribute the heat. Repeat this process 3 or 4 times, until the dough is very smooth and strong.

This is a very firm dough.

**FERMENTING
THE DOUGH**

Place the dough in a container at least 3 times its size and cover it tightly with plastic wrap. Let the dough ferment until doubled in bulk, about 2 hours.

**PREPARING
THE ONION**

Heap the ground onion into a mound in a small nonstick baking pan, or in a foil-lined and oiled pan. Bake it in a 350°F oven until light brown, about 1 hour, stirring it once or twice. The onion should be a moist, lightly caramelized paste. Let the onion cool.

**INITIAL SHAPING
AND PROOFING
THE DOUGH**

Cut the dough into 12 equal pieces, each 2.8 ounces (80 grams). Round the pieces (page 35) into smooth balls, cover them well with plastic wrap, and let proof until they are puffy and very light and deflate slightly when gently pressed, about 2½ hours.

**PREHEATING
THE OVEN**

About 45 minutes before the breads are fully proofed, arrange a rack on the oven's second-to-top shelf and place a baking stone on it. Clear away all racks above the one being used. Preheat the oven to 475°F (240°C).

**FINAL SHAPING
AND BAKING
THE BREAD**

Stretch each dough round out to look like a pizza 5 to 6 inches in diameter. Lightly pull out the center until it is very thin, leaving only a narrow membrane of dough at the center (you may have to push the center down with your thumbs to convince this not-very-extensible dough). Try to pull the dough rounds out as far as possible. Arrange 6 shaped rounds on a piece of parchment. Smear about ¼ teaspoon of the browned onion purée in the center of each round; it's just a tiny bit to give it a little flavor—don't overdo it. Slide the parchment onto the hot stone and bake the bialys until just spotted brown, 6 to 8 minutes, rotating them halfway into the bake for even browning. Transfer them to a rack to cool and bake the remaining bialys.

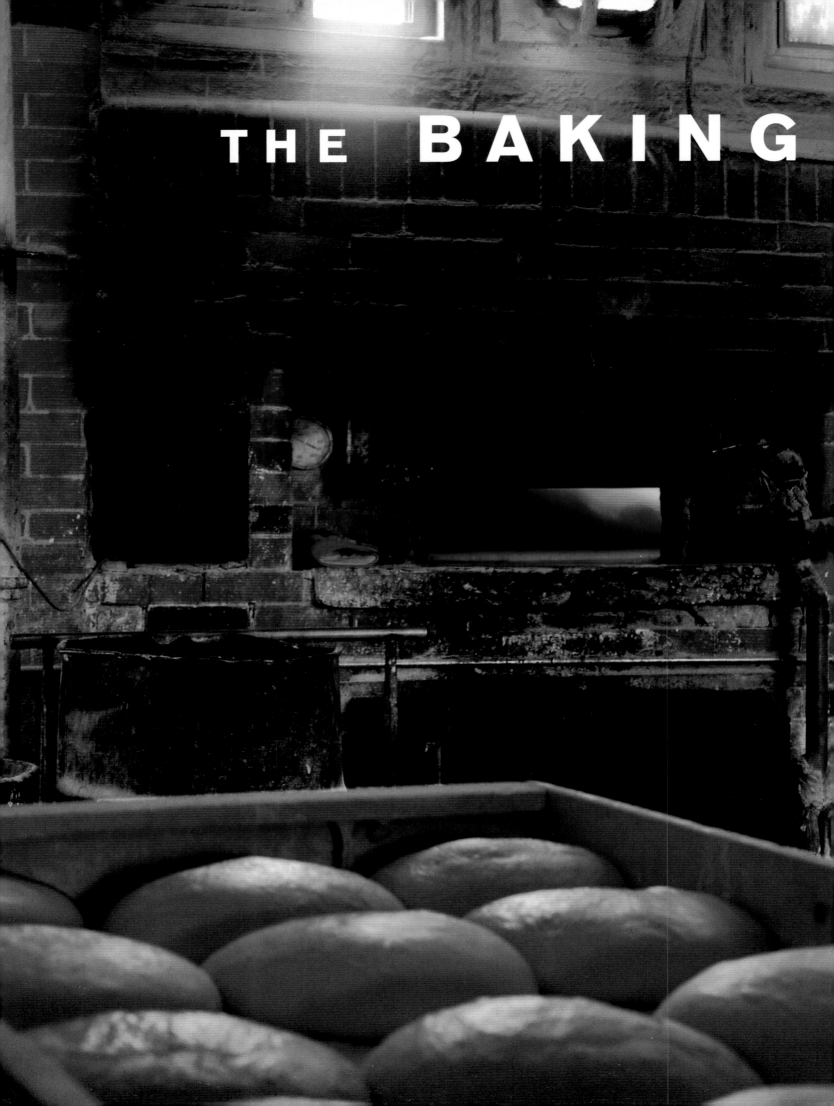

THE BAKING

LIFE

In the back of Royal Crown Bakery, Anthony Aprilano stirring coal in the firebox, causing a blaze to flame along the hearth's low ceiling. In the foreground, Tortano (page 203) proofing.

A BAKER'S TRAINING

GRACE BAKING COMPANY

ALBANY, CALIFORNIA

GLENN MITCHELL IS MY IDEA OF A MODEL ARTISAN BAKER. He's founder, CEO, and self-described head baker of Grace Baking of Albany, California, but his modest demeanor belies his tremendous accomplishments. He and his wife, Cindy Mitchell, built Grace Baking from scratch over ten years ago from a three-person market stall. Today, Grace employs more than two hundred people and comprises four retail bakeries as well as a nineteen-thousand-square-foot wholesale bakery that has both a bread and a pastry division. Glenn describes Grace as a full-service bakery with "probably more of a selection than any other bakery in the United States." His finesse with laminated and sweet doughs helped land the 1996 Baking Team USA its win in specialty breads at the Coupe du Monde de la Boulangerie, the World Cup of Bread Baking, a prestigious international bread-baking competition. Undoubtedly, Glenn is at the top of his profession, and I wanted to know how he arrived there.

I visited Glenn in December, when his bakery was in full swing meeting the holiday demand. We started early in the morning in the pastry department of his huge hangar-sized facility in what could have been a scene from Santa's workshop. All around us bakers were busy making a dizzying variety of decorated butter cookies. Grace's head pastry chef, Susan Merrill, worked next to us, brewing a giant cauldron of praline-flavored chocolate buttercream. Later she would use this ambrosial potion to fill Grace's beautiful bûches de Noël. Glenn and I made kugelhopf, a cake from Alsace, France, that he perfected for the Coupe du Monde competition. In a Hobart mixer, we blended the eggs, flour, milk, salt, and yeast, then slowly added the sugar, butter, and lastly rum-soaked raisins to make a silky dough. His secret is to butter the kugelhopf molds very heavily and sprinkle them with sliced almonds. As the cakes bake, the almonds sizzle in the butter, and perfume the bread with a "really yummy" (Glenn's favorite expression) browned-butter-and-almond scent.

After the breads were baked and cooling on racks, he told me about his training. Like most

OPPOSITE: Pugliese cooling on racks at Grace Baking. ABOVE: Glenn Mitchell, founder, CEO, and self-described head baker of Grace.

other bakers running large high-quality bakeries, he started baking early and worked in many bakeries before he ventured out on his own.

"I was fourteen when I started baking, in eighth grade. I just happened to walk by a bakery, and it looked like it would be fun, and started to work there. I did anything and everything there, from cleaning up to helping guys make bagels to delivering wedding cakes. I really liked it. It was the biggest single-standing retail bakery in Cleveland. It was called Sherwin's Bakery. At the time, we had all the temples in Cleveland for catering, so on a Saturday afternoon, we might be feeding twenty thousand people. It was really a big, super-busy place. You learned just everything."

He went on to eight years of college after that, never finishing, but baking all the while in different shops in Athens and Cleveland. Glenn eventually enrolled at the California Culinary Academy to learn pastry making. Then, diploma in hand, he immediately went to work in the Sheraton Palace kitchen after their pastry chef had a heart attack. Two months later, the Meridian Hotel offered him a position, and Glenn readily accepted.

The Meridian was a phenomenally stimulating place to work, according to Glenn. Alain Chapel oversaw the kitchen from his famed restaurant in France and circulated through it many French three-star chefs, such as Paul Bocuse. Glenn was sent to France twice, once to work under M. Monet at the Meridien Paris, "one of the best pastry chefs in France," and once to work for Alain Chapel himself in the Lyonnais.

By 1987, after five years at the Meridian, a wonderful opportunity arose. The Wilson Family wanted to create a new kind of market, called Rockridge Hall, in North Oakland, with the best purveyors and artisans owning and operating their own stalls. Tony Wilson, one of the brothers, found Glenn and helped him finance Grace Baking Company. Glenn began Grace with his soon-to-be wife, Cindy, as the pastry chef, himself as the bread and Danish baker, and a third partner (quickly bought out) to work the front. Grace boomed immediately, starting out with a very good wholesale account as well as a strong retail business at the market. Little wonder considering Glenn's talent and the huge, largely untapped market for artisan bread that existed then. (On their first day of business, Glenn guesses he baked about sixty loaves of bread. Today, by comparison, Grace bakes about fifteen thousand loaves a day.)

Glenn's training as a pastry chef has influenced his bread, giving him a unique perspective on flavors. "When you presented pastry, you'd always have something fruit, something chocolate, something cold, something warm, something crunchy, [something to appeal to] all the different senses. That's what I always thought about bread also. You can come to my bakery, and you can have something that's really crusty, like a baguette maybe; have something with a really wonderful flavor like pugliese; then we'll have a sourdough, then we'll have an herb bread, something with spinach. You know what I mean? Just a lot of sensations."

While his workload is overwhelming, he also told me he has the best job in the world. "I always liked the feeling of accomplishment. You know, you kind of walk in, and in the beginning you have all this flour, and then when you leave you have all this bread. That's always what I like about it. There's this immediate gratification. I always felt like, if I had a bad day, then the next day I got another chance."

Glenn Mitchell's Kugelhopf

- Makes one 2-pound (1000-gram) kugelhopf
- Time: At least 23 hours, with about 30 minutes of active work

Kugelhopf is a yeasted pound cake, a very simple, understated, but richly flavored cake with just a scattering of rum-soaked raisins. Mixing the dough is the main work, mostly because it is done in four stages. As with the other sweet doughs in the book, the dough is first developed without the butter and sugar. Once the dough is very smooth and strong, the sugar and then the butter are kneaded in separately. This allows the gluten to develop before the sugar can dehydrate it or the butter can coat it. The technique may be a hassle, but the high rise and silky texture of the cake make it worthwhile. Since the dough is refrigerated overnight, the messy and time-consuming work is gotten out of the way, then all that is left for bake day is to quickly shape the dough, let it proof, and bake it.

The original formula for this sweet dough called for a pre-ferment, but Glenn suggested that for home cooks it would be more convenient and actually more flavorful to eliminate the pre-ferment and just chill the partially fermented dough for 8 to 48 hours. This turns out to work really well and even intensifies the rum flavor.

RECIPE SYNOPSIS At least 6 hours before mixing the dough, macerate the raisins. Mix the dough and refrigerate it for 8 to 48 hours. Let it warm to room temperature and finish fermenting, 4 to 5 hours. Shape the dough, let it proof for 3½ hours, and bake it for about 1 hour.

	Macerated Raisins	volume	weight	metric	baker's percentages
6 HOURS BEFORE MIXING THE DOUGH MACERATING THE RAISINS	**Dark raisins**	¾ cup plus 2 tablespoons	4.6 ounces	130 grams	29%
	Good-quality dark rum	2 tablespoons	1 ounce	30 grams	7%

Toss the raisins with the rum in a small bowl, cover with plastic wrap, and let macerate for at least 6 hours. The raisins should completely absorb the rum.

	Dough	volume	weight	metric	baker's percentages
AT LEAST 8 HOURS AND UP TO 2 DAYS BEFORE BAKING MIXING THE DOUGH	**Milk, any kind**	1 cup	8 ounces	225 grams	50%
	Instant yeast	2 teaspoons	0.2 ounce	6 grams	1.4 %
	Unbleached all-purpose flour	3 cups	16 ounces	450 grams	100%
	Salt	1¾ teaspoons	0.3 ounce	9 grams	2%
	Eggs, chilled	1 large whole plus 1 egg yolk			15%
	Granulated sugar	6 tablespoons	2.5 ounces	70 grams	16%
	Unsalted butter, softened if mixing by hand or stand mixer, chilled if mixing by food processor	½ cup	4 ounces	113 grams	25%

continued

Microwave the milk on high power for 4 minutes or heat in a small saucepan on top of the stove until bubbles form around the edge, steam rises, and the milk smells cooked. Let it cool to 105° to 115°F, about the temperature of a comfortably hot bath. (Scalding the milk denatures a protein in the milk that attacks the gluten; if this step is skipped, the bread's texture will be coarser and denser.) Sprinkle the yeast over the warm milk, stir it in, and let stand for 5 to 10 minutes.

by hand: Add the flour and salt to a large bowl and stir them together briefly to mix. Add the yeast mixture and the egg and yolk. With a wooden spoon or your hand, mix the dough just until well combined. This dough is very stiff and may even seem crumbly. Turn the dough out of the bowl and knead until it is smooth but strong, 5 to 10 minutes. The dough will be gritty from the salt at first, but it will soon dissolve.

Add the sugar in 2 additions and knead the dough again until the sugar is fully incorporated and dissolved—a fairly messy task, a dough scraper will help—and the dough is very smooth. Add the softened butter in 2 additions, kneading each addition into the dough until it is fully incorporated (the dough will soften considerably with each addition of sugar and butter). Continue to knead the dough until it is satiny smooth, soft, and glossy. Fold in the macerated raisins and knead just until they are evenly distributed.

by stand mixer: Add the flour and salt to the mixing bowl, and stir them together briefly with your hand. Add the yeast mixture and the egg and yolk. With a wooden spoon, combine the ingredients until they are almost smooth. Using the dough hook, mix the dough on low speed just until it gathers on the hook and is well combined. This dough is so stiff that you may need to add 1 to 2 tablespoons water to get it to pick up on the hook. When the dough wraps around the hook, mix the dough on medium speed until it is very smooth and strong, about 3 minutes.

Add the sugar in 2 additions, then the butter in 2 additions, mixing each addition into the dough until it is fully incorporated and the dough cleans the bowl before adding the next. Continue to mix the dough until it is satiny smooth, soft, and glossy. Remove the dough from the bowl and knead in the macerated raisins by hand.

by food processor: Add the flour and salt to the workbowl fitted with the steel blade and pulse to combine them. Remove the cover and add the yeast mixture and the egg and yolk. Process the dough until it forms a smooth ball and begins to fog the workbowl. Remove the dough from the workbowl and knead it by hand to cool it and redistribute the heat. The dough will feel fairly stiff once it cools off. Return the dough to the workbowl, process it for 30 seconds, and hand knead to cool it. Repeat this process 2 or 3 more times until the dough is very smooth and strong.

With the machine running, slowly add the sugar to the dough through the feed tube and process until the sugar is dissolved and the dough is smooth. The dough will be very sticky at this point. Remove the dough and hand knead it to cool it again. Return the dough to the workbowl and add about half the butter, cut into chunks. Process the dough until the butter is incorporated, about 30 seconds. If the dough is very warm, hand knead it again to cool it. Add the rest of the butter, cut into chunks, and process it until it is fully incorporated, about 30 seconds. Remove the dough from the workbowl for the last time and knead in the raisins by hand. The dough should be very smooth, extensible, and silky.

FERMENTING
THE DOUGH

Roll the dough in flour, flatten it, and seal it in a large Ziploc bag. Immediately refrigerate it for 8 to 48 hours. When you are ready to continue, put the dough on a counter and let it finish fermenting in the Ziploc bag for 4 to 5 hours.

continued

	Garnish	volume	weight	metric	baker's percentages
BAKE DAY PREPARING THE MOLD AND SHAPING AND PROOFING THE DOUGH	**Unsalted butter**	3 tablespoons	1.5 ounces	45 grams	10%
	Sliced almonds	¼ cup	1 ounce	30 grams	7%
	Powdered sugar, **for dusting the top** **of the cake**				

Melt the butter and let it cool slightly, until it has thickened.

Lightly flour your work surface. Remove the dough from the bag, sprinkle it with flour, and press on it to deflate it. Gently round it into a very tight ball, replace it in the Ziploc bag, and let it rest until well relaxed, 20 to 25 minutes.

While the dough is relaxing, very heavily coat a 10-cup kugelhopf mold with the butter, using a pastry brush. (If you have smaller molds, just fill each mold to about half its volume with dough.) Be sure to put extra butter on the central cone, where the dough has a tendency to stick, and also leave a shallow pool of butter on the bottom of the mold. Sprinkle the sliced almonds on the pooled butter on the bottom of the mold.

Remove the dough from the bag and push your fingers through the center of the dough ball to make a hole. Let the dough rest again for 10 minutes, then enlarge the hole with your hands so that it fits the mold. Dampen your hands with water and pat the smooth top of the dough ring to make it tacky (this will help the almonds stick). Place the dough damp side down in the mold; it should fill it by half. Loosely cover the mold with plastic wrap. Let the dough proof until it is very well expanded and well domed over the mold, about 2 hours.

PREHEATING
THE OVEN

About 30 minutes before the dough is fully proofed, arrange a rack on the oven's bottom shelf and clear away all racks above the one being used. Preheat the oven to 350°F (180°C).

BAKING
THE CAKE

Bake the cake until it is well browned all around, 50 to 60 minutes, rotating it halfway into the bake. Remove it from the oven, immediately invert it onto a cooling rack, and let cool completely. The cake is best if stored for a day. Before serving it, sift a snowstorm of powdered sugar over it.

A GERMAN APPRENTICESHIP

In the United States, there is no national apprenticeship program, so that ambitious American bakers must create their own, as did Glenn Mitchell. Yet, in Europe, apprenticeship programs for all the manual trades have been in place for many centuries, teaching the trades and sometimes functioning as brotherhoods.

Carsten Kruse is one of the best-trained bakers I know. He is a German master baker and is now running the Dallas branch of Dutch Regale Bakery. I spoke with Carsten about his apprenticeship after I paid a late-night visit to his bakery to learn about their stollen and wonderful rye breads (see page 141, for more about the rye breads).

Carsten's family owns a large bakery in Hamburg, where he was "programmed to be a baker." He started his apprenticeship right after high school and finished four years later, a year longer than is normal for a trade because he added pastry making as well.

"During the week you have your practical work in the bakery, and you usually go once or twice during that week to school, to have all the technical background. You learn everything about the ingredients, the recipes, your formulations, and all that. That goes over two years in my case. And, in my case, I went to the North Sea coast to learn [to be a] pastry chef, and I actually stayed with the family. I lived above the bakery for two years. I was always there actually. . . . I had my meals there. I had my breakfast, my dinner, my lunch. I lived with the guy.

"After the apprenticeship, you have your test, which is the practical test, and then you have your written test, and once you pass that, you get a certificate that you are a professional journeyman of that trade. If you want to go on and make your master's degree in it, you have to have five years' proven journeymanship in different bakeries. In my case, I started traveling. I worked on a cruise liner; I worked in Switzerland and places like that to gain different experiences. I think I worked at ten or twelve different bakeries.

"And then I went to Master College, which was a full-time school, and I did that for almost a year. You go five or six days a week. You learn all about ingredients, how to train bakers or pastry chefs, even the business side of it. You have to learn accounting, equipment, everything. And then you do your test after that.

"What you do for the practical is you have certain categories of products you have to do. It means you have to do sourdough breads, rye sourdough, white sourdough, then you have to do a certain amount of pastry, croissants, Danishes. Then you have to lay all that out. You have to do all the costing for all the products, all the labeling. At the end of the day, at the end of the practical test, you have to arrange all these products in a display window, like you would do for a shop. And that display window has to have a certain theme, like summertime or Easter or Christmas. My theme was Thanksgiving. I made twenty-five different products in eight hours. You had the day before, I think, about two hours to start your sourdoughs or sponges or whatever you would like, but on the actual day you had only eight hours.

"I think for a lot of the young people, once they get out of high school and they don't want to go on to the university or something like that, it's really a good thing. They get kind of formed for another three years. And it really makes a big difference. It helps the young person kind of get a direction in life. They are not kind of thrown out in the street after high school."

Dutch Regale's Almond Stollen

- Makes four 1-pound (500-gram) stollen
- Time: About 17 hours, with about 1 hour of active work

Stollen is a very unusual cake—dense, fine-grained, and fragrant—and nothing like the typical sweet cake usually made in this country. It should contain very little milk and sugar, few if any eggs, but lots of butter and a complex array of flavorings. It is basically a yeasted shortbread dough. Its very low moisture content plus its special butter, sugar, and powdered sugar coating help it to keep for a long time, making it a great bread to give or send as holiday gifts.

This dough is mixed and fermented in three stages, to ensure a strong mix and fermentation. The key to success is to develop the dough thoroughly at each juncture. The preliminary dough needs to be mixed until very smooth and strong. The final dough will start out almost as crumbly as cookie dough but needs to be mixed until it is as shiny and elastic as the preliminary dough. A food processor is by far the fastest way to mix these doughs; a stand mixer will work as well, but it will take much, much longer.

If you can't buy compressed yeast cakes in your area, you will have to use osmotolerant yeast for this bread (see Sources, page 222), because of the dough's very low moisture. (The name of the yeast refers to its ability to thrive in liquids with high osmotic pressure—the condition found in sweet doughs—without dehydrating [see page 8].)

Stollen needs to be made with a bread flour, so use a flour with a 12.5% to 13% protein. I tried using all-purpose flour, thinking that the result would be more tender, but ended up with a dough that never came together and a lumpy, dense, and unsightly stollen.

Dutch Regale's stollen (see page 141) is made with a thick, syrupy, intensely orange flavoring called Orange Flavedo, which is not available to home bakers. Manager Eric Kastel suggested using orange juice concentrate, which I shore up with orange zest.

Dutch Regale formulated this stollen to appeal to American tastes, so it is light on the candied fruit and contains no rum. For a more European flavor, try the Rum Stollen variation on page 193.

RECIPE SYNOPSIS Mix the sponge and let it ferment for 1 hour. Meanwhile, beat the butter with the sugar and flavorings. Add the remaining flour and the sponge to the flavored butter mixture and mix until smooth. Let it ferment for 1 hour. Knead in the raisins and candied peel. Shape the dough, enclosing an almond-paste log. Let the dough proof for 1½ to 2 hours. Bake the stollen for 25 to 35 minutes. Remove them from the oven and brush them with butter. Let cool about 4 hours, then roll them in granulated sugar. Let stand for 8 hours, then dust heavily with powdered sugar and store in a plastic bag.

	Dough	volume	weight	metric	baker's percentages
	Milk, any kind	¾ cup plus 2 tablespoons	7 ounces	200 grams	33%
	Osmotolerant instant yeast, such as SAF Instant Gold	1 tablespoon plus 1 teaspoon	0.4 ounce	12 grams	2%
	OR compressed yeast	OR 1 cake	OR 1.3 ounces	OR 36 grams	OR 6%
	Unbleached bread flour	4 cups	21.2 ounces	600 grams	100%
	Unsalted butter, softened	1⅓ cups	10.6 ounces	300 grams	50%
	Granulated sugar, plus extra for coating	⅓ cup	2.3 ounces	70 grams	11%
	Salt	1½ teaspoons	0.3 ounce	8 grams	1.4%
	Ground cardamom	½ teaspoon			0.2%
	Almond paste,* soft, malleable	3 tablespoons	1.7 ounce	50 grams	8%
	Pure vanilla extract	1 teaspoon	0.2 ounce	5 grams	0.4%
	Orange juice concentrate	1 tablespoon	0.5 ounce	15 grams	2%
	Zest from 1 orange, minced	1 tablespoon plus 1 teaspoon	0.3 ounce	8 grams	1.4%

BAKE DAY
MIXING
THE DOUGH

* For best flavor, use an imported almond paste. I use Betty Crocker brand, which is imported from Germany and widely available.

Microwave the milk on high power for 4 minutes or heat in a small saucepan on top of the stove until bubbles form around the edge, steam rises, and the milk smells cooked. Let it cool to 105° to 115°F, about the temperature of a comfortably hot bath. To cool the milk faster, pour it into a heavy crockery bowl. (Scalding the milk denatures a protein in the milk that attacks the gluten; if this step is skipped, the bread's texture will be coarser and denser.) Sprinkle the yeast over the cooled milk, stir, and let stand for 5 minutes.

by stand mixer: Add 1¾ cups (9.3 ounces, 263 grams) flour to the yeast mixture in the mixing bowl and mix it together by hand just until it comes together. Using the dough hook, mix the dough on medium speed until it is smooth, very strong, and elastic, about 5 minutes. Do not skimp on the kneading here, for this preliminary dough will have to carry the rest of the ingredients. Move the dough to a small bowl, cover it tightly with plastic wrap, and let it ferment until well expanded, about 1 hour.

Add the butter, sugar, salt, cardamom, almond paste, vanilla, orange juice concentrate, and orange zest to the mixing bowl, fit the mixer with the paddle, and beat until the mixture is fluffy.

Add the fermented dough and the remaining 2¼ cups (11.9 ounces, 337 grams) flour to the but-ter mixture and mix the dough on medium-high speed with the paddle until it is very smooth, strong, and elastic, 20 to 30 minutes. The dough will be almost crumbly at first but will become strong and glossy after enough mixing. It is normal for this dough to be oily at the end of mixing. If the dough is just spinning with the paddle, increase the mixer's speed a notch or two to get the dough to fling off the paddle.

continued

LEFT: With all the ingredients added to the sponge, the dough looking crumbly. BELOW: After 20 to 30 minutes of mixing, the dough is cohesive and extensible.

RIGHT: Pressing a crease into the dough to carve out the third outside roll. BELOW: Butting an almond paste roll along the thick edge of the dough.

by food processor: Add 1¾ cups (9.3 ounces, 263 grams) flour to the yeast mixture in the work-bowl and process until this preliminary dough is smooth and very strong. Do not skimp on the processing here, for this preliminary dough will have to carry the rest of the ingredients. Transfer the dough to a small bowl, cover it tightly with plastic wrap, and let it ferment until it is well expanded, about 1 hour.

Add the butter, sugar, salt, cardamom, almond paste, vanilla, orange juice concentrate, and orange zest to the workbowl and process until well combined.

Add the fermented dough and the remaining 2¼ cups (11.9 ounces, 337 grams) flour to the butter mixture and process it in intervals until it is very smooth and strong: Process the dough for about 30 seconds, remove the dough from the workbowl and knead it by hand to cool it down (it tends to overheat), then return it to the workbowl, and process again for 30 seconds. Repeat this sequence 5 or 6 times, until the dough is very smooth, strong, and elastic. It is normal for this dough to be oily at the end of mixing.

FERMENTING THE DOUGH

Place the dough in a container at least 3 times its size and cover it tightly with plastic wrap. Let it ferment until it is light and about doubled in bulk, about 1 hour.

Filling	volume	weight	metric	baker's percentages
Candied lemon peel, diced	⅓ cup	1.7 ounces	50 grams	8%
Small dark raisins	3¾ cups	20 ounces	570 grams	95%
Almond paste, soft, malleable	1 cup	10.6 ounces	300 grams	50%

SHAPING AND PROOFING THE DOUGH

On a lightly floured work surface, roll out the dough into a thin sheet. Sprinkle with the lemon peel and raisins and roll the dough up. Fold the ends of the dough into the middle, just to better distribute the fruit, and let the dough rest for about 10 minutes. Cut the dough into 4 equal pieces, round them (page 17), then roll them into cylinders about 10 inches long. Cover and let rest for 20 minutes.

Cover 2 doubled or insulated baking sheets with sheets of parchment paper or aluminum foil, or butter the baking sheets well.

The cross-section of a stollen consists of 3 narrow rolls stacked to form a pyramid, 2 on the bottom supporting 1 on top. The stollen's bird's-eye view is oval, the whole effect symbolic of baby Jesus in his bunting. The shaping is very awkward to describe, so refer to the photographs if you get confused.

Clean off your work surface and lightly flour it. Place 1 dough piece smooth side down. Roll the piece out into a 10-inch square. Fold the top edge down and the bottom edge up to meet at a seam in the center. Now roll the dough into a 10 x 6-inch trough, leaving the top and bottom edges about ¾ inch thick and the middle quite thin.

Divide the almond paste into ¼-cup pieces. Knead 1 piece just until it is soft and oily, then roll it out into a log about 2 inches shorter than the dough.

continued

Place the log across the thin portion of the dough, butting it up against one thick edge. Dampen both thick edges of the dough with water to help seal them. Flip the opposite thick edge over to the center, to cover the almond log. This will now form the uppermost roll and should completely cover the almond log. The dough will now be a very narrow 3 x 10-inch rectangle. Press the thick edges together to seal the almond log into the dough. Crease the dough to define the uppermost roll and the remaining bottom roll: With the side of your hand, press a crease into the dough along the folded edge of the dough, which is also the backside of the almond log (it is quite narrow and will seem awkward). Now push your hands around the outline of the dough to tuck up the edges and push the outline of the dough into an oval shape. The shape may seem too narrow, but the dough spreads considerably as it proofs and bakes. Repeat with the remaining dough and almond paste.

Place 2 stollen on each prepared baking sheet, cover them loosely with plastic wrap, and let them proof just until they are very light and well expanded, 1½ to 2 hours.

PREHEATING THE OVEN

About 45 minutes before the dough is fully proofed, arrange 1 rack on the oven's second-to-top shelf and another on the bottom shelf. Clear away all racks above the one being used. Preheat the oven to 350°F (180°C).

	Coating	volume	weight	metric	baker's percentages
BAKING AND COATING THE STOLLEN	**Unsalted butter**	½ cup	4 ounces	113 grams	
	Granulated sugar				
	Powdered sugar				

Bake the cakes until well browned all around, 25 to 35 minutes, rotating them halfway into the bake. As the cakes are baking, place a cooling rack over a baking sheet or tray. Clarify the butter: Heat the butter over low heat until it melts, then skim off any foam and pour the clear yellow butter into a container, discarding the milky residue at the bottom.

Remove the cakes from the oven and immediately place them on the cooling rack.

Immediately brush the hot stollen on all sides, including the bottom, with the hot clarified butter. Let cool completely, then roll them in granulated sugar. Let stand for 8 hours, then sift powdered sugar over them. The stollen will keep for a month in a sealed bag.

Dutch Regale's Rum Stollen

- Makes four 13-ounce (400-gram) stollen
- Time: About 21 hours, with about 1 hour of active work

This is made identically to the preceding Almond Stollen, with dried and candied fruit macerated in rum and without the almond filling. I have included this variation because it is slightly simpler, and some might prefer the richer rum flavor.

RECIPE SYNOPSIS Mix the dried and candied fruits with the rum and let macerate for at least 6 hours. Mix the sponge and let it ferment for 1 hour. Meanwhile, beat the butter with the sugar and flavorings. Add the remaining flour and the sponge to the flavored butter mixture and mix until smooth; let it ferment for 1 hour. Knead in the macerated fruit, shape the dough, and let it proof for 1½ to 2 hours. Bake the stollen for 25 to 35 minutes. Remove them from the oven and brush them first with rum and then with butter. Let cool completely, about 4 hours, then roll them in granulated sugar. Let stand for 8 hours, dust with powdered sugar, and store in a plastic bag.

	Macerated Fruit	volume	weight	metric	baker's percentages
AT LEAST 6 HOURS BEFORE MIXING THE DOUGH **MACERATING THE FRUIT**	**Small dark raisins**	4⅓ cups	22.9 ounces	650 grams	108%
	Candied orange peel, diced	3 tablespoons	1.4 ounces	40 grams	7%
	Candied lemon peel, diced	¼ cup	1.8 ounces	50 grams	8%
	Flavorful dark rum	2 tablespoons	1 ounce	30 grams	5%

Combine the raisins, orange peel, lemon peel, and rum in a nonreactive container. Cover it tightly with plastic wrap and let macerate at room temperature for at least 6 hours.

BAKE DAY   Make the stollen as directed for Almond Stollen, substituting the macerated fruit mixture for the raisins and candied lemon peel and omitting the almond-paste log.

When the stollen come from the oven, generously brush them with rum (use ¼ cup [2 ounces, 20 grams] or more) before brushing them with the hot clarified butter. Coat with both sugars as directed for Almond Stollen.

A FRENCH APPRENTICESHIP

I visited with French master baker Lionel Vatinet, a ponytailed young Frenchman with a dreamy accent and a very French way of saying things like "*Bon,* a woman have a touch, you know?" Lionel is a member of the Compagnon de Devoir who was working as a teacher and consultant for the San Francisco Baking Institute when I met him, but who now co-owns La Farm Bakery in Cary, North Carolina.

Lionel generously and patiently gave me a private baguette lesson in an empty institute classroom. While smoking a hand-rolled cigarette during a break (he says it prevents him from overindulging),

he told me about his remarkable apprenticeship, which he calls "the most gifted thing in my life." To complete the program, Compagnons must bake in seven to ten bakeries all over France, along with taking classes and completing other requirements. This six-to-eight-year period of work and travel is called the Tour de France.

The traditions of the Compagnons are ancient and secret and full of mysterious symbols. In thirteenth-century France, workers were forbidden to "leave their masters without permission. Compagnon masons were the only exception: They alone had the right to travel from one work site to another and cockily wore a gold earring as a sign of their free

status" (*Smithsonian,* June 1996). Hence, Lionel's earring.

"People ask us if we are a sect, if we are an army. *Non,* we don't sign anything, it is more mental. You read the role, you accept it, say yes or no. If you say no, you don't stay; if you say yes, you are going to belong to the community. Is simple. It's to respect the person next to you; that's it. One of the principles is that the oldest teach the youngest, and for generations and generations we do that. And you have different step to graduate, to finish your Tour de France. It's great. You learn how to share, definitely. Where you sleep can be two to five to ten person in the same room. You eat together. *Bon,* you communicate. It is an apprenticeship of life."

ABOVE, LEFT TO RIGHT: Master baker Lionel Vatinet mixing rye dough in the San Francisco Baking Institute's classroom; Lionel painstakingly snipping thin rolls of dough to form elegant wheat ears. OPPOSITE: Fashioning a delicate rosebud.

FOLLOWING TRADITION

WHEN I THINK OF A BAKERY AS A NEIGHBORHOOD ANCHOR, a part of its rhythms and traditions, I think of the Royal Crown Bakeries in Brooklyn, New York. Owned by Giuseppe "Joe" and Franko Generoso, two Italian bakers originally from Calabria, these bakeries sustain a tradition I thought must have been long forgotten.

And their bread is some of the best I have tasted. Baked in two century-old coal-fired brick ovens, the loaves are leisurely spread with dark brittle crusts, and the dense crumb is honeycombed with mammoth air cells. Slightly yet not overly acidic, the flavor is unusually balanced in this time of fashionable sourness. But Royal Crown is about more than bread—it is about neighborhood and family.

On the Sunday that I visited, customers coming from church were lined up to buy bread and dessert for their 4:00 P.M. dinner. Generoso sisters and cousins waited on them behind the glass counters, filled with every manner of pastry, cake, and cookie. Friends dropped by to hear the latest, to comment on whatever was coming out of the oven, and even to lend a hand bringing fresh goods to the counter.

Joe's best friend, Glenn Galite, who owns the stained-glass shop next door and is finishing a degree in psychology, stopped in to pick up a loaf and ask, "How ya' doin'?" After being introduced, Glenn took me into the bakeshop at the back of the store to meet Joe's brother Franko and baker Anthony, both manning the oven that day. As Anthony peeled hot bread into an old shopping cart, Glenn and Franko told me stories about the bakery and neighborhood. The stories got even more colorful when Joe picked up Franko's thread.

Here are Joe and Glenn telling me one of their favorite stories. It begins with a talented young Italian baker named Massimo, who worked for Royal Crown for a short time before his visa expired. Massimo loved flour and secured his name in local legend by managing to cover himself and the bakery in flour whenever he worked:

OPPOSITE: Baker Joe Generoso gesturing "up to here"—as he presses out his rosettes. ABOVE: Tortano (page 203) and homemade sausages line the shelves behind the counter at Brooklyn's Royal Crown Bakery.

"I walked in the day of Christmas Eve. He was working the night shift," Joe begins. "I went to open the door, and from the door to where he is, I swear, you had to see mountains—it looked like it snowed in there. There was an inch and a half of flour on the floor. The whole floor—covered. Shovels were covered. When I swept it up, I think there was around maybe fifty, sixty pounds of flour. I actually filled up almost a hundred-pound bag. I could not believe how far he got flour. When I was walking—you know how you feel lumps of flour—I'm walking like this [mimes a tipsy snowman walking] and I was about to say to Massimo, and I just said, 'Forget it.'"

"Forget it, he's crazy, leave him alone," Glenn agrees.

"I'm not even going to say nothing. I'm going to start sweeping it up, and that's it."

"Was he mixing dough? What was he doing?" I ask.

"Massimo is very fast. He throws the flour, we all throw the flour on the bread."

"When you're shaping?" I am picturing a flour frenzy.

"No, not when we're shaping, when we're dusting to put in the oven. What happens is, you're supposed to use a little, but he's got . . . handfuls!"

Glenn interjects, "I want to make a video of him doing that, and I want to put like a Mass in there." He starts intoning *"In nomine Patris, et Filii, et Spiritus Sancti"* as he pretends to cross himself with thrown flour. We all dissolve into laughter.

Amazingly, all this bakery patina was created in only ten years. In 1987, Joe and Franko decided to open a pastry shop together. They had worked for their uncle Rocco at Rocco's Pastry Shop on Bleecker Street in the Village for more than fifteen years, with Franko baking pastry and Joe up front handling customers. With more than thirty years' experience between them, they felt that they knew the business well enough to start out on their own.

They bought a bakery on a street in Brooklyn dotted with pork shops—delis. It had a hundred-year-old oven and a horizontal mixer almost as ancient. To learn how to handle the oven, they enlisted several neighborhood old-timers to tutor them about operating the "key," or flue, that vents the steam and exhaust, firing the oven with coal and raising the heat with a timely addition of wood, taking the temperature of the oven not by looking at the thermostat, which turned out to be useless, but by looking at the color of the bricks or how fast the cornmeal thrown on the hearth burned. While the lessons took only a few hours, Franko says that really understanding and mastering the old behemoth took three years.

Originally they planned to sell only pastries, as their uncle still does. But the bakery had been known for good bread, and customers did not stop asking for it. The Generosos decided it was foolish to turn people away, so they started offering a few basic Italian American breads—panella, tortano, and brick-oven longs. They kept adding new breads and improving old ones, and now, ten years later, Royal Crown sells more than twenty types of bread, along with a complete line of cakes, pastries, and cookies.

When it came time to expand, they found a bakery less than a block away with another old oven, this one faced with white-glazed bricks, an old mixer, and an interesting provenance. The bakery had belonged to a baker with a bad gambling habit. He loved the horses and had squandered away all his earnings at the track. But one day his luck changed, and his horse actually came in. He was so astonished by this reversal of fortune that he had a heart attack and died on the spot. The winning ticket, by the way, was said to have been worth fifty dollars.

The bakeries have brought Joe and Franko much local acclaim, and they are ready to look for space to build a larger bakery. Unfortunately, any new bakery wouldn't have a coal-fired oven, because Joe is concerned about the long-term health risks associated with working with coal exhaust. Old-time bakers were said to develop "black lung" after only ten to fifteen years of daily exposure, and Joe wants to protect his workers, who are, after all, mostly family members. Joe thinks he can replicate the effect of the oven without hazarding his or anyone else's health.

Royal Crown's Fennel Taralli

- Makes 32 taralli
- Time: About 4 hours, with about 40 minutes of active work

Perfect for holiday gifts to send, these beautiful racetrack-shaped breadsticks are a labor of love; they last indefinitely if properly stored and taste fabulous. They are boiled before they are baked to preserve their shape and give them a beautiful sheen. Serve them with antipasti, cheeses, or sausage, or with afternoon tea.

RECIPE SYNOPSIS Mix the dough, then cut and shape the taralli. Let them rest for about 2 hours. Boil them for about 10 minutes, and bake for about 45 minutes.

	Dough	volume	weight	metric	baker's percentages
BAKE DAY **MIXING** **THE DOUGH**	**Active dry yeast**	½ teaspoon			0.2%
	Water, 110° to 115°F	1 cup plus 2 tablespoons	9 ounces	250 grams	44%
	Unbleached all-purpose flour	3 cups	16 ounces	450 grams	79%
	Durum flour*	¾ cup	4 ounces	120 grams	21%
	Salt	1¾ teaspoons	0.3 ounce	9 grams	1.6%
	Vegetable oil, such as corn	3 tablespoons	1.5 ounces	40 grams	7%
	White wine	¼ cup	2 ounces	60 grams	10%
	Fennel seeds	1 tablespoon	0.3 ounce	10 grams	2%
	Olive oil	2 tablespoons			

*Look for extremely fine, double-milled flour from durum wheat, which is sometimes called durum flour and sometimes extra fancy pasta or patent durum flour. Semolina, a more granular product, will not work here.

In a small pitcher, sprinkle the yeast over the warm water, stir, and let stand for 5 to 10 minutes.

by hand: Combine the all-purpose flour, durum flour, and salt in a large bowl. Add the vegetable oil, white wine, and yeasted water. Mix the dough together, then knead this incredibly stiff dough until it smooths out a little. Knead in the fennel seeds.

by food processor: Add the all-purpose flour, durum flour, salt, vegetable oil, and white wine to the workbowl fitted with the steel blade. With the machine running, add the yeasted water through the feed tube and process until a smooth but very firm dough is formed. Remove the dough from the workbowl and knead in the fennel seeds by hand.

continued

ABOVE, TOP TO BOTTOM: Pressing two ends of rolled out dough together to seal and form the narrow oval shape of taralli; breaking cooled sheets of cracker dough into pieces to serve. RIGHT: Baked Fennel Taralli.

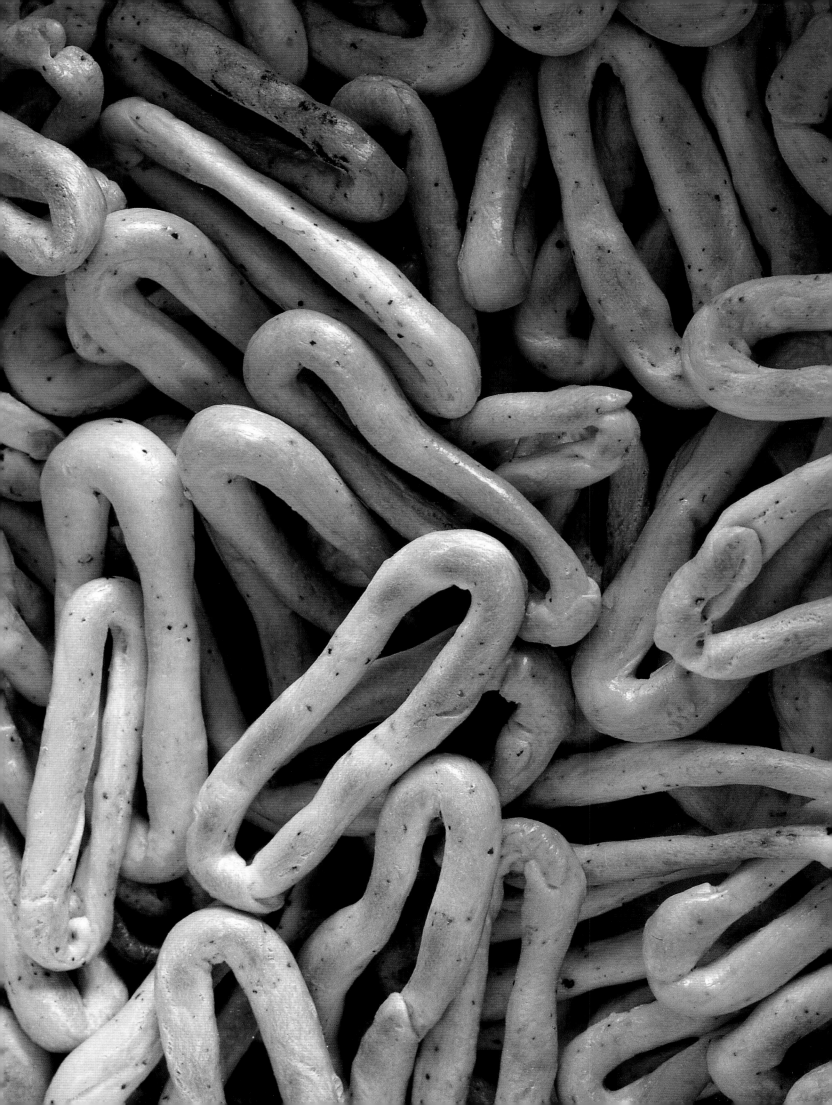

CUTTING AND SHAPING THE TARALLI	Immediately after mixing, cut the dough into 32 pieces, each a scant 2 tablespoons (1 ounce, 30 grams). Place a cup of water next to you to help you roll. Dampen your hands with just a few drops of water and roll a piece of dough into a rope about the thickness of a pen. It should be about 11 inches long. Pinch the ends together hard. Hold the rope ring together at the seal and let it drop into an elongated oval shape. Place it on a tray or on your work surface. The seal should be at the top curve. Continue to roll and shape the rest of the taralli.
RESTING THE TARALLI	Cover the taralli with plastic wrap and let them rest for 2 hours. They will not appear to rise at all.
PREHEATING THE OVEN	Arrange 2 racks on the oven's center shelves and clear away all racks above the ones being used. Preheat the oven to 400°F (205°C).
BOILING THE TARALLI	Fill a wide pot or deep saucepan three-quarters full of water, bring it to a boil, and then lower the heat so that the water simmers. Add the olive oil to the simmering water. Set a cooling rack over a baking sheet and place it near the water or line a baking sheet with some tea towels. Line 2 large baking sheets with parchment paper or oiled aluminum foil.

    Boil the taralli in batches small enough to fit comfortably in the pot. They will sink at first then quickly float. (If they do not float, let them continue to rest for another hour, then boil them.) After they float and puff up a bit, after about a minute of boiling, skim them from the pot and let them drain on the cooling rack. Boil the remaining taralli. After each batch has drained, move them to the paper-lined baking sheets. |
| **BAKING THE TARALLI** | When you have finished boiling the taralli, bake them until they are golden brown and very dry, about 45 minutes, rotating the baking sheets halfway into the bake. Let them cool on a rack and store them in a sealed container. |

Ben's Taralli Crackers

- Makes 8 to 10 jagged crackers
- Time: About 5 hours, with about 20 minutes of active work

	Photographer Ben Fink discovered that Fennel Taralli dough makes excellent crackers when it is rolled out into thin sheets and baked. The cooled sheets can then be broken up into smaller, serving-sized pieces. Of course, these are considerably less work than the taralli and are really delicious.
BAKE DAY FERMENTING THE DOUGH FOR CRACKERS	Make the taralli dough, place it in a bowl 3 times its size, and cover it tightly with plastic wrap. Let the dough ferment until it has risen slightly and is very extensible, 1 to 2 hours.
PREHEATING THE OVEN	While the dough is fermenting, arrange 2 oven racks on the oven's center shelves and clear away all racks above the ones being used. Preheat the oven to 400°F (205°C).
ROLLING OUT THE DOUGH AND BAKING THE CRACKERS	Line two 13 x 9-inch baking sheets with parchment paper. Cut the dough in half. On a floured work surface, roll out each half into a very thin sheet with a heavy-duty rolling pin. Lift the dough onto the lined baking sheets. Immediately bake them until golden brown and very dry, about 20 minutes, rotating the pans halfway into the bake. Peel the crackers from the paper and let cool on a rack. Break the crackers into serving-size pieces and store in a sealed container.

Royal Crown's Tortano

- Makes one 2¾-pound (1,200-gram) tortano
- Time: About 19 hours, with about 20 minutes of active work

This is the most beautiful bread Royal Crown makes, a huge round loaf filled with radish-size air cells, thanks to careful handling and lots of water in the dough. Joe adds potato for flavor and moistness and honey for color to this very wet, squishy dough. For extra flavor, the bread is leavened solely by its starter, so it rises very slowly and develops a nice but not aggressive acidity. To get authentic Italian flavor, you will need to bake this bread to a deep, dark brown, so don't skimp on the baking time—the bread will not burn!

RECIPE SYNOPSIS **THE EVENING BEFORE BAKING:** Make the starter and, if you like, the mashed potato. **THE NEXT MORNING:** Mix the dough and let it ferment for about 4 hours. Shape it, proof it for about 1 hour, and then bake the bread for about 45 minutes.

	Pre-ferment	volume	weight	metric	baker's percentages
THE EVENING BEFORE BAKING **MAKING** **THE PRE-FERMENT**	**Instant yeast**	¼ teaspoon			(eventually 0.3%)
	Water, 105° to 115°F	I cup			(eventually 73%)
	Unbleached bread flour	⅔ cup	3.5 ounces	100 grams	100%
	Potato	I small	3 ounces	85 grams	

Stir the yeast into the water in a glass measure and let it stand for 5 to 10 minutes. Add ⅓ cup of this yeasted water (discard the rest) to the flour and beat this very sticky starter until it is well combined. Cover with plastic wrap and let it ferment until it is full of huge bubbles and sharp tasting, about 12 hours. If your kitchen is very warm and the pre-ferment is fermenting very quickly, place it in the refrigerator after 3 hours of fermenting. In the morning, remove it and allow it to come to room temperature 30 minutes to an hour before beginning the final dough.

PREPARING THE POTATO

For efficiency, you may want to prepare the potato the night before. Quarter it, then boil it in water to cover until it can be easily pierced with a knife tip, about 20 minutes. Drain; if desired, reserve the water for the dough. Press the potato through a ricer or sieve to purée it and remove the skin. Store it in a covered container in the refrigerator. You will need only ¼ cup purée.

	Dough	volume	weight	metric	baker's percentages
BAKE DAY **MIXING** **THE DOUGH**	**Unbleached bread flour**	3¾ cups	20 ounces	575 grams	100%
	Water, including the potato water if desired, lukewarm	1¾ cups plus 3 tablespoons	14.6 ounces	420 grams	73%
	Pre-ferment				30%
	Honey	2 teaspoons	0.4 ounce	14 grams	2%
	Potato purée	¼ cup packed	2 ounces	60 grams	10%
	Salt	I tablespoon	0.5 ounce	15 grams	2.4%

continued

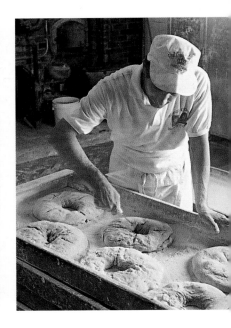

ABOVE, LEFT TO RIGHT:
Anthony Aprilano plunging
his hands into the center of
the tortano dough, then
whirling them around to
form a hole; widening the
hole by gently pulling the
dough out; slashing crosses
into floury, proofed tortanos.
RIGHT: Tortanos for sale.

by hand: Use your hands to mix the flour and water into a rough, very wet dough in a large bowl. Cover the dough and let rest (autolyse) for 10 to 20 minutes.

Add the pre-ferment, honey, potato, and salt, and knead the dough until it is smooth, 5 to 10 minutes. It will start off feeling rubbery, then break down into goo; if you persist, eventually it will come together into a smooth, shiny dough. If you do not have the skill or time to knead it to smoothness, the bread will not suffer. This is a tremendously wet and sticky dough, so use a dough scraper to help you, but do not add more flour, for it will ruin the texture of the bread.

by stand mixer: With your hands or a wooden spoon, mix the flour and water into a rough, very wet dough in the workbowl of your mixer. Cover the dough and let it rest (autolyse) for 10 to 20 minutes.

Fit the mixer with the dough hook. Add the pre-ferment, honey, potato, and salt and mix the dough on medium-high speed for 15 to 20 minutes, or until it is very silky and wraps around the hook and cleans the bowl before splattering back around the bowl. This dough is almost pourably wet.

FERMENTING AND TURNING THE DOUGH

Shape the dough into a ball and roll it in flour. Place it in a container at least 3 times its size and cover tightly with plastic wrap. Let it ferment until doubled in bulk and filled with large air bubbles, about 4 hours. Using plenty of dusting flour, turn the dough (page 16) 4 times in 20-minute intervals, that is, after 20, 40, 60, and 80 minutes of fermenting, then leave the dough undisturbed for the remaining time. Do not allow this dough to overferment or ferment to the point of collapse, for the flavor and structure of your bread will suffer.

SHAPING AND PROOFING THE DOUGH

Turn the fermented dough out onto a well-floured work surface, round it (page 17), and let it rest for 20 minutes. Sprinkle a couche or wooden board generously with flour. Slip a baking sheet under the couche, if you are using one, for support.

Sprinkle a generous amount of flour over the center of the ball. Push your fingers into the center to make a hole, then rotate your hand around the hole to widen it, making a large 4-inch opening. The bread should have about a 12-inch diameter.

Place the dough smooth side down on the floured couche or board and dust the surface with more flour. Drape it with plastic wrap and let it proof until it is light and slowly springs back when lightly pressed, about 1½ hours.

PREHEATING THE OVEN

Immediately after shaping the bread, arrange a rack on the oven's second-to-top shelf and place a baking stone on it. Clear away all racks above the one being used. Preheat the oven to 450°F (230°C).

BAKING THE BREAD

Unwrap the bread and flip it onto a floured peel or a sheet of parchment paper. Do not worry about damaging the bread as you handle it; it will recover in the oven as long as it is not overproofed. Slash it with 4 radial cuts in the shape of a cross. Slide the loaf onto the hot baking stone and bake until it is very dark brown, 40 to 50 minutes, rotating it halfway into the bake. Let the bread cool on a rack.

COMPETITION BAKING

BREAD BAKERS GUILD OF AMERICA

ANAHEIM, CALIFORNIA

DAWN WOODWARD BENDS OVER HER MIXER, SCRAPER IN HAND. Concentrating fiercely, she pushes the bowl around, jamming in her scraper sporadically to move the dough along.

This baker from Bread Alone Bakery in Boiceville, New York, is baking her heart out with two other bakers, each in a curtained-off booth, competing to be a 1999 Baking Team USA representative. We are in a corner of the Retail Bakers Association's annual convention in Anaheim, California, which the team's sponsor, the Bread Bakers Guild of America, has some-what miraculously turned into three complete artisan bakeries. The baking started early, before the convention opened, and I have had to talk my way past the security guards to be able to see the doughs being mixed.

Each competitor has won his or her respective regional competition but must capture this last round to make the team. The guild, in their third sponsorship, hopes this final competition of their first nationwide search will net a strong team. In February 1999 in Paris they will com-pete in the Coupe du Monde de la Boulangerie, the World Cup of Bread Baking, at Europain, a baking trade show. Competition will be more fierce than ever: The guild's last team startled the baking world by winning the specialty-breads category in 1996.

The two previous days' competitions yielded winners for two of the team's three slots. Thomas Gumpel, an instructor at the Culinary Institute of America at Greystone, won in the artistic design (bread sculpture) category, and Robert Jörin, also an instructor at the CIA Greystone, will represent the team in the viennoiserie category, which includes brioche, crois-sants, and Danish. The winner of today's specialty-breads competition will complete the team.

Soon, the hall doors open to conventioneers and activity starts to buzz around us. In the middle booth, Matt McDonald's timer is beeping: His ciabatta needs turning. Polished after a six-month internship at the National Baking Center in Minneapolis, Matt pulls the oozing dough from its tub, quickly folds it on the floured bench, and replaces it. His bench is stacked

OPPOSITE: Greg Mistell, director of the Bread Bakers Guild of America, helping contest winner Jan Schat into his Baking Team USA coat. ABOVE: Contestant Matt McDonald using a balance scale to weigh his dough.

LEFT TO RIGHT: Matt McDonald placing his twisted baguettes in a couche to proof; turning his proofed dough out of a coiled basket; judge Lionel Vatinet examining the shaping of the dough.

with fermentation tubs, each sporting its own timer. The other bakers seem to be relying more on their watches, but all are constantly checking plastic-enveloped schedules they have made for themselves.

Back in the first booth, Dawn is looking panicked. It seems that her doughs are failing to ferment. She signals for Craig Ponsford, the team's coach, who darts into her booth and checks the temperature of the proofer-retarder unit. Dawn has programmed it incorrectly, but a frantically hailed manufacturer's representative is able to reprogram it quickly. Yet Dawn's composure has been broken and her face is creased with anxiety.

In the third booth, baker Jan Schat is premolding his baguettes. The airy dough lies on the floured bench and Jan is swiftly cutting off pieces, weighing them with great care, and gently folding them into stubby logs. Bread weight must be spot on, which is not as easy as it sounds. Dough loses weight as it is baking, and bakers must correctly estimate the loss. Jan's dough is virtually airborne with huge bubbles, and he handles the dough delicately to preserve each one. A handsome man with serious sky-blue eyes set in a chiseled Nordic face, Jan is the managing partner at Accademia del Fornaio, baking chain Il Fornaio's private baking school in Burlingame, California. He moves with grace

and economy, and to us watching in the audience it is obvious that his seamless routine is founded on many years of experience.

Judge Rick Kirkby, of The Acme Bread Company, who represented the United States in the guild's first team in 1994, leans over the counter to question Matt. They have a brief conference and Rick writes a note on his clipboard. Rick, along with his fellow judges Lionel Vatinet, the French master baker and teacher, and Tom McMahon, founder and director emeritus of the guild, approach the contestants sporadically to question them about their formulas or techniques. While trying not to be intrusive, they do want to ruffle them a little to determine how well they can take the stress of competing and responding clearly to questions. In Paris, journalists and passersby will be peppering the contestants with questions, and they are expected to respond diplomatically.

Lionel in particular has been very relaxed about his judging, hardly even watching the action. He tells me in his beautifully accented English that, while the contestants' work habits are very important, the result is all that really counts: "The bread, it speaks for itself."

Checking our watches, the time for judging draws closer, and we see the bakers sweeping up, stacking up

LEFT TO RIGHT: Dawn Woodward transferring baguettes to a couche; Jan Schat shaping a baguette; Jan arranging finished breads for viewing.

their tubs, wiping down their benches, and even peeling bread into the ovens. Will all the bakers be ready in time? Somehow, by 3 P.M., each baker has made a beautiful sprawling display of bread.

Greg Mistell, director of the guild and owner of Pearl Bakery, finally announces that it is time for the judging to begin. After presenting the judges, he walks up to the bakers and has them introduce themselves, explain their baking background, and describe their breads to the crowd. With every effort expended, the tired bakers clear their booths.

Now the judges fan out to each booth, probing, smelling, holding, weighing, and tasting every batch, writing down their scores and impressions on clipboards. Tom lifts a baguette and turns it all around. He then weighs each one, noting the weight spread. Lionel cuts open a bread diagonally, looking at its hole structure. Rick picks up a cut bread and deeply smells the crumb. He then pulls out a piece from the loaf's center and slowly chews it, rolling it around in his mouth. Finally, having thoroughly dissected every batch, they retreat to a room behind the booths to compare their scores.

After a short discussion, the judges are ready. Greg produces a gratuitous envelope and dramatically opens

it: Jan has won, and the crowd cheers its approval. It's been a long day, but as Craig tells me later, the real work—training for the Coupe du Monde in Paris—has yet to begin. During the summer, the three California teammates will start their training with Craig and the other trainers. While the showing in Anaheim has been excellent, the bakers are not even close to being ready for the competition they will face in Paris.

"It's not a question of winning; it's a question of bringing out the best in people, through the intensity of a competition," Tom McMahon later explains to me. "And I think that was the entire Coupe du Monde experience for the guild itself. It was not about bringing home the cup to America for some nationalistic or just professional pride, but to engage in an overall effort to better the profession in the United States and to make us aware of international standards and the styles of baking in countries where they are known for their traditions. . . . It's really about bread for us."

P.S. The team chosen in Anaheim went on to win the Gold Cup at Coupe du Monde in Paris in February 1999.

ANALYSIS OF A BAGUETTE

The idea of judging bread is a curious concept, so I asked Craig Ponsford, the team coach, and judges Tom McMahon and Rick Kirkby to describe as best they can what goes through their heads while judging a baguette.

Tom says, "First and foremost, I have a rule that if it looks really good, then it probably is good. . . . I've never had a beautiful baguette that didn't taste good also." Craig adds, "Without cutting it open or smelling it, I just want to hold it and look at the color and the ears [the cuts] and the volume. I want to feel it. I want to pick it up and just feel how it feels, to feel if it's baked correctly."

Tom calls the cuts on the bread its most telling feature. "It has to stretch the surface of the bread underneath the cut. You can actually look at the gluten strands as they stretch across there. And when you see them going in the direction of the opening, stretching a lot before they break, it's generally a really healthy sign. What that means is that it's got good mix, good fermentation, and it's been handled properly along the way, and those things are going to mean that it tastes good."

Craig Ponsford examining crumb structure (holes) and color

Opening up the bread, the look of the crumb—its color, holes, and overall texture—is as critical as the bread's outer appearance. The crumb should be a creamy yellowish white, not dead white or gray. Craig checks to see if the baker took "good care of those flours" and didn't "bleach out the color by over mixing." He then checks to see if the holes are "relevant to the size of the baguette." According to Tom, "The hole structure should be irregular, with some large and some small holes, but more important to a trained eye is the look of the holes themselves. What you want is a nice thin cell membrane, where again the gluten has been stretched thin. You want

it translucent; you actually want to be able to see through it. You want to see them stretch for a long, long time before they break, sometimes leaving a very tissue-thin layer around the hole."

The cut breads are sniffed intensely. Says Craig, "I'm looking for a pretty nice smell of the wheat. I want the wheat to come across the fermentation. I want it to have a chardonnay-type of appeal to it, where you can still smell the fruit, yet it is complex."

Taste is perhaps the hardest to pin down. Tom says, "In a baguette, you're looking for almost a natural sweetness, without a sugariness." Rick mentions sweetness first, but describes "some very well-fermented baguettes" as tasting "slightly appley and nutty." Then he adds, "There is a way the crust interacts with that flavor, and if it's properly baked but not overly caramelized, that right level of caramelization is still nutty, without being bitter."

Besides flavor, the whole point of a baguette is its unique "mouthfeel," which Rick describes as "moist and substantial but with a crisp crust. I think it adds to the flavor without really being the flavor." Clearly a baguette is far more than the sum of its sensory parts.

Top, LEFT TO RIGHT: Examining breads with all the senses: Rick Kirkby checking aroma; Lionel Vatinet inhaling a bread's fragrance; Tom McMahon finally tasting. ABOVE: Judges McMahon *(left)*, Kirkby, and Vatinet observing Ponsford weighing finished breads.

COMPETITION GUIDELINES

Competition guidelines are rigid about timing, but a surprising amount is left up to the baker's discretion. Each baker has to make five different batches of bread in seven hours precisely, beginning at 7 A.M. and ending at 3 P.M. The first batch is baguettes, which must be based on 10 kilograms of flour, use a poolish (a liquid pre-ferment), and produce 250-gram baguettes. Batches two through four can be any traditional breads but should use a variety of flours and each must yield ten 400-gram breads. Batch five is called "Baker's Whim" and has "no restrictions on form, weight, or creation," but can weigh no more than 4 kilograms in total. All the breads are evaluated by a three-person panel for weight, volume, taste, and appearance. The challenge is steep, but the bakers have been practicing for weeks in preparation.

Baking Team USA Sweet Dough

- Makes 30 ounces (900 grams) dough, enough for 12 Baking Team USA Caps, 2 Macrina's Cinnamon Monkey Breads, or 2 Acme's Cinnamon-Currant Breads with Walnuts
- Time: At least 11 hours, with about 15 minutes of active work

This full-flavored sweet dough is very similar to the kugelhopf dough (page 181) except that it is slightly richer. It is also kneaded in four stages, which may seem tedious but will net a bread with a pillowy light, finely grained, tender yellow crumb and a tremendous rise in the oven. It has a richly fermented flavor, thanks to its long, cold fermentation. The original formula called for a pre-ferment, but on team member Glenn Mitchell's advice, I dropped it in favor of an extended chilling.

The two-part method of making bread—first kneading the dough, then chilling it to finish it up to two days later—is especially convenient. I like to make the dough at night after dinner, then finish it late the next afternoon or evening. That way, I can bake in the evening, with the main mess of ingredient gathering and kneading out of the way.

Once this dough is fully fermented, you can use it in your favorite recipe or try it in the delicious triad of sweet breads that follow: Baking Team USA Caps, Macrina's Cinnamon Monkey Bread, and Acme's Cinnamon-Currant Bread with Walnuts.

RECIPE SYNOPSIS Mix the dough, then chill it for 8 hours or up 2 days. Let it warm to room temperature for 2 hours. Shape, fill, and bake the bread as desired.

	Dough	volume	weight	metric	baker's percentages
AT LEAST 8 HOURS AND UP TO 2 DAYS BEFORE BAKING MIXING THE DOUGH	**Milk, any kind**	½ cup	4.4 ounces	125 grams	31%
	Instant yeast	2 teaspoons	0.2 ounce	6 grams	1.6%
	Unbleached all-purpose flour	2⅔ cups	14 ounces	400 grams	100%
	Eggs	3 large			35%
	Table salt	1½ teaspoons	0.3 ounce	8 grams	2%
	Granulated sugar	6 tablespoons	2.5 ounces	75 grams	18%
	Unsalted butter, softened if mixing by hand or stand mixer, chilled if mixing by food processor	½ cup	4 ounces	116 grams	29%
	Currants (if making cinnamon-currant bread, page 219)	1½ cups	5.6 ounce	160 grams	40%

Microwave the milk on high power for 4 minutes or heat in a small saucepan on top of the stove until bubbles form around the edge, steam rises, and the milk smells cooked. Let it cool to 105° to 115°F, about the temperature of a comfortably hot bath. (Scalding the milk denatures a protein in the milk that attacks the gluten; if this step is skipped, the bread's texture will be coarser and denser.) Sprinkle the yeast over the milk, stir, and let stand for 5 to 10 minutes.

by hand: Add the flour to a large bowl, then add the yeast mixture and the eggs. With a wooden spoon or your hand, mix the dough just until well combined. Cover the bowl tightly with plastic wrap and let rest (autolyse) for 15 to 20 minutes.

Add the salt to the dough and mix the dough in the bowl just until combined. Turn the dough out of the bowl and knead until it is smooth and strong, 5 to 10 minutes. The dough will first be gritty with the salt, but it will soon dissolve. Add half the sugar and knead the dough again until the sugar dissolves; add the remaining sugar and knead the dough until the sugar is fully incorporated and the dough is very smooth. Finally, add the butter in 2 additions and knead it into the dough until the dough is satiny smooth, soft, and glossy.

by stand mixer: Add the flour to the mixing bowl, then add the yeast mixture and the eggs. Mix the dough just until well combined. Cover the bowl tightly with plastic wrap and let rest (autolyse) for 15 to 20 minutes.

Add the salt to the dough and, using the dough hook, mix the dough on low speed until it is smooth, about 3 minutes. This is a soft dough that will never clean the bowl. Add the sugar in 2 additions then the butter in 2 additions, mixing until each addition is completely incorporated before adding the rest. Continue to mix the dough until it is satiny smooth, soft, and glossy.

by food processor: Add the flour and the salt to the workbowl fitted with the steel blade and pulse to combine them. Remove the cover and add the yeast mixture and eggs. Process the dough until it forms a smooth ball and begins to fog the workbowl. Remove the dough from the workbowl and knead it by hand to cool it and redistribute the heat. The dough will feel fairly stiff once it cools off. Return the dough to the workbowl, process it for 30 seconds, remove it again, and hand knead to cool it. Repeat this process 2 or 3 more times until the dough is very smooth and strong. Return the dough to the workbowl.

With the machine running, slowly add the sugar through the feed tube and process the dough until the sugar has dissolved and the dough is smooth. The dough will be very sticky at this point. Remove the dough and hand knead it to cool it again. Return the dough to the workbowl. Cut the butter into chunks and add about half to the workbowl. Process the dough until the butter is incorporated, about 30 seconds. If the dough is very warm, hand knead it again to cool it. Add the rest of the chunked butter and process it again until it is fully incorporated, about 30 seconds. The dough should be very smooth, extensible, and silky.

ADDING THE CURRANTS

If making Acme's Cinnamon-Currant Bread with Walnuts, knead the currants into the sweet dough until they are well dispersed.

FERMENTING THE DOUGH

Place the dough in a container at least 3 times its size and cover it tightly with plastic wrap, or after rolling it in flour, place the dough in a large plastic bag and seal the bag well. Refrigerate for at least 8 hours or up to 2 days. Let the dough warm to room temperature for 2 hours before shaping it.

FOLLOWING PAGES: Three sweet breads from one dough: Acme's Cinnamon-Currant Bread with Walnuts (page 219), Macrina's Cinnamon Monkey Bread (page 218), and Baking Team USA's Caps (page 216)

Baking Team USA Caps

- Makes 12 buns
- Time: About 5 hours from fermented dough to finished bread, with about 30 minutes of active work

Glenn Mitchell worked hard to develop this recipe for the competition, and it is very special. Fat, light buns enriched with kirsch-soaked dried cherries and chocolate chips, are topped with a sugar cookie before baking, which bakes into a crisp little cap—hence, the name. The cookies are frozen before baking to prevent them from cracking with the expanding rolls.

RECIPE SYNOPSIS Macerate the cherries for at least 6 hours while the dough is chilling. Remove the dough from the refrigerator the day of baking to warm up and finish fermenting. Roll out the sugar cookie dough and cut out disks. Freeze the disks for at least 1 hour. Roll the cherries and chocolate chips into the dough, shape it into buns, and let them proof for 1 to 2 hours. Place a cookie disk on each proofed bun and bake for about 35 minutes.

	Macerated Cherries	volume	weight	metric	baker's percentages
THE DAY OR EVENING BEFORE BAKING MACERATING THE CHERRIES	**Dried sweet cherries**	⅔ cup	3 ounces	85 grams	21%
	Kirsch	1 tablespoon	0.5 ounce	15 grams	4%

Coarsely chop the cherries and mix them with the kirsch in a small container. Cover and let macerate at room temperature for 6 to 12 hours.

	Sugar Cookie Dough	volume	weight	metric	baker's percentages
MAKING THE COOKIE DOUGH	**Unsalted butter, softened**	¼ cup	2.1 ounces	60 grams	50%
	Granulated sugar	⅓ cup	2.1 ounces	60 grams	50%
	Egg yolks	2 large			28%
	Unbleached all-purpose flour	¾ cup	4 ounces	115 grams	100%

Cream the softened butter with the sugar in a small bowl until light and fluffy, about 5 minutes. Stir in the egg yolks, then mix in the flour. Pat the dough into a ½-inch-thick block and wrap it well with plastic wrap. Refrigerate it until needed.

	Dough and Assembly	volume	weight	metric	baker's percentages
BAKE DAY **CUTTING** **AND FREEZING** **THE COOKIES**	**Chilled sugar cookie dough**				63%
	Fully fermented Sweet Dough (page 212), warmed to room temperature				
	Chocolate chips	scant ½ cup	3 ounces	85 grams	21%
	Macerated cherries				
	Egg, beaten	1 large			
	Cocoa powder, for garnishing				

Remove the cookie dough from the refrigerator and let it warm up for about 30 minutes.

On a well-floured work surface with a well-floured rolling pin, roll out the cooookie dough into a very thin sheet. Cut out large rounds using a 3½-inch round cookie cutter (or an empty tuna can). Place them on a parchment paper–lined cookie sheet and freeze until it is time to bake the rolls. They should be frozen hard by then.

SHAPING
THE BUNS

Line a half-sheet pan with parchment paper or butter it well. Lightly flour the top of the dough and the work surface. Turn the dough out and flour its exposed surface. Roll the dough out into a thin sheet. Sprinkle with the chocolate chips and macerated cherries, then roll the dough up into a tight cylinder. Fold the ends of the cylinder into the center, press the cylinder flat, fold it lengthwise in half into a thinner strip, and flatten it again. (The folding will help to better distribute the fruit and chocolate.)

Cut the cylinder into 12 equal pieces, each 2.5 ounces (70 grams). Sprinkle them with a little flour and round them lightly on an unfloured work surface. The dough is very sticky and should grip the work surface during rounding but should not stick to your hand. Cover them with plastic wrap and let rest until well relaxed, about 15 minutes. Shape the dough pieces into tight, very round rolls (page 35) and arrange them on the prepared baking sheet. Loosely cover them with plastic wrap and let proof until the buns are very soft, about doubled in size, and only slowly spring back when lightly pressed with a floured fingertip, 1 to 2 hours.

PREHEATING
THE OVEN

About 30 minutes before the dough is fully proofed, arrange a rack on the oven's second-to-top shelf and clear away all racks above the one being used. Preheat the oven to 325°F (160°C).

BAKING
THE BUNS

Retrieve the cookies from the freezer. Thoroughly brush each bun with the beaten egg, then center a frozen cookie disk on it and press it down lightly. Brush each cookie with the egg wash. Bake until the buns are browned all around, 30 to 35 minutes, rotating the baking sheet halfway into the bake. Let cool on a rack. Sift a bit of cocoa powder over the caps to garnish them before serving.

Macrina's Cinnamon Monkey Bread

- Makes two 9 x 5-inch pan breads
- Time: About 3½ hours from fermented dough to finished bread, with about 10 minutes of active work

Macrina Bakery & Café in Seattle is the little artisan bakery I wish I had just around the corner. In a suavely renovated room with a coffee bar and a scrumptious selection of homey baked goods, one morning I had a wonderful breakfast of excellent coffee served in a huge ceramic mug and this delicious and intricate-looking (but easily shaped) bread. Although it is called a monkey bread, it does not pull apart; instead, it is sliced to display a thick swirl of apple butter and cinnamon sugar. Leslie Mackie, the bakery's founder, writes, "The joy of this loaf is its delicious apple-cinnamon glaze. Apples being a staple here in Washington, it seemed a natural combination with the cinnamon sugar. This is a very popular morning bread at Macrina, shared with a steaming cup of joe."

RECIPE SYNOPSIS Shape and fill the fermented sweet dough, let it proof for 2 to 3 hours, then wash it with beaten egg and bake it for about 45 minutes.

	Dough and Filling	volume	weight	metric	baker's percentages
BAKE DAY **SHAPING** **THE BREAD**	**Brown sugar**	½ cup packed	3.5 ounces	100 grams	25%
	Granulated sugar	½ cup	3.5 ounces	100 grams	25%
	Cinnamon	1 tablespoon	0.3 ounce	7 grams	2%
	Nutmeg	½ teaspoon			0.3%
	Fully fermented Sweet Dough (page 212), warmed to room temperature				
	Apple butter	1 cup	10.2 ounces	290 grams	73%
	Unsalted butter, melted	¼ cup	2 ounces	60 grams	15%
	Egg, beaten	1 large			
	Sesame seeds	1 tablespoon	0.3 ounce	10 grams	2%

Butter two 9 x 5-inch baking pans and line them with 12 x 9-inch rectangles of parchment paper, leaving the 5-inch sides bare.

Combine the sugars and spices in a small bowl. Roll out the fermented dough into an 18 x 10-inch rectangle, about ½ inch thick. Spread it with an even layer of the apple butter, drizzle it with the melted butter, and then sprinkle it with the spiced sugar mixture.

Roll both long edges in so that they meet in the center in a very long and narrow double roll. The dough is very thick so you will be able to roll the sides only once. Flip the dough seam side down and cut it crosswise in half so that you have two 9-inch-long pieces. The top of the dough will retract when you cut it, exposing the filling. Place the loaves seam side down in the prepared baking pans, cover them well with plastic wrap, and let them proof until risen to the tops of the pans, 2 to 3 hours.

About 30 minutes before the dough is fully proofed, arrange a rack on the oven's bottom shelf and clear away all racks above the one being used. Preheat the oven to 325°F (160°C).

Brush the tops of the loaves with the beaten egg, and sprinkle with the sesame seeds. Bake until the breads turn a rich brown color, 40 to 45 minutes, rotating them halfway into the bake. Let cool for 10 minutes, then immediately remove them from the pans onto a rack, using a spatula to loosen the breads if necessary. (Do not allow the breads to cool in the pans or the sugar will harden and they will stick in the pans.) The breads will crack and seem to collapse as you remove them from the pans, but this is their correct final shape.

BEGINNER

Acme's Cinnamon-Currant Bread with Walnuts

- Makes two 8½ x 4½-inch pan breads
- Time: About 12½ hours from kneaded dough to finished bread, with about 20 minutes of active work

This rich bread is made in Acme's Division I (see essay, page 25), where I saw one leaving with almost every customer. This is a true monkey bread, with balls of currant-enriched dough deliciously stuck together in a walnut-punctuated cinnamon-caramel glaze.

RECIPE SYNOPSIS On baking day, let the dough warm up and finish fermenting for 1 to 2 hours. Cut the dough into small chunks, coat each one with cinnamon sugar, and layer them in loaf pans with more cinnamon sugar and walnuts. Let the loaves proof for 1 to 2 hours. Bake them for about 40 minutes, then remove them from the pans after 10 minutes to cool.

	Dough and Filling	volume	weight	metric	baker's percentages
BAKE DAY	**Fully fermented Sweet Dough (page 212), warmed to room temperature**				
	Granulated sugar	1½ cups	11.2 ounces	320 grams	80%
	Cinnamon	3 tablespoons	0.8 ounce	23 grams	6%
	Walnut halves	1⅓ cups	4.9 ounces	140 grams	35%

continued

Butter two 8½ x 4½-inch baking pans and line them with 12 x 8½-inch rectangles of parchment paper, leaving the 4½-inch sides bare. Combine the sugar and cinnamon in a small bowl. Fill a plant mister with water and have a bowl of water handy.

Flatten the dough into a rough rectangle. Roll it up into a cylinder, roll the cylinder out into a long snake, and cut it into 32 equal pieces. Round each piece (page 35) or leave them in squarish chunks.

Dip each piece of dough into the water and then coat it with the cinnamon sugar. Line each loaf pan with 8 pieces each and sprinkle each pan with 2 tablespoons cinnamon sugar. Scatter in the walnuts, dividing them equally between the pans and pushing them between the pieces of dough. Sprinkle each pan with another tablespoon of cinnamon sugar. Place the remaining cinnamon-sugar-coated dough pieces over the rest and press down on them lightly to scrunch them together.

Cover the loaves well with plastic wrap and let them proof until they dome over the pans, 1 to 2 hours.

**PREHEATING
THE OVEN**

About 30 minutes before the dough is fully proofed, arrange a rack on the oven's bottom shelf and clear away all racks above the one being used. Preheat the oven to 325°F (160°C).

**BAKING
THE BREAD**

Bake until the loaves are richly browned all around, 35 to 40 minutes, rotating them halfway into the bake. Let cool for just 10 minutes in their pans, then pull them out of the pans and invert them onto a rack to cool completely. (Do not allow the breads to get cold in the pans or the sugar will harden and it will be impossible to remove them without reheating them.) Serve the loaves upside down.

This is not an exhaustive list of equipment and ingredients suppliers but, instead, my personal list. You will need to call for catalogs, current prices, and shipping charges. Mail-ordering flour may seem extravagant because of shipping expenses, but it usually ends up costing no more than about double the price of supermarket flour, still just pennies per loaf. Also, buying flour in fifty-pound bags is well worth it if you are a frequent baker or can split it with a friend or two.

Joe Generoso of Royal Crown Bakeries

For diastatic malted barley flour, durum flour, whole white-wheat flour, 11.5% protein white flour (King Arthur all-purpose), osmo-tolerant instant yeast (SAF Gold), kitchen scales, dough scrapers, baking stones, and every other piece of baking equipment and ingredient under the sun:

> The Baker's Catalogue
> P.O. Box 876
> Norwich, VT 05055-0876
> (800) 827-6836
> www.kingarthurflour.com

For Hudson Cream white-wheat flour:

> Stafford County Flour Mills
> P.O. Box 21611
> Denver, CO 80221
> (800) 49-FLOUR
> www.flour.com

For Rhode Island jonnycake meal:

> Gray's Grist Mill
> P.O. Box 422
> Adamsville, RI 02801
> (608) 636-6075

For a variety of excellent flours, both commercial and organic, *to the trade only:*

Cook Natural Products
2109 Frederick Street
Oakland, CA 94606
(510) 534-2665
www.cooknaturally.com

For a variety of excellent flours, both commercial and organic, *to the trade only:*

Giusto's Specialty Foods, Inc.
344 Littlefield Avenue
South San Francisco, CA 94080
(650) 873-6566

For organic, all-winter, stone-ground, hard, red whole-wheat bread flour, and organic, all-winter, stone-ground, soft, red whole-wheat pastry flour (in fifty-pound bags only, shipped UPS):

Certified Foods, Inc.
1055 Montague Avenue
San Leandro, CA 94577
(510) 483-1177

For (fifty-pound bags only) organic 85%-extraction flour (wheat)—Alpine, organic hard-red-winter whole-wheat flour—Frontier, organic hard-red-winter 10.3% protein white flour—Aspen, and organic hard-red-winter 12% protein white flour—Columbine:

Rocky Mountain Flour Milling
P.O. Box 1110
Platteville, CO 80651
(970) 785-2794

For fine rye meal (dark rye flour), rye meal, and cracked rye:

Bob's Red Mill Natural Foods, Inc.
5209 S.E. International Way
Milwaukee, OR 97222
(503) 654-3215

For superb, super-ripe Kalamata olives (ask for "bulk Kalamatas" from the deli) and wonderful artisan breads and pastries, among other rare and unique foods:

Zingerman's
422 Detroit Street
Ann Arbor, MI 48104
(888) 636-8162

For couches in a variety of widths, flipping boards, and the largest selection of French and German proofing baskets:

F.B.M. Baking Machines
R.D. 3/Box 799
Cranbury, NJ 08512
(800) 449-0433

For measuring spoons and other equipment and cutlery:

Professional Cutlery Direct
242 Branford Road
North Branford, CT 06471
(800) 859-6994

For general baking equipment and an excellent selection of molds and pans:

Sur la Table
1765 Sixth Avenue South
Seattle, WA 98134-1608
(800) 243-0852

For general baking equipment and an excellent selection of molds and pans:

Williams-Sonoma
P.O. Box 7456
San Francisco, CA 94120-7456
(800) 541-2233

ADDRESSES

This is a directory of all the establishments featured in this book. However, there are many other bakers that I would have loved to include had time and space constraints not made it impossible. Please contact the Bread Bakers Guild of America, below, to find a more comprehensive listing of artisan bakers, equipment and ingredients suppliers, schools and baking classes.

The Acme Bread Company
2730 Ninth Street
Berkeley, CA 94710
(510) 843-2978

Artisan Bakers
750 West Napa Street
Sonoma, CA 95476
(707) 939-1765

Bread Bakers Guild of America
P.O. Box 22254
Pittsburgh, PA 15222
(412) 322-8275
www.bbga.org

Bruno Bakery
602 Lorimer Street
Brooklyn, NY 11211
(718) 349-6524

Della Fattoria
1159 Skillman Lane
Petaluma, CA 94952
(707) 762-1722

The Essential Baking Company
454 North 34th
Seattle, WA 98103
(206) 545-3804

Farm to Market Bread Company
216 West 73rd Street
Kansas City, MO 64114
(816) 363-3198

Gemelli
4 World Trade Center,
    Plaza Level
New York, NY 10048
(212) 488-2100

Grace Baking, Inc.
548 Cleveland Avenue
Albany, CA 94710
(510) 525-2253

Gray's Grist Mill, Inc.
P.O. Box 422
Adamsville, RI 02801
(508) 636-6075

The Hi-Rise Bread Company
208 Concord Avenue
Cambridge, MA 02138
(617) 876-8766

Kossar's Bialystoker Kuchen
367 Grand Street
New York, NY 10002
(212) 473-4810
www.kossarsbialys.com

La Farm Bakery
4248 Northwest Cary Parkway
Cary, NC 27513
(919) 465-2349

Macrina Bakery & Café
2408 First Avenue
Seattle, WA 98121
(206) 448-4089

Mennonite Heritage Museum
Box 231
Goessel, KS 67053
(316) 367-8200

National Baking Center
818 Dunwoody Boulevard
Minneapolis, MN 55403-1192
(612) 374-3303
www.nationalbakingcenter.com

Pearl Bakery, Inc.
102 Northwest Ninth Street
Portland, OR 97210
(503) 827-0910

Rocky Mountain Flour Milling
P.O. Box 1110
Platteville, CO 80651
(970) 785-2794
www.rmfm.cnchost.com

Royal Crown Bakery
6308 14th Avenue
Brooklyn, NY 11219
(718) 234-3208
and
6512 14th Avenue
Brooklyn, NY 11219
(718) 234-1002

Russ & Daughters
179 E. Houston Street
New York, NY 10002
(212) 475-4880
www.russ.com

San Francisco Baking Institute
390 Swift Avenue
South San Francisco, CA 94080
(415) 589-5784

Sullivan Street Bakery
73 Sullivan Street
New York, NY 10012
(212) 334-9435

Tom Cat Bakery
43-05 Tenth Street
Long Island City, NY 11101
(718) 786-4224

WheatFields bakery/café
904 Vermont
Lawrence, KS 66044
(913) 841-5553

Whole Foods Bakehouse
Dutch Regale Bakery
5531 East University
Dallas, TX 75206
(214) 369-0079

MORE ITALIAN BRICK-OVEN BAKERIES

A few bakeries on the East Coast still use their original brick ovens, firing them with wood, coal, or oil and have excellent bread, worth a detour for bread lovers:

In Philadelphia, Pennsylvania:
Faragalli's Bakery
1400 South 13th Street
Philadelphia, PA 19147
(215) 468-5197

Caccia Bakery
1526 Ritner Street
Philadelphia, PA 19145
(215) 334-1340

Lanci's Bakery
1716 Jackson Street
Philadelphia, PA 19145
(215) 336-2664

In Newark, New Jersey:
Original S. Giordano Bakery, Inc.
(This is where Frank Sinatra bought his panelle.)
33 7th Avenue
Newark, NJ 07104
(973) 483-1579
and
90 Franklin Street
Belleville, NJ 07109
(973) 751-9704

In Hoboken, New Jersey:
Marie's Bakery and Policastro Breads
261 2nd Street
Hoboken, NJ 07030
(201) 963-4281

Dom's Bakery Grand
506 Grand Street
Hoboken, NJ 07030
(201) 653-1948

Antique Bakery
122 Willow Avenue
Hoboken, NJ 07030
(201) 714-9323

In New York City:
Zito's Bakery
259 Bleecker Street
New York, NY 10014
(212) 929-6139

ACKNOWLEDGMENTS

ONE OF THE MOST GRATIFYING ASPECTS OF WRITING THIS BOOK has been my ability to feature many of the bakers who took an interest in me and my passion, opened up their bakeries, and discussed bread with me endlessly. I hope I did you all a smidgen of the justice you deserve.

There are, however, many others whom I also need to thank. Many years ago, Ron Wirtz, vice-president of information and distance learning at the American Institute of Baking, introduced me to the writings of Professor Raymond Calvel and started me off on my own long journey. Without the "motherly" (his words) Tom McMahon's fierce devotion to good bread and artisan baking, this book simply wouldn't exist. Professor Raymond Calvel, my inspiration and baking cornerstone, is a generous friend and avid long-distance mentor. Greg Mistell, who took Tom's place in the Bread Bakers Guild of America, has been deeply enthusiastic about this book from the beginning and was extremely generous with the guild's resources. Gina Piccolino, the guild's real director, has been useful beyond the call of duty, super-supportive, and a very important source of really good gossip. Didier Rosada, the absolute rock-bottom authority in all matters pertaining to bread, read and corrected parts of this manuscript and was very generous with his knowledge. Michel Suas, a kind man with a passion for great bread, opened up his San Francisco Baking Institute for an impromptu class for me.

For leads to some of the bakeries featured in this book, I would like to thank Anna Nurse, Annie Copps, George Greenstein, Maya Kaimal, Jill Van Cleave, Myra Chanin, and Ken Ayvazian.

Amy Albert is a true friend, a great editor, and an unwavering supporter. Susan Puckett, a great friend, plucked me from the slush piles and has ever since given me the most wonderful opportunities with *The Atlanta Journal-Constitution*.

P. J. Hamel and Brinna and Frank Sands of King Arthur Flour are some of the best people you could hope to meet in the baking industry. They are not only passionately interested in everything to do with artisan baking, they are fascinating, warm, and caring people. I am so very grateful that our paths have met.

Thank you, Lora Brody: Your matchmaker skills are as formidable as all your others.

Thank you to all the staff at Artisan—Deborah Weiss Geline, Dania Davey, Nancy Murray, Trish Boczkowski, and everyone there who made this the best-looking and most useful book it could possibly be. Barbara Ottenhoff and Judith Sutton polished and copyedited the manuscript: Thanks for doing such a sympathetic and comprehensive job. I am so grateful to have had Ann Bramson as an editor and publisher. Your eye for making beautiful books and your ear for language are really exceptional. I feel truly blessed to have been allowed to work with you.

Susan Ginsburg has been a writer's dream of an agent. Thanks for making this happen.

Ben Fink started out as a traveling companion, but ended up becoming a good friend. Ben, thanks not only for your simply fabulous work (sorry to use the f-word again, but it is just too perfect here), but for all the fun we had, even during the most arduous of the shoots. Rita Yeazel tirelessly tested every recipe until it was perfect. Thank you, Rita, for your assiduous reading, professional-quality testing, enthusiasm, and good cheer.

My mother, Bobbi Lee Caraway, my grandmother Ruth Marie Gorenstein, and her mother Grandma Kate Sherkow, Grandma Rivka Dennis, and Grandma Ruth Sue Coleman have been my fundamental sources of inspiration, guidance, love, and support. I could never thank any of you enough.

Finally, I need to thank my two children, Mathan Shlomo and Leia Kate Glezer, and my husband, Ari, who gave me the love and encouragement I needed to complete this work.

Pearl Bakery's best customer, Patrick Duncan Moore

INDEX

malted barley flour, 5

maltose, sourdough starters and, 89

margherita pizza, 152

    Gemelli, 153–55

Massimo (Royal Crown Bakeries), 197–98

May, Tony, 151–52

meal, rye, 5, 7

measuring ingredients, 9, 11, 15

measuring spoons, 9

medium rye flour, 5

    in Dutch Regale's Finnish rye bread, 146–49

    in Dutch Regale's korn bread, 143–45

    in The Pearl's walnut levain, 95–96

Mennonites, 45, 49–50, 130

Merrill, Susan, 179

miche, 34

microflora, 88, 89, 91

milk:

    in Baking Team USA sweet dough, 212–13

    in Dutch Regale's almond stollen, 186–90

    in Glenn Mitchell's kugelhopf, 181–84

    in Gray's Grist Mill thin jonnycakes, 68

    in Hi-Rise's Boston brown bread, 66

    in Judy Unruh's wedding zwieback, 53–54

milling, xi, 29, 42, 71, 76

    breaking rolls, 72

    long flow, 75

    reduction rolls, 72

    roller, 4, 71–76

    rye flour and, 5

    short flow, 71

    stone grinding, 57–61, 71

Mirsky, Shorty, 171

Mistell, Greg, 87, 209

misting of bread, 18

Mitchell, Cindy, 179, 180

Mitchell, Glenn, 77, 179–84, 185, 216

mixed starter, 103

mixing, 13

    see also kneading

moistening dough, 9

molasses, in Hi-Rise's Boston brown bread, 66

mold, storage and, 19

Monet, M., 180

mozzarella, in Gemelli pizza margherita, 153–55

muffins, 4

multi-grain breads, 21

    Della Fattoria's polenta bread, 118–19

    Dutch Regale's Finnish rye bread, 146–49

    Dutch Regale's korn bread, 143–45

    Essential's Columbia, 82–83

    Essential's Sweet Perrin, 77–80

    Gray's Grist Mill thin jonnycakes, 68

    Hi-Rise's Boston brown bread, 66

    Hi-Rise's corn bread, 64–65

    white-wheat rolls, 46–47

National Baking Center, 102, 207

Neapolitan pizza, xi, 151–52

nutmeg, in Macrina's cinnamon monkey bread, 218–19

Old dough, yeast pre-ferments and, 103

olive bread, Thom Leonard's Kalamata, 135–37

one-day breads, 20

    Dutch Regale's almond stollen, 186–92

    Dutch Regale's rum stollen, 193

    Gemelli pizza margherita, 153–55

    Gray's Grist Mill thin jonnycakes, 68

    Hi-Rise's Boston brown bread, 66

    Hi-Rise's corn bread, 64–65

    Judy Unruh's wedding zwieback, 53–54

    Kossar's bialys, 174–75

    Royal Crown's fennel taralli, 199–202

    Royal Crown's tortano, 203–5

    white-wheat rolls, 46–47

onions:

    in Kossar's bialys, 171, 174–75

    in Sullivan Street potato pizza, 156–59

orange juice concentrate, in Dutch Regale's almond stollen, 186–92

osmotolerant instant active dry yeast, 8

    in Bruno's pandoro, 164–67

    in Dutch Regale's almond stollen, 186–92

ovens, x, xii, 122

    coal-fired brick, 197, 198

    gas, 19

    placement of bread in, 18–19

    wood-fire, 129–31, 151

overfermentation, 102

overs, milling and, 72

oxidation, 12

oxygen, 12, 14

Pain au levain, x, 87, 88, 89, 91–94

    The Pearl's walnut levain, 95–96

    see also sourdough breads

pan bread, 53–55

    Hi-Rise's corn bread, 64–65

    Judy Unruh's wedding zwieback and, 53–54

pandoro, Bruno's, 161–67

panella, 198

panettone, 162

parchment paper, 18

pasta flour, 4

pastry scraper, 9

pâte fermentée, 103

pear bread, 77–80

Pearl Bakery, 87, 209

    fig-anise panini, 87, 98–99

    pane coi santi, 87, 98–99

    walnut levain, 87, 95–96

peeling bread onto baking stone, 18

peels, x, 4, 10, 18

percentages for ingredients, 6

Pichia saitoi, 89

pizza, 151–59

    margherita, Gemelli, 153–55

    Sullivan Street potato, 156–59

pizzaiolos, 151–59

plant mister, 10

Poilâne, Lionel, 3

polenta bread, Della Fattoria's, 118–19

Ponsford, Craig, 101, 102, 103, 208, 209, 210

poolish, 103, 211

potassium bromate, 73